Everyman, I will go with thee,
and be thy guide

William Shakespeare

MUCH ADO ABOUT NOTHING

Edited by
JOHN F. ANDREWS

Foreword by
KEVIN KLINE

EVERYMAN
J. M. DENT · LONDON
CHARLES E. TUTTLE
VERMONT

First published in Everyman by J. M. Dent 1996
Published by permission of GuildAmerica Books, an imprint
of Doubleday Book and Music Clubs, Inc.

J. M. Dent
Orion Publishing Group
Orion House
5 Upper St Martin's Lane
London WC2H 9EA
and
Charles E. Tuttle Co.
28 South Main Street, Rutland
Vermont 05701, USA

Photoset by Deltatype Ltd, Ellesmere Port, Cheshire
Printed in Great Britain by
The Guernsey Press Co. Ltd, Guernsey, C.I.

British Library Cataloguing-in-Publication Data is available
upon request

ISBN 0 460 87515 9

CONTENTS

ACKNOWLEDGEMENTS

The editor and publishers wish to thank the following for permission to use copyright material:

Cambridge University Press for material from Arthur Kirsch, *Shakespeare and the Experience of Love*, 1981, and Muriel C. Bradbrook, *Shakespeare and Elizabethan Poetry*, 1979;

Charles and John Van Doren for material from Mark Van Doren, *Shakespeare*, 1939;

The Johns Hopkins University Press for Northrop Frye, 'The Argument of Comedy', *English Institute Essays 1948*;

Longman Group UK Ltd for material from A. P. Rossiter, *Angel With Horns and Other Shakespeare Lectures*, 1961;

Manchester University Press for material from John Wain, 'The Shakespearian Lie-Detector in *Much Ado About Nothing*', *Critical Quarterly*, 1967;

Oxford University Press for material from Bertrand Evans, *Shakespeare's Comedies*, 1960. Copyright © Oxford University Press 1960;

Shakespeare Quarterly for material from Harry Berger Jr., 'Against the Sink-a-Pace: Sexual and Family Politics in *Much Ado About Nothing*', *Shakespeare Quarterly*, 34.3, 1982;

The Society of Authors on behalf of the Bernard Shaw Estate for material from Bernard Shaw, *Our Theatre in the Nineties*, 1932;

The University of Chicago Press for Harold C. Goddard, *The Meaning of Shakespeare*, 1951.

Every effort has been made to trace all the copyright holders but if any have been advertently overlooked the publishers will be pleased to make the necessary arrangement at the first opportunity.

NOTE ON THE AUTHOR AND EDITOR

WILLIAM SHAKESPEARE is held to have been born on St George's day, 23 April 1564. The eldest son of a prosperous glove-maker in Stratford-upon-Avon, he was probably educated at the town's grammar school.

Tradition holds that between 1585 and 1592, Shakespeare first became a schoolteacher and then set off for London. By 1594 he was a leading member of the Lord Chamberlain's Men, helping to direct their business affairs, as well as being a playwright and actor. In 1598 he became a part-owner of the company, which was the most distinguished of its age. However, he maintained his contacts with Stratford, and his family appears to have remained there.

From about 1610 he seems to have grown increasingly involved in the town's affairs, suggesting a withdrawal from London. He died on 23 April 1616, in his 53rd year, and was buried at Holy Trinity two days later.

JOHN F. ANDREWS has recently completed a 19-volume edition, *The Guild Shakespeare*, for the Doubleday Book and Music Clubs. He is also the editor of a 3-volume reference set, *William Shakespeare: His World, His Work, His Influence*, and the former editor (1974–85) of the journal *Shakespeare Quarterly*. From 1974 to 1984 he was director of Academic Programs at the Folger Shakespeare Library in Washington and Chairman of the Folger Institute. He now heads the Shakespeare Guild, which bestows the annual Sir John Gielgud Award for Excellence in the Dramatic Arts.

CHRONOLOGY OF SHAKESPEARE'S LIFE

Year[1]	Age	Life
1564		Shakespeare baptized 26 April at Stratford-upon-Avon
1582	18	Marries Anne Hathaway
1583	19	Daughter, Susanna, born
1585	21	Twin son and daughter, Hamnet and Judith, born
1590–1	26	*The Two Gentlemen of Verona* & *The Taming of the Shrew*
1591	27	*2 & 3 Henry VI*
1592	28	*Titus Andronicus* & *1 Henry VI*
1592–3		*Richard III*
1593	29	*Venus and Adonis* published
1594	30	*The Comedy of Errors. The Rape of Lucrece* published
1594–5		*Love's Labour's Lost*
1595	31	*A Midsummer Night's Dream, Romeo and Juliet,* & *Richard II.* An established member of Lord Chamberlain's Men
1596	32	*King John.* Hamnet dies
1596–7		*The Merchant of Venice* & *1 Henry IV*

[1] It is rarely possible to be certain about the dates at which plays of this period were written. For Shakespeare's plays, this chronology follows the dates preferred by Stanley Wells and Gary Taylor, the editors of The Oxford Shakespeare. Publication dates are given for poetry and books.

CHRONOLOGY OF HIS TIMES

Year	Literary Context	Historical Events
1565–7	Golding, Ovid's *Metamorphoses*, tr.	Elizabeth I reigning
1574	*A Mirror for Magistrates* (3rd ed.)	
1576	London's first playhouse built	
1578	John Lyly, *Euphues*	
1579	North, Plutarch's *Lives*, tr.	
	Spenser, *Shepheardes Calender*	
1587	Marlowe, *1 Tamburlaine*	Mary Queen of Scots executed
1588	Holinshed's *Chronicles* (2nd ed.)	Defeat of Spanish Armada
1589	Kyd, *Spanish Tragedy*	Civil war in France
	Marlowe, *Jew of Malta*	
1590	Spenser, *Faerie Queene*, Bks I–III	
1591	Sidney, *Astrophel and Stella*	Proclamation against Jesuits
1592	Marlowe, *Dr Faustus* & *Edward II*	Scottish witchcraft trials
		Plague closes theatres from June
1593	Marlowe killed	
1594	Nashe, *Unfortunate Traveller*	Theatres reopen in summer
1594–6		Extreme food shortages
1595	Sidney, *An Apologie for Poetry*	Riots in London
1596		Calais captured by Spanish
		Cadiz expedition

Year	Age	Life
1597	33	Buys New Place in Stratford
		The Lord Chamberlain's Men's lease to play at the Theatre expires; until 1599 they play mainly at the Curtain
1597–8		*The Merry Wives of Windsor* & *2 Henry IV*
1598	34	*Much Ado About Nothing*
1598–9		*Henry V*
1599	35	*Julius Caesar*. One of syndicate responsible for building the Globe in Southwark, where the Lord Chamberlain's Men now play
1599–1600		*As You Like It*
1600–1		*Hamlet*
1601	37	*Twelfth Night*. His father is buried in Stratford
1602	38	*Troilus and Cressida*. Invests £320 in land near Stratford[2]
1603	39	*Measure for Measure*. The Lord Chamberlain's Men become the King's Men. They play at court more than all the other companies combined
1603–4		*Othello*
c.1604	40	Shakespeare sues Philip Rogers of Stratford for debt
1604–5		*All's Well That Ends Well*
1605	41	*Timon of Athens*. Invests £440 in Stratford tithes
1605–6		*King Lear*
1606	42	*Macbeth* & *Antony and Cleopatra*
1607	43	*Pericles*. Susanna marries the physician John Hall in Stratford
1608	44	*Coriolanus*. The King's Men lease Blackfriars, an indoor theatre. His only grandchild is born. His mother dies
1609	45	*The Winter's Tale*. 'Sonnets' and 'A Lover's Complaint' published
1610	46	*Cymbeline*
1611	47	*The Tempest*
1613	49	*Henry VIII*. Buys house in London for £140
1613–14		*The Two Noble Kinsmen*
1616	52	Judith marries Thomas Quiney, a vintner, in Stratford. On 23 April Shakespeare dies; is buried two days later
1623		Publication of the First Folio. His widow dies in August

[2] A schoolmaster would earn around £20 a year at this time.

Year	Literary Context	Historical Events
1597	Bacon, *Essays*	
1598	Marlowe and Chapman, *Hero and Leander* Jonson, *Every Man in his Humour*	Rebellion in Ireland
1599	Children's companies begin playing Thomas Dekker's *Shoemaker's Holiday*	Essex fails in Ireland
1601	'War of the Theatres' Jonson, *Poetaster*	Essex rebels and is executed
1602		Tyrone defeated in Ireland
1603	Florio, Montaigne's *Essays*, tr.	Elizabeth I dies, James I accedes Raleigh found guilty of treason
1604	Marston, *The Malcontent*	Peace with Spain
1605	Bacon, *Advancement of Learning*	Gunpowder plot
1606	Jonson, *Volpone*	
1607	Tourneur, *The Revenger's Tragedy*, published	Virginia colonized Enclosure riots
1609		Oath of allegiance Truce in Netherlands
1610	Jonson, *Alchemist*	
1611	Authorised Version of the Bible Donne, *Anatomy of the World*	
1612	Webster, *White Devil*	Prince Henry dies
1613	Webster, *Duchess of Malfi*	Princess Elizabeth marries
1614	Jonson, *Bartholomew Fair*	
1616	Folio edition of Jonson's plays	

Biographical note, chronology and plot summary compiled by John Lee, University of Newcastle, 1996.

FOREWORD TO *Much Ado About Nothing*

George Bernard Shaw once suggested that trying to describe a theatre experience through words is as difficult as trying to describe the experience of a painting through dance.

Bearing that in mind, here are an actor's very subjective recollections of having prepared and performed the role of Benedick, opposite Blythe Danner's Beatrice, during the 1988 season at the Delacorte Theatre in Central Park. The New York Shakespeare Festival production was directed by Gerald Freedman and produced by Joseph Papp.

I had always believed *Much Ado About Nothing* to be a nearly indestructible crowd-pleaser, and I had wanted to play Benedick for many years, not so much from having read it in school as from having seen several productions over the past twenty years, both in the US and in Great Britain. Whenever I saw the play, I was struck not only by its unique interplay of comedy and romance but also by the scope of its tone, which fluctuates spasmodically between the very light and the quite dark. The trick to a successful production seemed to be in somehow reconciling these two extremes into one harmonious whole.

Taking our cue from the fact that most of the text is written in conversational prose rather than formal, heightened verse, we did not approach the play reverently in rehearsals. 'Screwball comedy' was a phrase which Gerald Freedman borrowed on a few occasions to describe the style of the production, which seemed to me very apt as it conjured images of those romantic, zany '30s movies in which the hero and heroine were strong-willed, high-strung, madly in love with one another, and locked in a battle of complete denial of that love . . . adversaries doomed to end up together.

During rehearsals the actors portraying Don John, Borachio, and Conrade explored the extremes of their characters' darkness – which extremity had the felicitous result of revealing their hidden but seldom-realized comic potential. Don John's paroxysms of jealousy and rage were both believable and laughable. The Act IV, Scene 1 denunciation of Hero was played straightforwardly for all its dramatic values (with the possible exception of Benedick's ironical interjection, 'This looks not like a nuptial,' a line whose comedic capabilities, however ill-timed or tasteless, I made no attempt to squelch).

In early rehearsals I began by playing Benedick as a loud, loutish, even braggart soldier – a sort of third cousin of *Miles Gloriosus* – with little of the courtier about him. This obvious 'type' slowly gained some dimension, I think, as I discovered that beneath his swagger, his posturing and soldierly machismo, there dwelt a rather confused adolescent in search of his identity and wishing desperately to be loved. It was Benedick's search for his identity, in fact, which eventually became for me the explanation or motivation, if you will, for all of his contradictory behavior. He seemed to me to be trying on different masks, or personalities, until he found one that fit.

I began to see that what commonly is referred to as Benedick's wit is in fact a series of buffoonish bids for attention. And whenever his 'wit' is directed at Beatrice, it is desperately defensive, and always protesting too much.

'She speaks poniards, and every word stabs,' Benedick howls. If we hear his description literally rather than dismiss it as mere irony, we can sense just how much she gets to him and therefore how desperate his defense must be. To me, their verbal swordplay is of the broadsword variety. It has little in common with the witty repartee of such Restoration lovers as Mirabell and Millamant in Congreve's *The Way of the World*, where subtlety and obliqueness of phrase are so prized. The world of *Much Ado* is Italian, not English, and our sets, costumes, and music appropriately reflected that passionate Mediterranean spirit.

I saw the central action of Benedick's story to be that of falling in love, and I began to notice in the trajectory of that fall a progress: from denial to adolescent infatuation through narcissistic love to mature love.

But while there is much potential humor in this evolution alone, the comedy is intensified by the attendant struggle Benedick undergoes as he tries to reconcile his longstanding public image of confirmed misogynous bachelor with his new private posture of romantic lover.

This struggle is compounded by Benedick's categorical refusal to do anything halfway. His unswerving absoluteness may be the character's most endearing quality, as well as his most ridiculous. He is as unequivocal and definitive in the oaths he swears against marriage in Act I as he is in his Act II decision to requite Beatrice's love for him ('I will be horribly in love with her'), and as he is in his ultimate Act V pronouncement that 'Man is a giddy thing, and this is my conclusion.' It is, in fact, this 'conclusion' that finally frees Benedick from the prison of his consistency. (In Elizabethan usage, 'giddy' also meant 'changeable'.)

I eventually reached a similar conclusion about the play – that it was as mercurial and giddy in tone as is human nature itself. And the key to playing it seemed to be in giving both the light and dark tones their full due, alternately, and also allowing for their simultaneity.

An example of this is the exchange between Beatrice and Benedick in Act IV, Scene 1, after the denunciation of Hero. Early in the run, we played this scene, regrettably, only for comedy. But as our performances matured, this encounter became not only a comic scene but also a dramatic love scene: the audience continued to laugh at Beatrice and Benedick but also began to get a sense of their genuinely caring for one another.

During the Central Park engagement rain interrupted several performances, but the audience refused to leave. They steadfastly waited out the weather, demanding a resolution to the play – a tribute to the power of Shakespeare's storytelling.

And whenever the play was allowed to reach its conclusion, and Beatrice and Benedick finally kissed, the audience cheered, for they fully apprehended the extent of the journey these characters had traveled. And in the meantime, Beatrice and Benedick had found not only one another but themselves as well.

Kevin Kline

KEVIN KLINE has appeared in a variety of leading roles with the New York Shakespeare Festival and The Acting Company, including Hamlet, Richard III, Henry V, and Benedick. Among his acting awards are two Tonys – Best Supporting Actor in a Musical for *On the Twentieth Century* (1978) and Best Actor in a Musical for *The Pirates of Penzance* (1980), The William Shakespeare Award for Classical Theatre (1989), and an Academy Award for *A Fish Called Wanda* (1989).

EDITOR'S INTRODUCTION TO
Much Ado About Nothing

Much Ado About Nothing has been described as the most down-to-earth of Shakespeare's romantic comedies. The universe it depicts is a 'familiar' one (V.iv.70), devoid of implausible features such as the allegorical quests of *The Comedy of Errors*, the fairy-world metamorphoses of *A Midsummer Night's Dream*, the magic caskets of *The Merchant of Venice*, the cross-dressed pages of *The Two Gentlemen of Verona* and *Twelfth Night*, and the 'strange Events' (V.iv.135) of *As You Like It*. Through special effects that parody the seemingly miraculous reversals in other plays of the same genre, the obstacles that impede erotic and spiritual fulfilment in *Much Ado About Nothing* are ultimately dissolved in 'Wonder'. But by permitting the audience to observe the contrivances that have been designed to produce a sequence of happy issues, Shakespeare ensures that none of us will depart from the theatre with any illusion that the 'Amazement' we've witnessed (V.iv.67–71) is a phenomenon which must be ascribed to supernatural causes.

Like *The Merry Wives of Windsor* but unlike most of the playwright's other works, which tend to alternate between a major 'verse plot' and a supporting 'prose plot', *Much Ado About Nothing* is predominantly in prose. Only rarely does its dialogue partake of the heightening of metre, let alone rhyme, and when it does so the characters defined by these dramaturgical media come across as comparatively 'artificial': reserved, formal, effete, or otherwise straitened by fashion's norms.

The personalities who command our keenest attention are Beatrice and Benedick. Their discourse scintillates with metaphorical flourishes, but under ordinary conditions it eschews the rhetorical resources of verse. The three significant exceptions to this rule occur in the final speech of III.i (where Beatrice responds to what she has just overheard in the second of the comedy's garden scenes), in the early segments of IV.i (where the solemnity of a ceremonial occasion bestows Sunday manners upon an entire congregation prior to the moment when Messina's sharpest critics of convention are left alone to revert to the prose they employ in all but the most constraining situations), and in everything but the culminating dialogue of V.iv (where the decorum befitting a climactic wedding ceremony imposes an uncommonly dignified bearing on Benedick and Beatrice as well as on the rest of the company).

Meanwhile, of the two dramatis personae who impress us as least capable of deviation from their traditionally prescribed roles, Claudio and Hero, one or the other participates in every scene that includes rhymed poetry or blank verse.

Nothing is a word of haunting ambiguity in Shakespeare (the playwright would later explore its potential most profoundly in the 'Nothing will come of Nothing' that constitutes the essence of *King Lear*), and in *Much Ado About Nothing* its implications include the possibilities inherent in the Elizabethan homonym, or near-homonym, *Noting*. Through the machinations of the surly Don John, who twice tricks Claudio into 'noting' things that undermine his faith in those he must learn to trust, an innocent maiden is spurned at the altar by a young lord who believes his honour to have been sullied. Fortunately, Don John's accomplices have themselves been 'noted' by the most ineffectual Watch that ever patrolled a precinct; and despite the incompetence of their asinine Constable, these dedicated but doltish servants of the Duke succeed in bringing the malefactors to justice. In the interim the Friar who was officiating at the truncated nuptial has 'noted' in the scorned bride a behaviour that persuades him of her chastity, and he sets in motion a process that will lead to reconciliation through ritual re-enactments of both the Crucifixion and the Resurrection.

The 'notings' that have always given the most delight to audiences, however, are the ones we see engineered by the friends of Benedick and Beatrice. Despite the 'merry War' (I.i.63) with which they try to mask their attraction to each other, these two wit-crackers convince their well-wishers that they belong together. Accordingly, in a brace of eavesdroppings that have never failed to set theatres aroar with laughter, the most stubborn of Love's heretics succumb to an 'inraged Affection' (II.iii.110) that neither can quite disclose to the other in a manner than would permit them to 'woo peaceably' (V.ii.77–78). Eventually Benedick concedes that 'the World must be peopled' (II.iii.257–58), and in due course Beatrice yields to his suit 'upon great Persuasion' (V.iv.95). But it is anything but clear that these charming competitors do so much as exchange a kiss before the dance that lightens their hearts and our own at the consummation of their final 'Skirmish of Wit' (I.i.65).

When Shakespeare wrote *Much Ado About Nothing*, evidently in 1598 or early 1599, he could have borrowed from a number of antecedents for the story of Hero and Claudio, among them passages in Lodovico Ariosto's *Orlando Furioso* (1516) that had been Englished by Sir John Harington (1591) and adapted by Edmund Spenser in Book II of *The Faerie Queene* (1590). But he probably drew principally upon a story in the *Novelle* of Matteo Bandello (1554) – either in the original Italian or in a French version included in François de Belleforest's *Histoires Tragiques* (1569) – and from *Fedele and Fortunato*, a 1585 English play (anonymous, but now widely attributed to Anthony Munday) that seems to have been a recasting of Luigi Pasaquaglio's *Il Fedele* (1579).

For the sparring of Benedick and Beatrice, Shakespeare may have derived some details from a passage in Baldasare Castiglione's *Il Cortegiano* (probably in Sir Thomas Hoby's 1561 translation of *The Courtier* from Italian). But it seems more than likely that the playwright also returned to Petruchio's wooing of the fiery Katherina in his own *Taming of the Shrew* (1593–94).

For Dogberry and the Watch, Shakespeare almost certainly profited either from his own observations or from conversations he would have had with his neighbours. According to one of his early biographers, the author of *Much Ado About Nothing* modelled his ineffable Constable upon an actual officer who lived in Buckinghamshire, not far from the Warwickshire that Shakespeare always regarded as his home.

THE TEXT OF THE EVERYMAN SHAKESPEARE

Background

THE EARLY PRINTINGS OF SHAKESPEARE'S WORKS

Many of us enjoy our first encounter with Shakespeare when we're introduced to *Julius Caesar* or *Macbeth* at school. It may therefore surprise us that neither of these tragedies could ever have been read, let alone studied, by most of the playwright's contemporaries. They began as scripts for performance and, along with seventeen other titles that never saw print during Shakespeare's lifetime, they made their inaugural appearance as 'literary' works seven years after his death, in the 1623 collection we know today as the First Folio.

The Folio contained thirty-six titles in all. Of these, half had been issued previously in the small paperbacks we now refer to as quartos.* Like several of the plays first published in the Folio, the most trustworthy of the quarto printings appear to have been set either from Shakespeare's own manuscripts or from faithful copies of them. It's not impossible that the poet himself prepared some of these works for the press, and it's intriguing to imagine him reviewing proof-pages as the words he'd written for actors to speak and embody were being transposed into the type that readers would filter through their eyes, minds, and imaginations. But, alas, there's no indisputable evidence that Shakespeare had any direct involvement with the publication of these early editions of his plays.

What, then, about the scripts that achieved print for the first

---

* Quartos derived their name from the four-leaf units of which these small books were comprised: large sheets of paper that had been folded twice after printing to yield four leaves, or eight pages. Folios, volumes with twice the page-size of quartos, were put together from two-leaf units: sheets that had been folded once after printing to yield four pages.

time in the Folio? Had the dramatist taken any steps to give the permanency of book form to those texts before he died? We don't know. All we can say is that when a fatal illness seized him in 1616, Shakespeare was denied any opportunities he might otherwise have taken to ensure that his 'insubstantial Pageants' survived the mortal who was now slipping into the 'dark Backward and Abysm of Time'.

Fortunately, two of the playwright's colleagues felt an obligation, as they put it, 'to procure his Orphans Guardians'. Sometime after his death John Heminge (or Heminges) and Henry Condell made arrangements to preserve Shakespeare's theatrical compositions in a manner that would keep them vibrant for posterity. They dedicated their endeavour to two noblemen who had helped see England's foremost acting company through some of its most trying vicissitudes. They solicited several poetic tributes for the volume, among them a now-famous eulogy by fellow writer Ben Jonson. They commissioned an engraved portrait of Shakespeare to adorn the frontispiece. And they did their utmost to display the author's dramatic works in a style that would both dignify them and make them accessible to 'the great Variety of Readers'.

As they readied Shakespeare's plays for the compositors who would set them into stately Folio columns, Heminge and Condell (or editors and scribes designated to carry out their wishes) revised and augmented many of the entrances, exits, and other stage directions in Shakespeare's manuscripts. They divided most of the works into acts, and many into both acts and scenes.* For a number of plays they appended 'Names of the Actors', or casts of characters. Meanwhile they made every effort to guarantee that the Folio printers had reliable copy-texts for each of the titles: authoritative manuscripts for the plays that had not been published previously, and good quarto printings (annotated in some instances to insert staging details, mark script changes, and add supplementary material) for the ones that had been issued prior to the Folio. For several titles they supplied texts that were

---

* The early quartos, reflecting the unbroken sequence that probably typified Elizabethan and Jacobean performances of the plays, had been printed without the structural demarcations usual in Renaissance editions of classical drama.

substantively different from, if not always demonstrably superior to, the quarto versions that preceded them.

Like even the most accurate of printings that preceded it, the Folio collection was flawed by minor blemishes. But it more than fulfilled the purpose of its generous-minded compilers: 'to keep the memory of so worthy a Friend and Fellow alive as was our Shakespeare'. In the process it provided a publishing model that remains instructive today.

MODERN EDITIONS OF THE PLAYS AND POEMS

When we compare the First Folio and its predecessors with the usual modern edition of Shakespeare's works, we're more apt to be impressed by the differences than by the similarities. Today's texts of Renaissance drama are normally produced in conformity with twentieth-century standards of punctuation and usage; as a consequence they look more neat, clean, and, to our eyes, 'right' than do the original printings. Thanks to an editorial tradition that extends back to the early eighteenth century, if not before, most of the rough spots in the early printings of Shakespeare have long been smoothed away. Textual scholars have ferreted out redundancies and eradicated inconsistencies. They've mended what they've perceived to be errors and oversights in the playscripts, and they've systematically attended to what they've construed as misreadings by the copyists and compositors who transmitted these playscripts to posterity. They've added '[Within]' brackets and other theatrical notations. They've revised stage directions they've judged incomplete or inadequate in the initial printings. They've regularized disparities in the speech headings. They've gone back to the playwright's sources and reinstated the 'proper' forms for many of the character and place names which a presumably hasty or inattentive author got 'wrong' as he conferred identities on his dramatis personae and stage locales. They've replaced obsolete words like *bankrout* with their modern heirs (in this case *bankrupt*). And in a multitude of other ways they've accommodated Shakespeare to the tastes, interests, and expectations of latter-day readers.

The results, on the whole, have been splendid. But interpreting the artistic designs of a complex writer is always problematical, and the task is especially challenging when that writer happens to have been a poet who felt unconstrained by many of the 'rules' that more conventional dramatists respected. The undertaking becomes further complicated when new rules, and new criteria of linguistic and social correctness, are imposed by subsequent generations of artists and critics.

To some degree in his own era, but even more in the neoclassical period (1660–1800) that came in its wake, Shakespeare's most ardent admirers thought it necessary to apologise for what Ben Jonson hinted at in his allusion to the 'small Latin, and less Greek' of an untutored prodigy. To be sure, the 'sweet Swan of Avon' sustained his popularity; in fact his reputation rose so steadily that by the end of the eighteenth century he'd eclipsed Jonson and his other peers and become the object of near-universal Bardolatry. But in the theatre most of his plays were being adapted in ways that were deemed advisable to tame their supposed wildness and bring them into conformity with the decorum of a society that took pride in its refinement. As one might expect, some of the attitudes that induced theatre proprietors to metamorphose an unpolished poet from the provinces into something closer to an urbane man of letters also influenced Shakespeare's editors. Persuaded that the dramatist's works were marred by crudities that needed expunging, they applied their ministrations to the canon with painstaking diligence.

Twentieth-century editors have moved away from many of the presuppositions that guided a succession of earlier improvers. But a glance at the textual apparatus accompanying virtually any modern publication of the plays and poems will show that emendations and editorial procedures deriving from such forebears as the sets published by Nicholas Rowe (1709), Alexander Pope (1723–5, 1728), Lewis Theobald (1733, 1740, 1757), Thomas Hanmer (1743–5, 1770–1), Samuel Johnson (1765), Edward Capell (1768), George Steevens (1773), and Edmond Malone (1790) retain a strong hold on today's renderings of the playwright's works. The consequence is a 'Shakespeare' who offers the tidiness we've come to expect in our libraries of treasured authors, but not necessarily the playwright a 1599 reader of the Second Quarto of *Romeo and Juliet* would still be able to recognize as a contemporary.

OLD LIGHT ON THE TOPIC

Over the last two decades we've learned from art curators that paintings by Old Masters such as Michelangelo and Rembrandt look a lot brighter when centuries of grime are removed from their surfaces – when hues that had become dulled with soot and other extraneous matter are allowed to radiate again with something approximating their pristine luminosity. We've learned from conductors like Sir Neville Marriner and Christopher Hogwood that there are aesthetic rewards to be gained from a return to the scorings and instruments with which Renaissance and Baroque musical compositions were first presented. We've learned from twentieth-century experiments in the performance of Shakespeare's plays that an open, multi-level stage, analogous to that on which the scripts were originally enacted, does more justice to their dramaturgical techniques than does a proscenium auditorium devised for works that came later in the development of Western theatre. We've learned from archaeological excavations in London's Bankside area that the foundations of playhouses such as the Rose and the Globe look rather different from what many historians had expected. And we're now learning from a close scrutiny of Shakespeare's texts that they too look different, and function differently, when we accept them for what they are and resist the impulse to 'normalize' features that strike us initially as quirky, unkempt, or unsophisticated.

The Aims that Guide the Everyman Text

Like other modern editions of the dramatist's plays and poems, The Everyman Shakespeare owes an incalculable debt to the scholarship that has led to so many excellent renderings of the author's works. But in an attempt to draw fresh inspiration from the spirit that animated those remarkable achievements at the outset, the Everyman edition departs in a number of respects from the usual post-Folio approach to the presentation of Shakespeare's texts.

RESTORING SOME OF THE NUANCES OF
RENAISSANCE PUNCTUATION

In its punctuation, Everyman attempts to give equal emphasis to sound and sense. In places where Renaissance practice calls for heavier punctuation than we'd normally employ – to mark the caesural pause in the middle of a line of verse, for instance – Everyman sometimes retains commas that other modern editions omit. Meanwhile, in places where current practice usually calls for the inclusion of commas – after vocatives and interjections such as 'O' and 'alas', say, or before 'Madam' or 'Sir' in phrases such as 'Ay Madam' or 'Yes Sir' – Everyman follows the original printings and omits them.

Occasionally the absence of a comma has a significant bearing on what an expression means, or can mean. At one point in *Othello*, for example, Iago tells the Moor 'marry patience' (IV.i.90). Inserting a comma after 'marry', as most of today's editions do, limits Iago's utterance to one that says 'Come now, have patience.' Leaving the clause as it stands in the Folio, the way the Everyman text does, permits Iago's words to have the additional, agonizingly ironic sense 'Be wed to Patience'.

The early texts generally deploy exclamation points quite sparingly, and Everyman follows suit. Everyman also follows the early editions, more often than not, when they use question marks in places that seem unusual by current standards: at the conclusion of what we'd normally treat as exclamations, for example, or at the ends of interrogative clauses in sentences that we'd ordinarily denote as questions in their entirety.

The early texts make no orthographic distinction between simple plurals and either singular or plural possessives, and there are times when the context doesn't indicate whether a word spelled *Sisters*, say, should be rendered *Sisters*, *Sisters'*, or *Sister's* in today's usage. In such situations the Everyman edition prints the word in the form modern usage prescribes for plurals.

REVIVING SOME OF THE FLEXIBILITY OF
RENAISSANCE SPELLING

Spelling had not become standardized by Shakespeare's time, and that meant that many words could take a variety of forms. Like

James Joyce and some of the other innovative prose and verse stylists of our own century, Shakespeare revelled in the freedom a largely unanchored language provided, and with that in mind Everyman retains original spelling forms (or adaptations of those forms that preserve their key distinctions from modern spellings) whenever there is any reason to suspect that they might have a bearing on how a word was intended to be pronounced or on what it meant, or could have meant, in the playwright's day. When there is any likelihood that multiple forms of the same word could be significant, moreover, the Everyman text mirrors the diversity to be found in the original printings.

In many cases this practice affects the personalities of Shakespeare's characters. One of the heroine's most familiar questions in *Romeo and Juliet* is 'What's in a Name?' For two and a half centuries readers – and as a consequence actors, directors, theatre audiences, and commentators – have been led to believe that Juliet was addressing this query to a Romeo named 'Montague'. In fact 'Montague' *was* the name Shakespeare found in his principal source for the play. For reasons that will become apparent to anyone who examines the tragedy in detail, however, the playwright changed his protagonist's surname to 'Mountague', a word that plays on both 'mount' and 'ague' (fever).* Setting aside an editorial practice that began with Lewis Theobald in the middle of the eighteenth century, Everyman resurrects the name the dramatist himself gave Juliet's lover.

Readers of *The Merchant of Venice* in the Everyman set will be amused to learn that the character modern editions usually identify as 'Lancelot' is in reality 'Launcelet', a name that calls attention to the clown's lusty 'little lance'. Like Costard in *Love's Labour's Lost*, another stage bumpkin who was probably played by the actor Will Kemp, Launcelet is an upright 'Member of the Commonwealth'; we eventually learn that he's left a pliant wench 'with Child'.

Readers of *Hamlet* will find that 'Fortinbras' (as the name of the Prince's Norwegian opposite is rendered in the First Folio and in

---

* For anyone who doubts that Shakespeare's alteration of Romeo's family name was part of a conscious artistic plan, it may be worth noting that 'Capulet', like 'Capilet' in *Twelfth Night* and *All's Well That Ends Well*, means 'small horse'.

most modern editions) appears in the earlier, authoritative 1604 Second Quarto of the play as 'Fortinbrasse'. In the opening scene of that text a surname that meant 'strong in arms' in French is introduced to the accompaniment of puns on *brazen*, in the phrase 'brazon Cannon', and on *metal*, in the phrase 'unimprooued mettle'. In the same play readers of the Everyman text will encounter 'Ostricke', the ostrich-like courtier who invites the Prince of Denmark to participate in the fateful fencing match that draws *Hamlet* to a close. Only in its final entrance direction for the obsequious fop does the Second Quarto call this character 'Osrick', the name he bears in all the Folio text's references to him and in usual modern editions of Shakespeare's most popular tragedy.

Readers of the Everyman *Macbeth* will discover that the fabled 'Weird Sisters' appear only as the 'weyward' or 'weyard' Sisters. Shakespeare and his contemporaries knew that in his *Chronicles of England, Scotland, and Ireland* Raphael Holinshed had used the term 'weird sisters' to describe the witches who accost Macbeth and Banquo on the heath; but presumably because he wished to play on *wayward*, the playwright changed their name to *weyward*. Like Samuel Johnson, who thought punning vulgar and lamented Shakespeare's proclivity to seduction by this 'fatal Cleopatra', Lewis Theobald saw no reason to retain the playwright's weyward spelling of the witches' name. He thus restored the 'correct' form from Holinshed, and editors ever since have generally done likewise.

In many instances Renaissance English had a single spelling for what we now define as two separate words. For example, *humane* combines the senses of 'human' and 'humane' in modern English. In the First Folio printing of *Macbeth* the protagonist's wife expresses a concern that her husband is 'too full o'th' Milke of humane kindnesse.' As she phrases it, *humane kindnesse* can mean several things, among them 'humankind-ness', 'human kindness', and 'humane kindness'. It is thus a reminder that to be true to his or her own 'kind' a human being must be 'kind' in the sense we now attach to 'humane'. To disregard this logic, as the protagonist and his wife will soon prove, is to disregard a principle as basic to the cosmos as the laws of gravity.

In a way that parallels *humane*, *bad* could mean either 'bad' or 'bade', *borne* either 'born' or 'borne', *ere* either 'ere' (before) or 'e'er' (ever), *least* either 'least' or 'lest', *lye* either 'lie' or 'lye', *nere* either 'ne'er' or 'near' (though the usual spellings for the latter were *neare* or *neere*), *powre* either 'pour' or 'power', *then* either 'than' or 'then', and *tide* either 'tide' or 'tied'.

There were a number of word-forms that functioned in Renaissance English as interchangeable doublets. *Travail* could mean 'travel', for example, and *travel* could mean 'travail'. By the same token, *deer* could mean *dear* and vice versa, *dew* could mean *due*, *hart* could mean *heart*, and (as we've already noted) *mettle* could mean *metal*.

A particularly interesting instance of the equivocal or double meanings some word-forms had in Shakespeare's time is *loose*, which can often become either 'loose' or 'lose' when we render it in modern English. In *The Comedy of Errors* when Antipholus of Syracuse compares himself to 'a Drop / Of Water that in the Ocean seeks another Drop' and then says he will 'loose' himself in quest of his long-lost twin, he means both (a) that he will release himself into a vast unknown, and (b) that he will lose his own identity, if necessary, to be reunited with the brother for whom he searches. On the other hand, in *Hamlet* when Polonius says he'll 'loose' his daughter to the Prince, he little suspects that by so doing he will also lose her.

In some cases the playwright employs word-forms that can be translated into words we wouldn't think of as related today: *sowre*, for instance, which can mean 'sour', 'sower', or 'sore', depending on the context. In other cases he uses forms that do have modern counterparts, but not counterparts with the same potential for multiple connotation. For example, *onely* usually means 'only' in the modern sense; but occasionally Shakespeare gives it a figurative, adverbial twist that would require a nonce word such as 'one-ly' to replicate in current English.

In a few cases Shakespeare employs word-forms that have only seeming equivalents in modern usage. For example, *abhominable* (derived, however incorrectly, from *ab*, 'away from', and *homine*, 'man'), which meant 'inhuman', 'nonhuman', or 'subhuman' to the poet and his contemporaries, is not the same word as our *abominable* (ill-omened, abhorrent). In his advice to the visiting players Hamlet complains about incompetent actors who imitate 'Humanity so abhominably' as to make the characters they depict seem unrecognizable as men. Modern readers who don't realize the distinction between Shakespeare's word and our own, and who see *abominable* on the page before them, don't register the full import of the Prince's satire.

Modern English treats as single words a number of word-forms that were normally spelled as two words in Shakespeare's time. What we render as *myself*, for example, and use primarily as a reflexive or intensifying pronoun, is almost invariably spelled *my self* in Shakespeare's works; so also with *her self*, *thy self*, *your self*, and *it self* (where *it* functions as *its* does today). Often there is no discernible difference between Shakespeare's usage and our own. At other times there is, however, as we are reminded when we come across a phrase such as 'our innocent self' in *Macbeth* and think how strained it would sound in modern parlance, or as we observe when we note how naturally the self is objectified in the balanced clauses of the Balcony Scene in *Romeo and Juliet*:

> Romeo, doffe thy name,
> And for thy name, which is no part of thee,
> Take all my selfe.

Yet another difference between Renaissance orthography and our own can be exemplified with words such as *today*, *tonight*, and *tomorrow*, which (unlike *yesterday*) were treated as two words in Shakespeare's time. In *Macbeth* when the Folio prints 'Duncan comes here to Night', the unattached *to* can function either as a preposition (with *Night* as its object, or in this case its destination) or as the first part of an infinitive (with *Night* operating figuratively as a verb). Consider the ambiguity a Renaissance reader would have detected in the original publication of one of the most celebrated soliloquies in all of Shakespeare:

> To morrow, and to morrow, and to morrow,
> Creeps in this petty pace from day to day,
> To the last Syllable of Recorded time:
> And all our yesterdayes, have lighted Fooles
> The way to dusty death.

Here, by implication, the route 'to morrow' is identical with 'the way to dusty death', a relationship we miss if we don't know that for Macbeth, and for the audiences who first heard these lines spoken, *to morrow* was not a single word but a potentially equivocal two-word phrase.

RECAPTURING THE ABILITY TO HEAR WITH OUR EYES

When we fail to recall that Shakespeare's scripts were designed initially to provide words for people to hear in the theatre, we sometimes overlook a fact that is fundamental to the artistic structure of a work like *Macbeth*: that the messages a sequence of sounds convey through the ear are, if anything, even more significant than the messages a sequence of letters, punctuation marks, and white spaces on a printed page transmit through the eye. A telling illustration of this point, and of the potential for ambiguous or multiple implication in any Shakespearean script, may be found in the dethronement scene of *Richard II*. When Henry Bullingbrook asks the King if he is ready to resign his crown, Richard replies 'I, no no I; for I must nothing be.' Here the punctuation in the 1608 Fourth Quarto (the earliest text to print this richly complex passage) permits each *I* to signify either 'ay' or 'I' (*I* being the usual spelling for 'ay' in Shakespeare's time). Understanding *I* to mean 'I' permits additional play on *no*, which can be heard (at least in its first occurrence) as 'know'. Meanwhile the second and third soundings of *I*, if not the first, can also be heard as 'eye'. In the context in which this line occurs, that sense echoes a thematically pertinent passage from Matthew 18:9: 'if thine eye offend thee, pluck it out'.

But these are not all the implications *I* can have here. It can also represent the Roman numeral for '1', which will soon be reduced, as Richard notes, to 'nothing' (0), along with the speaker's title, his worldly possessions, his manhood, and eventually his life. In Shakespeare's time, to become 'nothing' was, *inter alia*, to be emasculated, to be made a 'weaker vessel' (1 Peter 3:7) with 'no thing'. As the Fool in *King Lear* reminds another monarch who has abdicated his throne, a man in want of an 'I' is impotent, 'an O without a Figure' (I.iv.207). In addition to its other dimensions, then, Richard's reply is a statement that can be formulated mathematically, and in symbols that anticipate the binary system behind today's computer technology: '1, 0, 0, 1, for 1 must 0 be.'

Modern editions usually render Richard's line 'Ay, no; no, ay; for I must nothing be'. Presenting the line in that fashion makes good sense of what Richard is saying. But as we've seen, it doesn't make total sense of it, and it doesn't call attention to Richard's paradoxes in the same way that hearing or seeing three undifferentiated *I*'s is likely to have done for Shakespeare's contemporaries. Their culture was more attuned than ours is to the oral and aural dimensions of language, and if we want to appreciate the special qualities of their dramatic art we need to train ourselves to 'hear' the word-forms we see on the page. We must learn to recognize that for many of what we tend to think of as fixed linkages between sound and meaning (the vowel 'I', say, and the word 'eye'), there were alternative linkages (such as the vowel 'I' and the words 'I' and 'Ay') that could be just as pertinent to what the playwright was communicating through the ears of his theatre patrons at a given moment. As the word *audience* itself may help us to remember, people in Shakespeare's time normally spoke of 'hearing' rather than 'seeing' a play.

In its text of *Richard II*, the Everyman edition reproduces the title character's line as it appears in the early printings of the tragedy. Ideally the orthographic oddity of the repeated *I*'s will encourage today's readers to ponder Richard's utterance, and the play it epitomizes, as a characteristically Shakespearean enigma.

OTHER ASPECTS OF THE EVERYMAN TEXT
Now for a few words about other features of the Everyman text.

One of the first things readers will notice about this edition is its bountiful use of capitalized words. In this practice as in others, the Everyman exemplar is the First Folio, and especially the works in the Folio sections billed as 'Histories' and 'Tragedies'.* Everyman

---

* The quarto printings employ far fewer capital letters than does the Folio. Capitalization seems to have been regarded as a means of recognizing the status ascribed to certain words (*Noble*, for example, is almost always capitalized), titles (not only King, Queen, Duke, and Duchess, but Sir and Madam), genres (tragedies were regarded as more 'serious' than comedies in more than one sense), and forms of publication (quartos, being associated with ephemera such as 'plays', were not thought to be as 'grave' as the folios that bestowed immortality on 'works', writings that, in the words of Ben Jonson's eulogy to Shakespeare, were 'not of an age, but for all time').

makes no attempt to adhere to the Folio printings with literal exactitude. In some instances the Folio capitalizes words that the Everyman text of the same passage lowercases; in other instances Everyman capitalizes words not uppercased in the Folio. The objective is merely to suggest something of the flavour, and what appears to have been the rationale, of Renaissance capitalization, in the hope that today's audiences will be made continually aware that the works they're contemplating derive from an earlier epoch.

Readers will also notice that instead of cluttering the text with stage directions such as '[Aside]' or '[To Rosse]', the Everyman text employs unobtrusive dashes to indicate shifts in mode of address. In an effort to keep the page relatively clear of words not supplied by the original printings, Everyman also exercises restraint in its addition of editor-generated stage directions. Where the dialogue makes it obvious that a significant action occurs, the Everyman text inserts a square-bracketed phrase such as '[Fleance escapes]'. Where what the dialogue implies is subject to differing interpretations, however, the Everyman text provides a facing-page note to discuss the most plausible inferences.

Like other modern editions, the Everyman text combines into 'shared' verse lines (lines divided among two or more speakers) many of the part-lines to be found in the early publications of the plays. One exception to the usual modern procedure is that Everyman indents some lines that are not components of shared verses. At times, for example, the opening line of a scene stops short of the metrical norm, a pentameter (five-foot) or hexameter (six-foot) line comprised predominantly of iambic units (unstressed syllables followed by stressed ones). In such cases Everyman uses indentation as a reminder that scenes can begin as well as end in mid-line (an extension of the ancient convention that an epic commences *in media res*, 'in the midst of the action'). Everyman also uses indentation to reflect what appear to be pauses in the dialogue, either to allow other activity to transpire (as happens in *Macbeth*, II.iii.87, when a brief line 'What's the Business?' follows a Folio stage direction that reads, '*Bell rings. Enter Lady.*') or to permit a character to hesitate for a moment of reflection (as happens a few seconds later in the same scene when Macduff responds to a demand to 'Speak, speak' with the reply 'O gentle Lady, / 'Tis not for you to hear what I can speak').

Readers of the Everyman edition will note that many word-forms are printed with apostrophes to indicate contractions (*to't* for 'to it', for example, or *o'th'* for 'of the') or syllabic elisions (*look'd* for 'looked', for instance, or *nev'r* or *ne'er* for 'never'). In many cases these departures from ordinary spelling occur in verse contexts that call for the deletion of syllables which if voiced would result in minor violations of the metrical norm. Thus in *Twelfth Night*, II.iv.107, *loved* is syncopated to *lov'd* in Viola's statement 'My Father had a Daughter lov'd a Man'. On the other hand, in *A Midsummer Night's Dream*, II.i.26, *loved* is treated as a fully voiced two-syllable word in 'But she, perforce, withholds the loved Boy'. In situations such as these Everyman almost invariably retains the word-forms to be found in the early printings that have been adopted as control texts. At times this policy results in lines whose metre can be construed in different ways by different interpreters. In *A Midsummer Night's Dream*, III.ii.292, to cite one line for illustrative purposes, it could be argued that the first *Personage* should be syncopated to *Pers'nage* when Hermia says, 'And with her Personage, her tall Personage'. By the same token it could be maintained that words such as *even*, *Heaven* and *whether* should be syncopated in pronunciation when, as is usual, they occur in positions that would normally demand a sound with the metrical value of a single syllable. The frequency with which syllabic elisions crop up in the original editions of Shakespeare's works would seem to suggest that the playwright and his colleagues placed a premium on metrical regularity. At the same time, the frequent absence of syncopated or contracted word-forms in settings where the metre would lead us to expect them (*I am* is only rarely rendered as *I'm*, for example, though it continually appears in positions that invite compression to one syllable) could be viewed as evidence that Shakespeare was anything but rigid in such matters, and may even have consciously opted for the subtle variations that derive from occasional unstressed syllabic additions to an otherwise steady march of iambic feet. Given the metrical ambiguity of the early texts, it is difficult if not impossible to determine how 'smooth' the verse-speaking was intended to be in the theatres for which Shakespeare wrote his scripts. Rather than impose a fixed order that might be incompatible with the poet's own aesthetic principles, then, the Everyman text merely preserves the metrical inconsistencies to be observed in the Quarto and Folio printings of Shakespeare's plays and poems.

Everyman also retains many of the other anomalies in the early texts. In some instances this practice affects the way characters are depicted. In *A Midsummer Night's Dream*, for example, the ruler of Athens is usually identified in speech headings and stage directions as 'Theseus', but sometimes he is referred to by his title as 'Duke'. In the same play Oberon's merry sprite goes by two different names: 'Puck' and 'Robin Goodfellow'.

Readers of the Everyman edition will sometimes discover that characters they've known, or known about, for years don't appear in the original printings. When they open the pages of the Everyman *Macbeth*, for example, they'll learn that Shakespeare's audiences were unaware of any woman with the title 'Lady Macbeth'. In the only authoritative text we have of the Scottish tragedy, the protagonist's spouse goes by such names as 'Macbeth's Lady', 'Macbeth's Wife', or simply 'Lady', but at no time is she listed or mentioned as 'Lady Macbeth'. The same is true of the character usually designated 'Lady Capulet' in modern editions of *Romeo and Juliet*. 'Capulet's Wife' makes appearances as 'Mother', 'Old Lady', 'Lady', or simply 'Wife'; but she's never termed 'Lady Capulet', and her husband never treats her with the dignity such a title would connote.

Rather than 'correct' the grammar in Shakespeare's works to eliminate what modern usage would categorize as solecisms (as when Mercutio says 'my Wits faints' in *Romeo and Juliet*), the Everyman text leaves it intact. Among other things, this principle applies to instances in which archaic forms preserve idioms that differ slightly from related modern expressions (as in the clause 'you are too blame', where 'too' frequently functions as an adverb and 'blame' is used, not as a verb, but as an adjective roughly equivalent to 'blameworthy').

Finally, and most importantly, the Everyman edition leaves

unchanged any reading in the original text that is not manifestly erroneous. Unlike other modern renderings of Shakespeare's works, Everyman substitutes emendations only when obvious problems can be dealt with by obvious solutions.

The Everyman Text of Much Ado About Nothing

The earliest and most authoritative text of *Much Ado About Nothing* is a lightly punctuated quarto that came off the press in 1600. From all indications this edition was set primarily, if not entirely, from the playwright's 'foul papers' (in this case a relatively clean draft of the comedy that would have antedated any of the refinements and clarifications which occurred as the script was adapted for use as a performance promptbook), and an annotated exemplar of Q1 was almost certainly what lay behind the largely derivative *Much Ado* that emerged a couple of decades later in the First Folio.

The compilers of the 1623 Folio inserted act divisions – though they neglected to provide scene designations – in a theatrical score that had been published without segmentation in the Quarto. They deleted five brief passages from the Q1 text: I.i.319–20 ('and . . . her'), III.ii.35–38 ('or . . . Doublet'), IV.i.20 ('not . . . do'), IV.ii.19–22 ('BOTH . . . Villains.'), and V.iv.33 ('Here . . . Claudio.'). They added a handful of stage directions and modified several others, for the most part capably but at times erroneously. Meanwhile they incorporated dozens of small changes, among them an assortment of what were evidently intended as corrections of misreadings, omissions, or inconsistencies in the phrasing and punctuation of the 1600 printing. But few if any of the alterations the Folio editors and typesetters introduced would lead one to infer that they had access to a trustworthy roster of revisions either from the author or from the acting company that staged the original productions of Shakespeare's witty love-fest.

Notwithstanding some minor anomalies in its identification of the *dramatis personae*, the First Quarto appears to have been a conscientious and generally accurate rendering of the copy that issued from Shakespeare's pen. For that reason, and to a degree that sets Everyman apart from other twentieth-century redactions of the play, the *Much Ado About Nothing* in the present volume adheres with unusual fidelity to Q1, even in passages where that text seems to reflect the provisional first thoughts and the sometimes incompatible second thoughts of a theatre artist who, in his typical fashion, was still formulating and reformulating many aspects of the play he was devising as he committed ink to paper.

Everyman preserves in unaltered form the vast majority of Q1's speech headings and stage directions. Among other things, Everyman retains the two Quarto references to Leonato's wife; although Shakespeare never gives 'Innogen' a line of dialogue, he nevertheless includes her in the entrances that commence Acts I and II. By the same token Everyman reproduces Quarto speaker assignments that modern editions usually emend in II.i.105–8 (where the masked Benedick dances with Margaret prior to his encounter with Beatrice), in III.iii.188 (where Conrade can be construed as satirizing the illiterate watchmen who have just arrested him and Borachio), in V.iii.22 (where an unspecified 'Lord' pledges himself to a ritual that would seem most appropriate for Claudio), and in V.iv.98 (where, in an utterance that is perfectly in character for him, Leonato – rather than Benedick – tells Beatrice, 'Peace, I will stop your Mouth'). Everyman keeps Quarto forms such as 'Brother' and 'Old Man' for Antonio, 'Balthaser' for the singer whose name is usually spelled 'Balthasar' in today's editions, 'Counte' as well as 'County' for Count Claudio, 'Francis' and 'Friar' for Friar Francis, 'Bastard', 'Dun John', and 'John' for Don John, 'Pedro', 'Peter', and 'Prince' for Don Pedro, and 'Ursley' for Ursula.

To avoid confusion in III.v, IV.ii, and V.i, Everyman regularizes to 'Dogberry' and 'Verges' a variety of references to the Constable and his elderly Headborough (parish officer). In several instances the Quarto identifies members of the Watch either by type – for example, 'Keeper' (gaoler or police warden) and 'Andrew' (Merry Andrew, a generic name for a clown) – or by the surnames of the actors who would have portrayed them in Shakespeare's theatre (Kemp and Cowley). In a similar way Everyman normalizes to 'Margaret' a 'Margarite' spelling in V.ii.25.

In accordance with its usual practice, Everyman retains such

Elizabethan orthographic forms as *affoord*, *boorded*, *Coosins*, *counsaile*, *Coze*, *daunce*, *dispight*, *Divel*, *doest*, *doost*, *dooth*, *foorth*, *Lanthorn*, *Maister*, *no body*, *shew*, *sixt*, *spight*, *valiaunt*, *vildly*, *woont*, and *woorth*. In its text of *Much Ado About Nothing* Everyman also preserves a number of *im-* and *in-* prefixes for words that normally begin with *em-* or *en-* today: *imbrace*, *imployer*, *Imployment*, *incounter*, *indear'd*, *Indurance*, *indure*, *inraged*, *intirely*, and *intreat*.

In a few passages Everyman emends the First Quarto text. For each item in the following list the first entry is the reading adopted by Everyman (with a parenthetical reference to F1, F2, or F3 if the non-Q1 reading derives from the 1623 First Folio, the 1632 Second Folio, or the 1663 Third Folio), and the second entry is the reading to be found in the 1600 Quarto.

I.i.		
	66	**that;** (that. F1) that,
	73	**Creature.** (F1) creature,
	178	**High** hie
	311	**War-thoughts** war-thoughts,
	312	**vacant,** vacant:
I.iii.	50	**Brother's** (F1) bothers
	76	*Exeunt* (F1) *exit*
II.i.	90	*Maskers . . . Drum.* This stage direction appears only in F1.
	93	**So** So,
	209	**Fowl,** foul?
	231	**Bird's** birds (so also in II.i.239)
	272	*Enter . . . Hero.* (F1) *Enter Claudio and Beatrice.*
	314	**obtained.** obtained,
	392	**too,** too
II.ii.	58	*Exeunt exit*
II.iii.	27	**an** (F1) and
	148–49	**us of** (F1) of us
	233	*Exeunt* (F1) Omitted from Q1.
III.i.	107	*Exeunt* (F2) *Exit* F1; omitted from Q1.
III.ii.	55	PRINCE (F1) BENE.
	135	*Exeunt* (F2) *Exit* F1; omitted from Q1.
III.iii.	87	**Statues** (F1) statutes
	95	**Fellows'** fellows

III.iv.	18	**in** (F1) it
III.v.	3	DOGBERRY CONST. DOG. (so also, or 'CONST. DO.', in III.v.7, 10, 18, 21, 27, 37, 48, 50, 57)
	8	VERGES HEADB. (so also, or 'HEAD.', in III.v.15, 32, 34, 66)
IV.i.	146	**not,** not
	156	**Lady;** lady, **mark'd** mark'd,
	178	**Mercy.** (F1) mercy,
	204	**Family's** families
	220	**ours.** ours,
	236	**Lady's** ladies
	253	*Exeunt* exit
	272	**not;** not,
IV.ii.	1	DOGBERRY KEEPER
	2	VERGES COWLEY (so also in IV.ii.5)
	4	DOGBERRY ANDREW
	10	DOGBERRY KEMP (so also, or 'KE.,' in IV.ii.13, 17, 20, 28, 33, 39, 45, 49, 55, 61, 75, 80)
	56	VERGES CONST.
	73	DOGBERRY CONSTABLE
	74	CONRADE COULEY (so also in IV.ii.79)
	95	*Exeunt Exit*
V.i.	6	**Ear,** ear
	114	**Brother,** (F1) brother
	171	**there's** theirs
	184	**on** (F1) one
	210	DOGBERRY CONST. (so also in V.i.219, 260, 312, 324, 328, 331)
	265	VERGES CON. 2
V.ii.	25	*Margaret* (F3) *Margarite*
	43	*Enter Beatrice.* Placed as in F1; Q1 provides an entrance for Beatrice after Benedick addresses her.
	51	**pass'd** past
	95	**Praiseworthy** praise worthy
	112	**Uncle's** uncles *Exeunt* (F1) *exit*
V.iii.	10	**domb** (F1) dead

In a number of passages that distinguish it from other modern editions, the Everyman text retains First Quarto readings, spelling forms, or punctuation styles. For each listing below, the first entry, in boldface, is the reading to be found in Everyman; the second entry, in regular type, is the reading adopted by some if not most of today's editions.

I.i.   0 **Innogen his Wife** Omitted from most editions
                 (compare II.i.0).
             1 **Peter** Pedro (so also in I.i.11)
             9 **self,** self
            10 **here,** here
            23 **shew** show (compare I.ii.7, II.i.51, 232, II.iii.117,
                 199, 232, III.i.102, III.ii.6, 122, 131, III.iii.64, 126,
                 IV.i.35, 40, 52, 219, 262, IV.ii.71, V.i.95, V.ii.37)
            29 **,then** than (compare I.iii.28, 30, III.i.116, III.iii.150,
                 IV.ii.65, V.i.248, V.ii.86, V.iii.33)
            42 **Burbolt** bird-bolt
            51 **Vittaile** victual
         52–53 **Trencher Man** trencherman
            60 **Stuffing well** stuffing – well,
            91 **Benedict** Benedick
            96 **hote** hot (F1)
            97 **John** [Don] John
            99 **Trouble:** trouble?
           100 **incounter** encounter (compare I.i.335, III.iii.163)
           113 **full Benedick** full, Benedick
           122 **deer** dear (so also in I.i.133, 153, IV.i.45, 338)
           126 **Curtesy** courtesy (so also in I.i.128)
           129 **onelie** only (so also in I.i.179; compare I.i.305)
           144 **Parrat** parrot-
           152 **all.** all,
                 Leonato, Leonato –
           153 **Benedick,** Benedick –
           155 **Moneth** month
           163 **you,** you;
           181 **unhansome** unhandsome (compare IV.ii.93,
                 V.iv.104)
           182 **other,** other
           186 **enquier** inquire
           212 **Enter ... Bastard.** Most editions omit '*John the
                 Bastard*'.
           244 **despight** despite (compare II.i.402)
           245 **Part,** part
           260 **loose** lose (so also in III.i.32)
           279 **Horn** horn-
           289 **you.** you –

290 **House** house, *or* house –
291 **it.** it –
305 **onely** only (so also in II.i.406, II.ii.31, III.i.17, 23, 92,
          III.iii.44, III.iv.76, IV.i.1, V.ii.53; compare I.i.129)
330 **to night** tonight (compare II.i.177, 374, II.iii.92, 97,
          III.i.101, 103, III.ii.34, 35, 89, 113, 115, 124, 125,
          III.iii.102, 103, 155, III.v.34, V.i.293, 294, 304,
          305, 338, 339, 340, V.iv.37, 130)

I.ii.
      4 **dreampt** dreamt (so also in II.i.363)
      6 **Events** event (F1)
      9 **thick** thick-
     23 **withall** withal
     28 **Shill** skill (F1)

I.iii.
      1 **goodyear** good-year
     11 **bornc** born (so also in II.i.350, 353, V.ii.42)
     12 **Medicine,** medicine
     33 **plain** plain-
     34 **Mussel** muzzle
     42 *Enter Borachio.* Usually placed after 'here?'
     50 **Mary** marry, (compare I.iii.55, II.i.291, II.iii.90,
          III.iii.88, III.v.3, 7, 34, IV.i.80, 208, IV.ii.4, 10, 27,
          39, 52, V.i.53, 55, 219)
     55 **one** on
     65 **Countc** Count (compare II.i.1, 13, 219, 298, 300,
          305, 306, 316, 319, II.ii.1, 34, III.iv.63, IV.i.10, 17,
          88, 318, V.i.238)
     70 **me.** me?

II.i.
      0 **his Wife,** Omitted in most editions (compare I.i.0).
          Niece, Most editions follow this word with '[*Marga-
          ret, Ursula*]'.
     43 **Berrord** bearward *or* bearherd
     64 **Metal** mettle
     69 **Kinred** kindred
     90 *Enter . . . Drum. Enter Prince, [Don] Pedro, Claudio,
          and Benedick, and [Don] John, [and Borachio as
          Maskers, with a Drum].*
     91 **about** a bout
     96 **company.** company?
    105 BENEDICK [BALTHASAR] *or* [BORACHIO] (so also in
          II.i.108, 110)
    122 **ill well** ill-well
    190 **Claudio.** Claudio?
    205 **Blindman** blind man
    225 **Goodwill** good will

247 **Indurance** endurance (compare II.i.286, 365,
II.iii.255, III.iii.39)
253 **huddleing** huddling
283 **Imployment** employment (compare V.ii.32)
319 **Qu** cue
320 **Herault** herald
322 **much?** much.
329 **it,** it –
351 **No** No,
402 **dispight** despite (so also in II.ii.32, III.ii.68, III.iv.90,
V.i.75; compare I.i.244)

II.ii.   28 **enough,** enough
33 **Hour,** hour
38 **Match)** match,

II.iii.   21 **Ortography** orthography
45 **Kid-Fox** hid-fox
65 **more:** more,
88 **live** lief
90 **hear Balthaser** hear, Balthasar
99 **Foul** fowl
110 **inraged** enraged
170 **End: he** end? He

III.i.   0 *Ursley Ursula* (so also in III.i.4)
37 **intirely** entirely
38 **new** new-
40 **intreat** entreat (compare V.iv.18)
56 **indear'd** endear'd
60 **featured** featur'd (F1)
61 **fair** fair-
63 **Antique** antic (compare V.i.95)
83 **counsaile** counsel (compare III.i.102, III.iii.95,
IV.i.100, V.i.3, 5, 21, 23, 31)
96 **bearing** bearing,
109 **adew** adieu

III.ii.   29 **cannot** can
36 **Germaine** German
Waste waist
97–98 **(I . . . Heart),** I . . . heart
115 **her, then** her then,
125 **her** her,

III.iii.   11 WATCH 1 1 WATCH.
17 WATCH 2 2 WATCH. (so also in III.iii.28)
Maister master (compare III.iii.179, IV.ii.8, 17, 18,

		22, 69, 82, V.i.232, V.iii.24)
	25	**Lanthorn** lantern
	40	WATCH [2] WATCH. (so also in III.iii.48, 53, 59, 74, 97, 106, 116, 135)
	85	**birlady** By'r Lady (so also in III.iii.92, III.iv.83)
	117	**Dun** Don
	137	**gentle Man** gentleman
	148	**Club.** club?
	175	**o'er night** o'er-night
	177	WATCH 1 [2] WATCH. (so also in III.iii.183, 186)
	179	WATCH 2 [1] WATCH.
	181	**Lechery,** lechery
	188	CONRADE [2 WATCH.]
III.iv.	16	**Millaine's** Milan's
	17	**exceeds** cxcccds,
	22	**blewish** blueish
	23	**fine** fine,
		queint quaint,
		graceful graceful,
	33	**saving** 'saving
	35	**Husband.** husband'.
	54	**hey** heigh
	81	**holy** holy-
III.v.	11	**of** off (compare IV.ii.74, V.i.96)
	12	**blunt, as** blunt as,
	27	**and't** and
	38	**talking** talking,
	44	**worshipp'd,** worshipp'd:
	69	**Noncome** non-come
IV.i.	1	**brief,** brief —
	5	**Lady.** lady?
	7	**her.** (her; Q1, F1) her,
		Friar, Friar; *or* Friar.
	10	**Counte.** count?
	49	**imbrace** embrace
	52	**shewed** show'd
	55	**thee seeming,** thee, Seeming!
		it, it:
	67	**True,** True!
	76	**me how** me. How
		beset. beset! *or* beset?
	94	**named** nam'd
	100	**Heart?** heart!

90 **Anthony.** Antony – (so also in V.i.98)
95 **antiquely** anticly (compare III.i.63)
96 **of** off (compare III.v.11)
97 **Enemies** enemies –
   durst. durst –
98 **all.** all –
105 **Lord.** lord –
106 **No** No, *or* No?
108 **See** See,
120 **high** high –
124 **Doest** Dost
134 **me,** me.
139 **more,** more:
144 **ieast** jest
154 **Calve's** calf's
181 **All** All,
185 **Yea** Yea,
187 **Mind,** mind;
189 **Braggards** braggarts
190 **which** which,
   thanked thankcd,
202 **is,** is
203 **Hose,** hose
207 **up** up,
211 **nere** ne'er
253 **dronk** drunk
285 **Waight** weight
301 **over Kindness** over-kindness
308 **Hired** Hir'd
320 **hard** hard-

V.ii.   2 **Hands,** hands
         9 **me,** why me? Why,
        10 **Stairs.** stairs?
        32 **Imployer** employer
        40 **babling** babbling
        49 **Then,** 'Then'
           now, and now. And
        51 **is,** is
        62 **him,** him
        70 **Epithite** epithet
        86 **rings,** rings

V.iii.   2 LORD [A] LORD
         3 **Done** [CLAUDIO] Done
        10 **domb** dumb

11 CLAUDIO **Now** Now
17 **groan.** groan,
22 LORD [CLAUDIO]
23 **Right** rite
32 **speeds** speed's

V.iv.   0 Most of today's editions also add Beatrice to the roster
of *dramatis personae* in this entrance direction.
5 **appears,** appears
7 **sorts** sort (F1)
12 **masked** mask'd (F1)
26 **Claudio** Claudio, (F1)
Prince, but prince. But
40 **matter?** matter,
42 **Cloudiness.** cloudiness?
56 **No** No,
60 **liv'd** liv'd,
Wife, wife;
61 **loved** lov'd (F1)
73 **Name, what** Name. What
75 **Claudio,** Claudio
78 **Cousin** cousin,
82 **matter, then** matter. Then
88 **Fashioned** Fashion'd
98 LEONATO [BENEDICK]
102 **Humour, dost** humour. Dost
107 **it, and** it; and
120 **Friends, let's** friends. Let's
124 **Word, therefore** word. Therefore
126 **Wife, there** wife. There
132 *Dance. Dance.* [*Exeunt.*]

MUCH ADO ABOUT NOTHING

NAMES OF THE ACTORS

LEONATO, Governor of Messina
INNOGEN, his Wife
ANTONIO, his Brother
HERO, his Daughter
BEATRICE, his Niece

DON PEDRO, Prince of Aragon
DON JOHN, his bastard Brother
BENEDICK, a Lord of Padua
CLAUDIO, a young Lord of Florence

BALTHASER [BALTHASAR], a Singer, attendant on Don Pedro

BORACHIO
CONRADE } Followers of Don John

MARGARET
URSULA [URSLEY] } Gentlewomen attendant on Hero

FRIAR FRANCIS
DOGBERRY, Master Constable
VERGES, a Headborough
FIRST WATCH
SECOND WATCH

SEXTON
BOY
LORD

MESSENGERS
MUSICIANS
ATTENDANTS

I.i. This scene takes place near the house of Leonato, the Governor of Messina, a seaport in northeastern Sicily.

S.D. **Innogen, his Wife** Since this character is given no lines and is never referred to in the dialogue of the play, editors normally omit her from the two stage directions in which she appears (the other is at the beginning of II.i). It may be, however, that Shakespeare intended to present Leonato as a governor whose wife puts in at least two ceremonial appearances, even though she has no speaking role in the ensuing action.

1 **Don Peter** an anglicized version of Don Pedro, a nobleman from Arragon (Aragon, a region in northeastern Spain). Only here and in line 11 does this form of the name occur. Evidently Shakespeare decided, shortly after he began composing the text, to use the Spanish form of the name (though he retained Don John rather than reverting to Don Juan). By the time the play was ready for performance, the two initial references to 'Don Peter' may have been regularized to 'Don Pedro'; it is possible, however, that Shakespeare wished to introduce this character to the audience by the English version of his name.

3 **by this** by this time.

4 **three Leagues** nine miles.

6 **Action** military engagement.

7 **sort** rank or degree.

8 **Name** prominence, rank.

10 **find here** read in this letter.

13–14 **equally rememb'red** borne in mind and rewarded in a manner that matches his merit.

15 **beyond . . . Age** in a way that surpasses what one of his youthfulness would have been expected to do.

15–16 **in . . . Lamb** while appearing to be no more ferocious (lion-like) than a lamb (proverbial for gentleness). *Lion* plays on *Leonato* ('lionate'), the name of the Governor the Messenger addresses.

17 **bett'red Expectation** exceeded what was anticipated from him.

23 **modest enough** sufficiently maiden-like in its restraint and humility. Here as elsewhere, *shew* (show) hints at an apthetic form of *eschew* (shun); compare III.ii.130–31.

ACT I

Scene 1

Enter Leonato, Governor of Messina, Innogen his Wife, Hero
his Daughter, and Beatrice his Niece, with a Messenger.

LEONATO I learn in this Letter, that Don Peter of
Arragon comes this Night to Messina.

MESSENGER He is very near by this, he was not
three Leagues off when I left him.

LEONATO How many Gentlemen have you lost in this   5
Action?

MESSENGER But few of any sort, and none of
Name.

LEONATO A Victory is twice it self, when the
Achiever brings home full Numbers. I find here,   10
that Don Peter hath bestowed much Honour on a
young Florentine called Claudio.

MESSENGER Much deserv'd on his part, and equally
rememb'red by Don Pedro, he hath borne himself
beyond the Promise of his Age, doing in the   15
Figure of a Lamb of Feats of a Lion; he hath
indeed better bett'red Expectation than you
must expect of me to tell you how.

LEONATO He hath an Uncle here in Messina will
be very much glad of it.   20

MESSENGER I have already delivered him Letters,
and there appears much Joy in him, even so much
that Joy could not shew it self modest enough

24   **a Badge of Bitterness**   a response (weeping) that would
        normally signify that the recipient had received bad news
        rather than the 'better' tidings (line 17) that Claudio's uncle
        did in fact enjoy.

26   **Measure**   quantity (with a reminder that the outburst did not
        exhibit 'measure' in another sense: moderation).

27   **kind**   in kind, true to the nature of that kind of man.

29–30   **How . . . Weeping**   Reverberations of this statement will sound
        through much of the later action of the play.

29   **then**   Leonato probably means 'than'; but the Quarto spelling
        and punctuation are also compatible with the usual modern
        sense of *then*.

31   **Mountanto**   an Italian name that refers to (a) an upright thrust
        in duelling (the *montanto*), and (b) a mounting or strutting
        posture. Compare *Love's Labour's Lost*, IV.i.1–4. In the early
        printings of *Romeo and Juliet* Romeo's surname is spelled
        Mountague.

35   **What**   what man; who. See the note to II.i.137.

36   **Benedick**   a name that derives from *Benedictus*, 'blessed', and is
        thus related to *Beatrice*, from *Beatrix*, 'she who blesses'.
        Beatrice was probably pronounced 'Bettris', and thus may
        have been hinted at in lines 16–19.

37   **pleasant**   jocular, mirthful.

39   **Bills**   public notices, placards, with wordplay on (a) a
        long-staved weapon, (b) a farm implement, and (c) a bird's
        bill (beak).

40   **at the Flight**   (a) in the shooting of light arrows, and (b) in
        fleeing, taking wing like a mounting Cupid.

41   **Fool**   professional court jtester.

41–42   **subscrib'd for Cupid**   undertook the challenge, signing up in the
        name of Cupid, the God of Love.

42   **Burbolt**   a blunt-headed arrow, a bird-bolt, (a) to be used to
        shoot fowl at short distances, and (b) harmless enough to be
        handled by fools and children. Compare *Twelfth Night*,
        I.v.102–3.

46   **tax**   take to task, chide, censure, charge.

47   **meet with you**   even (meted) with you. Leonato puns on *mate*
        and on the kind of *meat* ('Killing') Beatrice was referring to in
        lines 43–45. Compare line 125, and see the note to line 36.

without a Badge of Bitterness.

LEONATO   Did he break out into Tears?   25

MESSENGER   In great Measure.

LEONATO   A kind Overflow of Kindness; there are
no Faces truer than those that are so wash'd;
how much better is it to weep at Joy, then to
joy at weeping.   30

BEATRICE   I pray you, is Signior Mountanto
return'd from the Wars or no?

MESSENGER   I know none of that Name, Lady, there
was none such in the Army of any sort.

LEONATO   What is he that you ask for, Niece?   35

HERO   My Cousin means Signior Benedick of Padua.

MESSENGER   O he's return'd, and as pleasant as
ever he was.

BEATRICE   He set up his Bills here in Messina,
and challeng'd Cupid at the Flight, and my   40
Uncle's Fool reading the Challenge subscrib'd
for Cupid, and challeng'd him at the Burbolt.
I pray you, how many hath he kill'd and eaten
in these Wars? But how many hath he kill'd? for
indeed I promised to eat all of his Killing.   45

LEONATO   Faith, Niece, you tax Signior Benedick
too much, but he'll be meet with you, I doubt
it not.

MESSENGER   He hath done good Service, Lady, in
these Wars.   50

BEATRICE   You had musty Vittaile, and he hath
holp to eat it; he is a very valiaunt Trencher

---

51   **musty Vittaile**   stale victuals (food), with wordplay on *meet*.

52   **holp**   helped.

52–53 **valiaunt Trencher Man**   (a) a man who serves with (line 49) or
partakes plentifully of the trencher (a wooden serving platter),
or (b) a common soldier who digs trenches, as opposed to (c)
a knightly gentleman who uses and defends trenches valiantly
in the heat of battle.

53   **Stomach**   (a) appetite, with word play on (b) courage ('guts'), a sense Beatrice denies to Benedick.

55   **to a**   Beatrice plays on *too*; her phrase can mean either (a) in combat with, or (b) in comparison to. She is probably alluding as well to other kinds of manliness 'to a Lady'.

60   **stuff'd Man**   the kind of man a taxidermist might make for mounting as a game trophy. In III.iv.65–66 *stuff'd* will take on additional senses.

        Stuffing well   both (a) 'stuffing, well', and (b) 'fitting or filling up well [properly]'. Most of today's editions supply a comma or a dash between these words; the early texts contain no punctuation.

61   **mortal**   either (a) subject to being killed, stuffed, and mounted like a game animal, or (b) limited to the frailties of the human condition.

62   **mistake**   mis-take, misconstrue. In the exchange that follows (lines 63–73) Benedick and Beatrice are compared to jousting knights.

67   **five Wits**   either (a) five senses, or (b) faculties of memory, fantasy, judgment, imagination, and common wit (both common sense, as in line 69, and an ability to utter witticisms).

68   **halting**   limping, wounded.

70   **Difference**   defining distinction. Beatrice's phrasing is a reminder of the kind of *Difference* (quarrel) that typifies her dealings with Benedick. It is also an allusion to a heraldic term for a variation that distinguishes the coat of arms of a junior member or branch of a family from the arms of the main line.

72   **hath left**   both (a) has inherited or bequeathed (see the note to line 70), and (b) has remaining.

        known   either (a) acknowledged for, and (b) recognizable as. Beatrice may also be punning on carnal knowledge, a sense that would befit a genital meaning of *Wit* (line 69).

74   **sworn Brother**   confirmed brother-in-arms, one who has vowed to assist his fellow knight in all contingencies, even in an expedition to Hell (lines 82–84).

Man, he hath an excellent Stomach.

MESSENGER And a good Soldier too, Lady.

BEATRICE And a good Soldier to a Lady, but what   55
is he to a Lord?

MESSENGER A Lord to a Lord, a Man to a Man,
stuff'd with all honourable Virtues.

BEATRICE It is so indeed, he is no less than a
stuff'd Man; but for the Stuffing well, we are   60
all mortal.

LEONATO You must not, Sir, mistake my Niece;
there is a kind of merry War betwixt Signior
Benedick and her, they never meet but there's a
Skirmish of Wit between them.   65

BEATRICE Alas he gets nothing by that; in our
last Conflict, four of his five Wits went
halting off, and now is the whole Man govern'd
with one, so that if he have Wit enough to keep
himself warm, let him bear it for a Difference   70
between himself and his Horse, for it is all
the Wealth that he hath left to be known a
reasonable Creature. Who is his Companion now?
he hath every Month a new sworn Brother.   75

MESSENGER Is't possible?

BEATRICE Very easily possible; he wears his
Faith but as the Fashion of his Hat, it ever
changes with the next Block.

---

77 **Faith** (a) fidelity to his vows, loyalty, and (b) religion.

78 **Block** wooden mould for the shaping (fashioning) of hats.
Beatrice is implying that anyone who would be the 'sworn
Brother' of such a man as Benedick is a blockhead.

79–80 **in your Books** in your favour (good books). Beatrice gives the phrase a literal twist in her reply (line 81). The Messenger's phrase pertains to (a) fellowship (referring to members enrolled in the books of a college), (b) heraldry (referring to names listed in a register of knights and other members of the noble classes), (c) credit-worthiness (referring to a tradesman's roster of reliable customers), and (d) virtue (referring to those inscribed in the 'book of life' in Revelation 3:5).

81 **and** if. *Study* means 'library'.

83 **Squarer** quarrelsome brawler (one prone to squaring off in skirmishes). Beatrice is probably punning on (a) the kind of 'Block' referred to in line 78, and (b) *Squire* (young armour-bearing attendant to a knight). Lines 82–84 anticipate II.i.274–84.

86 **Claudio** In light of what Beatrice has said in lines 66–68, it is amusing that Benedick's companion has a name that means 'halting' or 'lame' in Latin.

89 **presently** instantly.

91 **Benedict** Beatrice puns on Benedick's name. See the note to line 36. She may be referring (a) to a *benedict* as a mild laxative or purge, and suggesting that his association with Benedick has afflicted Claudio with the 'runs' (line 89), hinting both at diarrhoea and at the flight of a coward. She may also be alluding (b) to the Benedictine order, which specialized in the exorcizing of demonic spirits (thought to be the cause of madness); if so, she is suggesting that Claudio will be in need of a *benedict* (exorcist) if he spends too much time with Benedick. It is also conceivable that she is referring (c) to the *carduus benedictus*, a 'blessed thistle' thought to be a panacea (a cure for all the afflictions Benedick might visit on his companion). Compare III.iv.74–82. By 'mad', Beatrice may be suggesting that Benedick is addicted to whoremongering, paying 'a thousand pound' a year to 'pound' harlots; she may also be calling attention to the insanity caused by syphilis, one byproduct of whoring.

94 **hold friends with you** do my best to remain on amicable terms with you [to avoid incurring the danger of your displeasure].

95 **run mad** become infatuated with love's passions and yield to wantonness. See the note to line 91.

MESSENGER   I see, Lady, the Gentleman is not in
your Books.   80
BEATRICE   No, and he were, I would burn my Study.
But I pray you, who is his Companion? Is there
no young Squarer now that will make a Voyage
with him to the Divel?
MESSENGER   He is most in the company of the   85
right noble Claudio.
BEATRICE`   O Lord, he will hang upon him like a
Disease; he is sooner caught than the
Pestilence, and the Taker runs presently mad.
God help the noble Claudio, if he have caught   90
the Benedict, it will cost him a thousand
Pound ere 'a be cured.
MESSENGER   I will hold friends with you, Lady.
BEATRICE   Do, good Friend.
LEONATO   You will never run mad, Niece.   95
BEATRICE   No, not till a hote January.
MESSENGER   Don Pedro is approach'd.

Enter Don Pedro, Claudio, Benedick, Balthasar,
and John the Bastard.

PEDRO   Good Signior Leonato, are you come to
meet your Trouble: the Fashion of the World is
to avoid Cost, and you incounter it.   100
LEONATO   Never came Trouble to my House in the
Likeness of your Grace, for Trouble being

---

96   **hote**   hot (perhaps with wordplay on the French word *haut*,
         'high' or 'haughty'), both in temperature and in the lusts
         overheated weather can induce.

99   **meet your Trouble**   meet those who will cause you trouble
         (inconvenience). Don Pedro's words will prove prophetic in a
         way he little suspects.

100   **incounter**   encounter, embrace. See the note to line 335.
         Fashion (line 99) echoes line 77; *Cost* echoes lines 90–92.

104 **abides** stays, remains.

106 **Charge** (a) burden, duty (as a gracious host), and (b) cost.

112 **a Child** too young to jeopardize my wife's chastity.

113 **have it full Benedick** have been replied to in kind, and with a full measure of Benedick's 'pleasant' manner (line 37). Compare lines 47, 60.

114 **what you are** what kind of threat you are to the husbands of the world (as implied in lines 111–12). *Man* echoes lines 54–61.

115 **fathers her self** provides herself with a father (proclaims her father's identity) through her own appearance and manner (as explained in the sentence that follows, lines 115–16), so much so indeed that she seems identical with, or on an equal footing with, her own father. In line 116 *Father* can mean 'spiritual authority', 'priest'.

118 **his Head** both (a) his exact appearance (that of a white-haired man), and (b) his wisdom (the ornament of his age). Benedick may also be saying that Beatrice is too wilful to allow any man, even one so noble as Messina's governor, to be her 'Head' in marriage (an echo of Ephesians 5:23, where the Apostle Paul says that 'the husband is the head of the wife, even as Christ is the head of the church').

121 **marks you** pays any attention to you, takes you seriously.

122 **Disdain** contemptuous aloofness.
deer both (a) deer (here a doe), and (b) dear. See the note to line 133, and compare line 153.

125 **meet Food** suitable nourishment. Like her uncle, Beatrice puns on *meat*. Compare lines 44–53, 64–65, 98–99.

126 **convert** both (a) be transformed, and (b) experience a conversion (change of heart). *Curtesy* (courtesy) plays on *cur*, a word that is associated with fawning flatterers in *Julius Caesar*, III.i.35–43, and in *The Merchant of Venice*, I.iii.112–30.

128 **Turncoat** traitor (like the 'base Spaniel' curs who kneel before Caesar as they prepare to assassinate him), person who shifts allegiance by reversing the side of his coat that he displays. Benedick puns on *convert* (line 126), whose Latin roots yield the sense 'turn with'.

129 **onelie** only, but here with a Quarto spelling that may indicate worldplay on *one* and *lie*.

gone, Comfort should remain: but when you
depart from me, Sorrow abides, and Happiness
takes his leave.   105

PEDRO   You embrace your Charge too willingly: I
think this is your Daughter.

LEONATO   Her Mother hath many times told me so.

BENEDICK   Were you in doubt, Sir, that you ask'd
her?   110

LEONATO   Signior Benedick, no, for then were you
a Child.

PEDRO   You have it full Benedick, we may guess
by this what you are, being a Man. Truly the
Lady fathers her self. — Be happy, Lady, for   115
you are like an honourable Father.

BENEDICK   If Signior Leonato be her Father, she
would not have his Head on her Shoulders for
all Messina, as like him as she is.

BEATRICE   I wonder that you will still be talking,   120
Signior Benedick, no body marks you.

BENEDICK   What, my deer Lady Disdain! are you
yet living?

BEATRICE   Is it possible Disdain should die,
while she hath such meet Food to feed it as   125
Signior Benedick? Curtesy it self must convert
to Disdain if you come in her Presence.

BENEDICK   Then is Curtesy a Turncoat. But it
is certain I am loved of all Ladies, onelie you
excepted: and I would I could find in my Heart   130

131   **hard Heart** a heart inured against conversion [to love]. Benedick alludes to the biblical sense of this phrase (as in Exodus 4:21, John 12:40, and Romans 9:18), to imply that he cannot be converted from disdain to 'Curtesy'. The mock prayer in lines 130–32 will soon be answered in a way the speaker little recognizes himself to intend.

133   **deer Happiness** dear (priceless) benefit. Here *deer* plays sardonically on the sense of *dear* that relates to endearment. It may also allude to the sense of *deer* that is synonymous with *hart*; compare line 122.

134   **else** otherwise.
      pernicious ruinous, malign.

135   **cold Blood** dispassionate nature. The humour Beatrice describes would have been classified as either phlegmatic (cold and moist) or melancholic (cold and dry). See the note to II.i.359–60.

136   **Humour** disposition, temperament, 'Mind' (line 140).

139   **still** yet, forever.

141   **predestinate** predestined, inevitable. Benedick's phrasing echoes the theological doctrine (associated with Calvinism) that whatever happens in human life is preordained.

143   **and 'twere** if it were.

144   **rare Parrat Teacher** extraordinary tutor of parrots, both (a) in their ability to scratch and (b) in their habit of reiterating trite sayings.

145   **Tongue** both (a) ability to speak, and (b) comprehension of the language.

146   **Beast of yours** beast with your ability to speak (with the implication that Benedick is just as incapable of articulation as a beast). Beatrice's words apply with more justice to Don John (see line 163).

148   **and . . . Continuer** and a stamina that would make it as capable of running on tirelessly.

149– **Keep your Way** proceed on the course you've chosen [without
50   benefit of any further company from me].

150   **Jade's Trick** a device for avoiding further effort or competition. Jades, worn-out horses, were proverbial for slipping out of collars. Beatrice implies that Benedick is a cowardly knight who pretends that it is his horse, rather than himself, who retreats from a 'Skirmish' (line 65) in which he has suffered a broken lance.

that I had not a hard Heart, for truly I love
none.

BEATRICE   A deer Happiness to Women, they would
else have been troubled with a pernicious
Suitor. I thank God and my cold Blood, I am   135
of your Humour for that; I had rather hear my
Dog bark at a Crow than a Man swear he loves
me.

BENEDICK   God keep your Ladyship still in that
Mind, so some Gentleman or other shall scape a   140
predestinate scratch'd Face.

BEATRICE   Scratching should not make it worse,
and 'twere such a Face as yours were.

BENEDICK   Well, you are a rare Parrat Teacher.

BEATRICE   A Bird of my Tongue is better than a   145
Beast of yours.

BENEDICK   I would my Horse had the Speed of your
Tongue, and so good a Continuer; but keep your
Way, a' God's name, I have done.

BEATRICE   You always end with a Jade's Trick, I   150
know you of old.

PEDRO   That is the Sum of all. – Leonato, Signior
Claudio, and Signior Benedick, my deer Friend
Leonato hath invited you all. I tell him we
shall stay here at the least a Moneth, and he   155
heartily prays some Occasion may detain us
longer: I dare swear he is no Hypocrite, but
prays from his Heart.

LEONATO   If you swear, my Lord, you shall not be

150–   **I . . . old**   lengthy experience has made me thoroughly familiar
51   with you.

152   **That . . . all**   That settles it. Don Pedro is concluding a private
         conversation with Leonato in which the latter insists on
         playing the gracious host even when his guests threaten to
         stay a month (line 155). *Deer* (line 153) echoes lines 122, 133.

155   **Moneth**   month.

160   **forsworn**   proven a perjurer (one who lies under oath). In lines 159–60 Leonato is saying that he will make it impossible for Don Pedro to unswear what he has just sworn. Lines 160–62 are addressed to the morose and laconic Don John, a man of genuinely 'cold Blood' (line 135).

161   **being**   inasmuch as you have been.

S.D.   *Manent*   remain.

169   **noted her not**   failed to mark her in any special way (compare line 121).

170   **modest**   seemly in her manner (acting the part of a chaste maiden). An actor is said to be 'modest' when playing a role decorously and consistently (see *The Taming of the Shrew*, Induction, i.94–98). Compare lines 23–24.

173   **Custom**   habitual pracatice, normal trade in discourse.

174   **Tyrant**   cruel persecutor.

177   **Low**   short.

178   **Fair**   blonde (synonymous with 'beautiful' in the Renaissance).

180   **affoord**   afford, spare for. In line 179, as in line 129, *onelie* is the Quarto spelling for 'only'.

182–   **like her**   find her appealing. *Unhansome* (unhandsome, line
83   181) means 'lacking in beauty'.

186   **enquier**   inquire.

190   **Sad Brow**   serious demeanour. See the note on *Case* (line 189) at line 251.

191   **flouting Jack**   satirical fellow, speaking with sarcastic irony.

191–   **Cupid . . . Hare-finder**   the blind God of Love is adept at spying
92   out hares. Benedick probably refers to Cupid's ability to instil misguided love of the unlovely, whether a brown hare or an ugly whore. (For more explicit wordplay on *hare/whore*, see *Romeo and Juliet*, II.iii.138–47.)

192   **Vulcan . . . Carpenter**   Vulcan, blacksmith of the Gods, was also the prototype of cuckolds; his one exploit as a 'Carpenter' was to make a net to catch Venus in bed with Mars and expose the lovers publicly; in the process he subjected himself to ridicule. Benedick may be alluding to the kind of 'Construction' noted in III.iv.50.

193–   **in . . . Song?**   in what key are you singing, so that one who
94   wishes to join you may do so harmoniously?

forsworn. – Let me bid you welcome, my Lord,   160
being reconciled to the Prince your Brother:
I owe you all Duty.

JOHN   I thank you, I am not of many Words, but I
thank you.

LEONATO   Please it your Grace lead on?   165

PEDRO   Your Hand, Leonato, we will go together.
                Exeunt. Manent Benedick and Claudio.

CLAUDIO   Benedick, didst thou note the Daughter
of Signior Leonato?

BENEDICK   I noted her not, but I look'd on her.

CLAUDIO   Is she not a modest young Lady?   170

BENEDICK   Do you question me as an honest Man
should do, for my simple true Judgement? or
would you have me speak after my Custom, as
being a professed Tyrant to their Sex?

CLAUDIO   No, I pray thee speak in sober   175
Judgement.

BENEDICK   Why i'faith me thinks she's too Low
for a High Praise, too Brown for a Fair Praise,
and too Little for a Great Praise; onelie this
Commendation I can affoord her, that were she   180
other than she is, she were unhansome, and
being no other, but as she is, I do not like
her.

CLAUDIO   Thou thinkest I am in sport, I pray
thee tell me truly how thou lik'st her.   185

BENEDICK   Would you buy her, that you enquier
after her?

CLAUDIO   Can the World buy such a Jewel?

BENEDICK   Yea, and a Case to put it into. But
speak you this with a Sad Brow? or do you play   190
the flouting Jack, to tell us Cupid is a good
Hare-finder, and Vulcan a rare Carpenter. Come,
in what Key shall a man take you to go in the
Song?

198 **and**   if. So also in line 209.

199 **possess'd . . . Fury**   inhabited and controlled by one of the
        Furies (the three snake-haired goddesses in Greek myth who
        pursued the perpetrators of unavenged crimes).

200 **dooth**   doeth, doth.

202 **turn**   convert to. Compare lines 126–28.

203 **trust my self**   feel confident of my bachelor's resolve. Lines
        203–5 are a reminder that Benedick *has* 'sworn the contrary'.

207–8 **but . . . Suspicion**   who will not keep his hat on at all times,
        fearing that if he doesn't he will be exposing the horned
        brows of a cuckold (a husband whose wife is unfaithful).

209 **Threescore**   sixty years of age.
        Go to   come now (an expression of dismissal).

211 **the Print of it**   the imprint of it on your unmanly neck.
        sigh away Sundays   spend your leisure in tedium with your wife
        [who restricts your freedom in ways that parallel the
        Elizabethan prohibitions against Sabbath amusements].

s.d **Enter . . . Bastard**   Since 'John the Bastard' has no dialogue in
        the passage that follows, most editions omit the Quarto
        reference to him. But it is conceivable that he enters at the
        same time as Don Pedro (perhaps from a different stage-door)
        and hovers in the background. If so, he is probably out of
        earshot, for in I.iii his responses to Borachio (who *does*
        eavesdrop on a later portion of this scene) suggest that he is
        hearing for the first time what transpires here.

215 **constrain**   command, force, 'charge' (line 217, echoing line
        106).

217 **I . . . Allegiance**   I command you to prove your loyalty to me,
        both as a friend and as your superior officer, by disclosing
        what you know.

218 **You hear**   you note that I am ordered to tell your secret (so I'm
        not to be blamed for betraying your confidence).

219 **a Dumb Man**   a man who seems incapable of speech (like the
        silent Don John). If Don John has in fact entered here with his
        brother, he may be left to stand to one side or depart at this
        point.

221 **now . . . part**   that is your line to speak (your question).

CLAUDIO   In mine Eye, she is the sweetest Lady   195
that ever I look'd on.

BENEDICK   I can see yet without Spectacles, and
I see no such Matter. There's her Cousin, and
she were not possess'd with a Fury, exceeds her
as much in Beauty as the first of May dooth the   200
last of December. But I hope you have no intent
to turn Husband, have you?

CLAUDIO   I would scarce trust my self, though I
had sworn the contrary, if Hero would be my
Wife.   205

BENEDICK   Is't come to this? In faith hath not
the World one Man but he will wear his Cap
with Suspicion? Shall I never see a Bachelor
of Threescore again? Go to, i'faith, and
thou wilt needs thrust thy Neck into a Yoke,   210
wear the Print of it, and sigh away Sundays.
Look, Don Pedro is returned to seek you.

Enter Don Pedro, John the Bastard.

PEDRO   What Secret hath held you here, that you
followed not to Leonato's?

BENEDICK   I would your Grace would constrain me   215
to tell.

PEDRO   I charge thee on thy Allegiance.

BENEDICK   You hear, Count Claudio. – I can be as
secret as a Dumb Man; I would have you think so;
but on my Allegiance, mark you this, on my Allegiance,   220
he is in love. With who? now that is your Grace's part.

222 **short** brief. Benedick is employing understatement; but he is
also punning on another sense of 'Answer', namely 'Leonato's
short Daughter'.

224 **so were it utt'red** it would [and should] be exposed (literally,
'let out') in just this manner (by his violating my trust).

225 **the old Tale** Apparently Benedick refers to the tale of a
murderer whose crimes are disclosed by a witness who
pretends that she is describing a dream. The murderer repeats
the words cited in lines 225–27 until finally she says, 'But it is
so.'

232 **fetch me in** lure me into a full confession.

235 **Troths** faiths (truths), with allusion to the betrothal vows that
unite a man and a woman in marriage. Benedick refers to
'two' of each because, in being faithful to his 'Allegiance' to
Don Pedro (line 217), he has betrayed his loyalty to Claudio.

241 **melt . . . me** force me to forswear (melting with fear), even if I
am threatened with being burned at the stake as a heretic. In
due course Benedick's willingness to be burned at the stake
will be fulfilled in a way that plays on the coital sense of *die*
(compare III.ii.64–69) and the virile sense of *Stake*. Benedick's
imagery echoes lines 79–80.

243 **obstinate Heretic** unyielding opponent of the true faith (in this
case faith in the God of Love). The literal meaning of
obstinate is 'standing against'.

244 **despight** contempt.

245 **maintain his Part** sustain his role as a heretic. Like *Stake*, *Will*,
and *Bugle* (lines 242, 246, 251), *Part* is here a word with
phallic innuendo. Claudio's phrasing hints that Benedick's
'Will' (a word that can refer not only to 'intent' but also to
'desire' and to the genitalia of both genders) may eventually
'maintain his Part' in a way that pertains to the performance
of a man who 'will die in it' (line 242).

250 **Rechate winded** recheat (a series of horn notes) sounded. Here
Rechate implies 'horn', and *winded in* plays on *wound in*,
screwed (ratcheted) into.

251 **Baldrick** a leather belt worn diagonally across the shoulder and
chest to house a horn or sword. A cuckold's 'Baldrick' would
be worn across his brow. In either instance a baldrick would
constitute 'a Case to put it into' (line 189).

Mark how short his Answer is: with Hero, Leonato's
short Daughter.

CLAUDIO   If this were so, so were it utt'red.

BENEDICK   Like the old Tale, my Lord, it is not   225
so, nor 'twas not so: but indeed, God forbid it
should be so.

CLAUDIO   If my Passion change not shortly, God
forbid it should be otherwise.

PEDRO   Amen, if you love her: for the Lady is   230
very well worthy.

CLAUDIO   You speak this to fetch me in, my Lord.

PEDRO   By my troth, I speak my Thought.

CLAUDIO   And in faith, my Lord, I spoke mine.

BENEDICK   And by my two Faiths and Troths, my   235
Lord, I spoke mine.

CLAUDIO   That I love her, I feel.

PEDRO   That she is worthy, I know.

BENEDICK   That I neither feel how she should be
loved, nor know how she should be worthy, is the   240
Opinion that Fire can not melt out of me, I
will die in it at the Stake.

PEDRO   Thou wast ever an obstinate Heretic in the
despight of Beauty.

CLAUDIO   And never could maintain his Part, but   245
in the force of his Will.

BENEDICK   That a Woman conceived me, I thank
her; that she brought me up, I likewise give
her most humble Thanks; but that I will have a
Rechate winded in my Forehead, or hang my   250
Bugle in an invisible Baldrick, all Women shall

253 **mistrust**   either (a) trust inappropriately (because the object of
trust is not trustworthy), or (b) mistrust, suspect of infidelity.
Before long what Benedick says about husbands will be borne
out in the behaviour of a would-be husband.

right   both (a) correct, virtuous behaviour, and (b) privilege,
civil right. *Right* can mean 'upright', 'erect', and in time
Benedick's words will prove ironic.

254 **Fine**   conclusion (finish of my little sermon on women).

255 **go the finer**   proceed the more elegantly and simply, without the
scorn horns (or the paranoid fear of horns) would earn me.

256 **ere I die**   before I expire. *Die* echoes lines 241–42.

260 **loose**   both (a) release, and (b) lose. Benedick alludes to the
notion that sighing (either for love or for other reasons)
depleted the blood, whereas imbibing alcohol, particularly red
wine, restored it to its original strength and colour.

262 **Ballad-maker's Pen**   here, the pen of one who composes
satirical ballads about cuckolds.

265 **notable Argument**   noteworthy instance of apostasy
(abandonment of one's religion or principles). Like *Pen*,
Argument is often used with genital innuendo. *Notable* echoes
lines 167–68.

266 **Bottle**   both (a) wicker basket, and (b) container for liquids.
Benedick refers to archery practice; his image will prove apt,
because in addition to its occasional use as a target, a cat was
proverbial as a creature which could easily be induced to talk
if it were given strong drink; see *The Tempest*, II.ii.90, and
All's Well That Ends Well, IV.iii.266–69.

268 **Adam**   the first (and hence foremost) of men; possibly a
reference to Adam Bell, a legendary archer.

270 **savage Bull**   here a symbol of (a) yoked oxen, and (b) horned
cuckolds. When Zeus wooed Europa as a bull, he bore her off
on his back.

274 **vildly**   vilely, in a way that is both disrespectful and hideous in
its crudity.

279 **Horn mad**   as furious as a frustrated bull using his horns as
savage weapons. Compare *The Comedy of Errors*, II.i.56–58.
Mad echoes line 95.

280 **spent . . . Quiver**   shot his quiverful of arrows to make men
quiver with the fever caused by love.

pardon me. Because I will not do them the wrong
to mistrust any, I will do my self the right to
trust none: and the Fine is (for the which I
may go the finer) I will live a Bachelor.   255

PEDRO   I shall see thee, ere I die, look pale
with Love.

BENEDICK   With Anger, with Sickness, or with
Hunger, my Lord, not with Love: prove that ever
I loose more Blood with Love than I will get   260
again with Drinking, pick out mine Eyes with a
Ballad-maker's Pen, and hang me up at the Door
of a Brothel-house for the Sign of blind Cupid.

PEDRO   Well, if ever thou dost fall from this
Faith, thou wilt prove a notable Argument.   265

BENEDICK   If I do, hang me in a Bottle like a
Cat, and shoot at me, and he that hits me, let
him be clapp'd on the Shoulder, and call'd Adam.

PEDRO   Well, as Time shall try: in time the
savage Bull doth bear the Yoke.   270

BENEDICK   The savage Bull may, but if ever the
sensible Benedick bear it, pluck off the Bull's
Horns, and set them in my Forehead, and let me
be vildly painted, and in such great Letters
as they write 'Here is good Horse to hire', let   275
them signify under my Sign, 'Here you may see
Benedick the Married Man.'

CLAUDIO   If this should ever happen, thou wouldst
be Horn mad.

PEDRO   Nay, if Cupid have not spent all his Quiver   280

281 **Venice** a city proverbial for 'the Sign of blind Cupid' (line 263). Since blindness was one of the consequences of syphilis, a disease frequently acquired in brothels, Cupid's traditional image was doubly apt in the signboards to which it was applied during the Renaissance.

283 **temporize ... Hours** be brought to terms (tempered) in time. If Don Pedro is punning on *hours/whores*, he is hinting that in the meantime Benedick will spend his idle hours with women he doesn't wish to marry. See the notes to lines 91, 191–92.

284 **repair** resort, proceed.

288 **Matter** substance (ability or intelligence). Compare lines 197–98.

289 **Embassage** embassy, mission (conveying your regards and your acceptance of his invitation to supper). See lines 82–84.
commit you pledge you to acceptance, warrant your word that you will 'not fail' to be his honoured guest (line 286). In line 290 Claudio twists *commit you* ('commend you', 'hand you over') into a phrase that mocks the conventional closing for a letter, 'To the Tuition of God'.

290 **Tuition** tutelage, watchful protection.
from my House from my entire household.

292 **sixt** sixth (the normal Shakespearean spelling).

294– **the ... Fragments** the text of your conversation is occasionally
96 decorated, and thereby shielded from close scrutiny, by formulaic phrases [such as those you mock in my 'Discourse']. Benedick puns on (a) the body of a letter, (b) a body clothed with 'Fragments' (line 296), and (c) a bodice (vest or upper part of a woman's dress) 'guarded' (both ornamented and protected) with pieces of trim ('Guards', line 296).

297 **basted on neither** loosely sewn on in any case.
flout old Ends mock (a) old fragments of cloth, (b) traditional endings (for letters), and (c) and formulaic tags, to ornament or conclude a conversation (such as 'and so I commit you' and 'examine your Conscience').

298 **examine your Conscience** look into your own thoughts [to be sure that you are not just as perfunctory or satirical in your appropriation of pious phrases as you imply I am].

301 **teach** instruct (in what it may do to help you). At this point the discourse shifts into the more formal medium of verse.

304 **Hath ... Son** This question recalls lines 186–87.

in Venice, thou wilt quake for this shortly.

BENEDICK I look for an Earthquake too then.

PEDRO Well, you will temporize with the Hours;
in the mean time, good Signior Benedick, repair
to Leonato's, commend me to him, and tell him I   285
will not fail him at Supper, for indeed he hath
made great Preparation.

BENEDICK I have almost Matter enough in me for
such an Embassage, and so I commit you.

CLAUDIO To the Tuition of God: from my House if   290
I had it.

PEDRO The sixt of July: your loving Friend
Benedick.

BENEDICK Nay mock not, mock not; the Body of
your Discourse is sometime guarded with   295
Fragments, and the Guards are but slightly
basted on neither; ere you flout old Ends any
further, examine your Conscience; and so I
leave you.   *Exit.*

CLAUDIO My Liege, your Highness now may do me
good.   300

PEDRO My Love is thine to teach; teach it but
how,
And thou shalt see how apt it is to learn
Any hard Lesson that may do thee good.

CLAUDIO Hath Leonato any Son, my Lord?

PEDRO No Child but Hero: she's his onely Heir.   305
Doost thou affect her, Claudio?

CLAUDIO   O my Lord,
When you went onward on this ended Action,
I look'd upon her with a Soldier's Eye,
That lik'd, but had a rougher Task in hand,

305 **onely** only, sole. Compare lines 129, 179.

306 **affect her** like her, feel attracted to her.

307 **ended Action** just-concluded military expedition. *Action*
echoes lines 5–6.

311   **that**   now that.

312   **Rooms**   vacated spaces, here evocative of 'soft and delicate'
      interiors (line 313), that contrast with the 'rougher' hardships
      (line 309) of what the Moor calls 'the flinty and steel Coach
      of War' in *Othello*, I.iii.229.

314   **prompting me**   reminding me, bringing forth to me [like a stage
      prompter in the theatre].

315   **I lik'd ... Wars**   These words could well be placed in quotation
      marks, as the thoughts of Claudio's personified 'Desires' (line
      313).

316   **presently**   forthwith, immediately, as in lines 89, 338. *Book*
      ('volume', line 317) echoes lines 79–80.

317   **tire**   both (a) weary, and (b) attire, clothe.

319   **break**   broach the matter as your broker (matrimonial agent).
      In keeping with the tacit implication of Claudio's question in
      line 304, Don Pedro approaches marriage not merely as an
      affair of the heart but as a social and financial transaction to
      be negotiated with Hero's father.

320   **End**   purpose. But for other pertinent senses of *End*, see *All's
      Well That Ends Well*, IV.ii.68 and IV.iv.35–36. Don Pedro's
      phrasing echoes lines 297–98 and 307.

321   **twist**   spin, form into twine. Compare lines 294–99, and see the
      note to line 325.
      fine   both (a) thin (like thread), and (b) excellent. In his reply
      Claudio gives *fine* a third sense: (c) [too] brief. Meanwhile he
      plays on *End*: compare lines 254–55.

323   **Grief**   both (a) sadness, deprivation, and (b) grievance,
      complaint.

325   **salv'd**   both (a) softened, soothed [as with an ointment], and (b)
      salvaged, remedied (with play, on 'selvage', cloth border).

326   **What ... Flood?**   Why does the bridge (the 'Treatise' or
      discourse) need to be any longer than the width of the river to
      be crossed (the 'End' to be achieved)?

327   **The ... Necessity**   the best benefit (grant, gift) is what meets
      the need.

328   **Look ... fit**   Whatever will serve the purpose is suitable. In II.ii
      of *All's Well That Ends Well*, the word *fit* has a copulative
      sense that is only hinted at in lines 328–29.

330   **to night**   both (a) to [in honour of] night, and (b) tonight.

Than to drive Liking to the name of Love: 310
But now I am return'd, and that War-thoughts
Have left their Places vacant, in their Rooms
Come thronging soft and delicate Desires,
All prompting me how fair young Hero is,
Saying I lik'd her ere I went to Wars.   315
PEDRO   Thou wilt be a Lover presently,
And tire the Hearer with a Book of Words;
If thou dost love fair Hero, cherish it,
And I will break with her, and with her Father,
And thou shalt have her; was't not to this End   320
That thou began'st to twist so fine a Story?
CLAUDIO   How sweetly you do minister to Love,
That know Love's Grief by his Complexion!
But lest my Liking might too sudden seem,
I would have salv'd it with a longer Treatise.   325
PEDRO   What need the Bridge much broader than
   the Flood?
The fairest Graunt is the Necessity;
Look what will serve is fit; 'tis once thou
   lovest,
And I will fit thee with the Remedy.
I know we shall have Revelling to night;   330
I will assume thy Part in some Disguise,
And tell fair Hero I am Claudio,
And in her Bosom I'll unclasp my Heart,
And take her Hearing prisoner with the Force
And strong Incounter of my amorous Tale;   335

---

335   **strong encounter**   overwhelming eloquence. Don Pedro uses a
         martial metaphor that plays on a vulgar English derivative
         from the Latin word *cunnus* (female pudendum) and carries
         implications that frequently relate to the encounter (literally,
         'in-count-'er') of a male's private 'Part' (line 331, an echo of
         lines 13, 221, 245). Don Pedro's language in lines 331–38
         depicts a virile 'Persuasion' (V.iv.95) that borders on rape;
         Tale (story) hints at a 'tail' (*penis* in Latin) that is 'amorous'
         in the fierce manner of a 'savage Bull' (line 270) intent on
         entering a 'Bosom' and capturing it with a strong 'Conclusion'
         (clasping together).

338 **Practice** application. *Practice* often means 'trickery' or 'stratagem', and that sense is pertinent to a plot (lines 331–35) that anticipates a later development in the events to be dramatized.

I.ii This scene takes place at Leonato's house in Messina.

2 **provided this Music** Evidently Leonato has asked the son of his brother (the 'Old Man' who is later identified as Antonio) either to be the musician or to handle the musical arrangements for the evening. It may be that *this Music* refers to sounds the audience can hear, and perhaps to musicians who can be seen.

4 **dreampt** dreamt.

6 **they** the 'News' (here treated as plural) referred to in line 4.

7 **As ... them** as the outcome determines. Most editors emend *Events* to *event* or *stamps* to *stamp*; but what we would regard as errors of agreement are common in Elizabethan usage.

8 **shew well outward** appear 'good' to the eye [at the moment]. The *Cover* imagery echoes I.i.23–24, 128, 249–55, 316–17, 328–29, 331–37.

9–10 **thick pleached Alley** a walkway between hedges of densely intertwined branches.

11 **over-heard ... mine** This is the first of the play's numerous instances of 'noting' by an eavesdropper. What *we* should note is that the account the Old Man provides does not accord with what we have just heard ourselves. Here *Man* means 'serving man'.

12 **discovered** disclosed.

14 **accordant** in accord with his inclinations; the affections of her heart (*cor* or *cordis* in Latin) harmonizing with his.

15 **take ... Top** seize the present occasion by the top of its head (its forelock). Leonato's brother alludes to a proverbial emblem of the proper way to prevail upon Fortune. Here Elizabethans might have heard an echo of *The Prince* (1532), where Machiavelli depicts Fortune as a woman who favours bold, spirited men who win her forcibly and treat her harshly, if necessary, to keep her from becoming unruly. See the note to I.i.335, where Don Pedro outlines a procedure that Shakespeare dramatized at length in *The Taming of the Shrew*.

Then after to her Father will I break,
And the Conclusion is, she shall be thine.
In Practice let us put it presently.   *Exeunt.*

Scene 2

Enter Leonato and an Old Man, Brother to Leonato.

LEONATO   How now, Brother, where is my Cousin
your Son? Hath he provided this Music?

OLD MAN   He is very busy about it. But Brother, I
can tell you strange News you yet dreampt not
of.

LEONATO   Are they good?   5

OLD MAN   As the Events stamps them, but they
have a good Cover: they shew well outward. The
Prince and Count Claudio, walking in a thick
pleached Alley in mine Orchard, were thus much   10
over-heard by a Man of mine: the Prince
discovered to Claudio that he loved my Niece
your Daughter, and meant to acknowledge it this
Night in a Daunce, and if he found her accordant,
he meant to take the present Time by the Top,   15
and instantly break with you of it.

LEONATO   Hath the Fellow any Wit that told you
this?

OLD MAN   A good sharp Fellow, I will send for
him, and question him your self.   20

LEONATO   No, no, we will hold it as a Dream

---

17   **Wit**   common sense; reliability as a witness. Compare
        I.i.66–74.

20   **question**   you may interrogate.

21   **hold . . . Dream**   treat it as if it were only a dream.

30

22 **appear it self**   manifest its as yet hidden features (see lines 7–8) in all their nakedness.

23 **withall**   with all [of this information].

24 **peradventure**   by chance. *Prepar'd* echoes I.i.284–87; *Answer* recalls I.i.221–22.

25 **Coosins**   Leonato probably addresses this remark to both his brother and the 'Cousin' (nephew) referred to in line 1. It may be that Antonio's son has just arrived for his part in the evening's festivities.

26 **cry you mercy**   beg your pardon.

27 **Friend**   Leonato probably addresses a musician.
    use   put to good use, employ.

28 **Shill**   a dialectical form of *skill* (the First Folio reading). Here *Shill* can function as a gerund-like variant of the verbs *skill* ('separate', 'curdle', or 'make a difference', as in the phrase 'It skills not much' in *Twelfth Night*, V.i.291) and *shrill* (one of whose meanings is 'sound loudly'). *I will use your shill* can thus carry the implication 'Through your ability to provide musical sounds I will sever the hearts of my guests from any thoughts or feelings that are incompatible with a festive atmosphere'.
    have a Care   be attentive and industrious. *Busy* echoes line 3.

I.iii   This scene evidently takes place elsewhere in Leonato's house.

1   **What . . . goodyear**   an expression similar to 'what the devil'. The phrase *goodyear* may here be used to mean 'plague' (from the French *goujères*, 'pox'), as in *King Lear* V.iii.24; but it could also refer to a year (corresponding in the Pharaoh's dream to an ear) of plenty and allude to Genesis 41.

2   **out . . . sad**   immoderately melancholy.

3   **Measure**   moderation, restraint. Lines 2–3 echo I.i.25–26.

4   **breeds**   begets it, brings it about.

9   **patient Sufferance**   endurance (suffering) of affliction without complaint. *Remedy* recalls I.i.322–38.

11 **borne under Saturn**   both (a) carried and (b) born under the influence of the planet that was thought to cause a sombre disposition. See the notes to I.i.135, 146.

till it appear it self: but I will acquaint my
Daughter withall, that she may be the better
prepared for an Answer, if peradventure this be
true. Go you and tell her of it. – Coosins, you   25
know what you have to do. – O I cry you mercy,
Friend, go you with me and I will use your
Shill. Good Cousin, have a Care this busy
Time.   *Exeunt.*

Scene 3

*Enter Sir John the Bastard, and Conrade his
Companion.*

CONRADE   What the goodycar, my Lord, why are
  you thus out of measure sad?
JOHN   There is no Measure in the Occasion that
  breeds, therefore the Sadness is without Limit.
CONRADE   You should hear Reason.   5
JOHN   And when I have heard it, what Blessing
  brings it?
CONRADE   If not a present Remedy, at least a
  patient Sufferance.
JOHN   I wonder that thou (being, as thou say'st   10
  thou art, borne under Saturn) goest about to
  apply a moral Medicine, to a mortifying
  Mischief. I cannot hide what I am: I must be
  sad when I have Cause, and smile at no man's
  Jests, eat when I have Stomach, and wait for   15

12–13 **a moral . . . Mischief**   a philosophical solution to a deadly
  physical disease. Don John will later allude to the
  mortification (humiliation) that irks him. *Cause* (line 14) is
  here synonymous with 'a Case' (since the Latin *causa* is at the
  root of both words); compare I.i.188–89.

15   **Stomach**   appetite. Compare I.i.53.

17   **tend ... Business**   be subject to no one else's priorities or
       'Leisure' (schedule), serve no one but myself.

18   **claw**   stroke or scratch (cajolingly or flatteringly).
       in his Humour   to humour him (improve his mood or win his
       good will).

19–20 **make ... this**   display this attitude openly.

21   **Controlment**   restraint.

21–22 **stood out against**   opposed, rebelled against.

23   **Grace**   favour. Theologically, *grace* refers to undeserved mercy.
       Compare I.i.101–2, 165, 215–16, 221.

24   **take true Root**   become firmly and justly implanted.

26–27 **frame ... Harvest**   devise a growing 'Season' [by your
       responsiveness to the sunlight of your brother's 'Grace'] that
       will yield you the benefits of both your own and his 'fair
       Weather'.

28   **Canker**   either (a) a wild rose (that is, a weed rather than a true
       'Rose', line 29), or (b) a cankerworm (caterpillar eating away
       at the 'Hedge').
       then   than. But here as in line 30 (compare I.i.29), the usual
       modern sense of *then* could also be construed as applicable.

29   **Blood**   both (a) breeding (here a deficiency in the noble 'Blood'
       of his legitimate brother Don Pedro), and (b) humour,
       disposition, passion. Compare I.i.135–36, 259–63.

31   **Carriage**   bearing, attitude.

34   **trusted ... Mussel**   trusted so long as I wear a muzzle (like a
       vicious dog) and do not have 'my Mouth' to use (lines
       36–37).

35   **enfraunchis'd ... Clog**   given all the freedom of movement
       permitted an animal whose legs are hobbled with a clog (a
       heavy block of wood). What Don John probably means is that
       he has been 'enfranchised' (released from captivity) only on
       the condition that he accept certain restrictions upon his
       liberty. See lines 19–21.

36   **decreed**   decided, determined (or perhaps agreed in response to
       my victorious brother's decrees).

38   **my Liking**   what I choose. Compare I.i.308–10.

39   **alter me**   both (a) change me, and (b) bring me to the altar in a
       spirit of Christian grace.

no man's Leisure, sleep when I am drowsy, and
tend on no man's Business, laugh when I am
merry, and claw no man in his Humour.

CONRADE   Yea, but you must not make the full
Show of this till you may do it without   20
Controlment; you have of late stood out
against your Brother, and he hath ta'en you
newly into his Grace, where it is impossible
you should take true Root, but by the fair
Weather that you make your self; it is   25
needful that you frame the Season for your
own Harvest.

JOHN   I had rather be a Canker in a Hedge, then a
Rose in his Grace, and it better fits my Blood
to be disdain'd of all, then to fashion a   30
Carriage to rob Love from any: in this (though
I cannot be said to be a flattering honest Man)
it must not be denied but I am a plain dealing
Villain. I am trusted with a Mussel, and
enfraunchis'd with a Clog, therefore I have   35
decreed not to sing in my Cage. If I had my
Mouth, I would bite; if I had my Liberty, I
would do my Liking; in the mean time, let me
be that I am, and seek not to alter me.

CONRADE   Can you make no use of your Discontent?   40
JOHN   I make all use of it, for I use it only;
Who comes here? – What News, Borachio?

Enter Borachio.

BORACHIO   I came yonder from a great Supper;

---

41   **use it only**   make use of nothing else.

43   **great Supper**   huge feast. Borachio's name (from the Spanish
          borracho, drunkard) fits the overindulgence implied by the
          occasion he describes.

45   **Intelligence of**   secret information about.

47   **Model**   architectural plan (as in 2 *Henry IV*, I.iii.42). *Mischief*
      (line 48) echoes lines 10–14.

48   **What . . . Fool**   what sort of fool is he.

49   **betrothes . . . Unquietness**   pledges himself to a life of turmoil.
      Compare I.i.206–12, 247–77.

50   **Mary**   indeed, truly (from an oath, often spelled *marry* in
      Shakespeare's time, that originally referred to the Virgin
      Mary); here a reminder that Claudio wishes to 'marry one
      Hero'. So also in line 55.

53   **proper Squire**   handsome (here, excessively refined) young
      courtier.

57   **forward March-chick**   premature chick (a precocious maiden,
      but one who is too young to marry).

59–60 **Being . . . Room**   while I was being treated with the indifference
      customary for a servant who was engaged in fumigating a
      stale room.

60   **comes me**   in comes toward me. Borachio uses a construction
      that grammarians call an ethical dative.

61   **sad Conference**   solemn conversation.

65   **Counte**   an anglicization of the Italian *conte*, count (often
      spelled, and no doubt pronounced, *County*, as in II.i.195).
      Lines 63–65 show that Borachio is a better spy than
      Leonato's informant; compare I.ii.1–25.

67   **Start-up**   upstart (since Claudio has subdued his elder's
      rebellion and supplanted him in the hierarchy of Don Pedro's
      favoured companions).

69   **bless**   bring bliss to, bestow grace upon. Here *cross* means
      'thwart' or 'impede'; but in time it will mean 'make cross' or
      'infuriate'.

70   **sure**   loyal; securely on my side.

72   **Cheer**   both (a) enjoyment of the cheer (generous supply of
      food, drink, and warm entertainment) they are given, and (b)
      high spirits.

the Prince your Brother is royally entertain'd by
Leonato, and I can give you Intelligence of an   45
intended Marriage.

JOHN   Will it serve for any Model to build
Mischief on? What is he for a Fool that
betrothes himself to Unquietness?

BORACHIO   Mary it is your Brother's right Hand.   50

JOHN   Who, the most exquisite Claudio?

BORACHIO   Even he.

JOHN   A proper Squire, and who, and who, which
way looks he?

BORACHIO   Mary one Hero, the Daughter and Heir   55
of Leonato.

JOHN   A very forward March-chick, how came you
to this?

BORACHIO   Being entertain'd for a Perfumer, as
I was smoking a musty Room, comes me the Prince   60
and Claudio, Hand in Hand in sad Conference:
I whipp'd me behind the Arras, and there heard
it agreed upon that the Prince should woo Hero
for himself, and having obtain'd her, give her
to Counte Claudio.   65

JOHN   Come, come, let us thither, this may prove
Food to my Displeasure. That young Start-up
hath all the Glory of my Overthrow: if I can
cross him any way, I bless my self every way.
You are both sure, and will assist me.   70

CONRADE   To the Death, my Lord.

JOHN   Let us to the great Supper. Their Cheer is

73   **that**   in that, because.

74   **a' my Mind**   of my disposition (compare I.i.139–41). If so, the cheer (hospitality) Leonato bestows upon Don Pedro and his companions in their 'Cheer' (festivity, line 72) would poison their celebration of my defeat. From what Don John says in this scene, we are probably to infer that the 'Action' referred to in I.i.6 was directed against him and his allies, and that the 'Honor' bestowed on 'a young Florentine called Claudio' (I.i.11–12) was in recognition of Claudio's role in putting down the Bastard's 'Turncoat' (I.i.128) uprising against his pure-bred brother, the Prince of Aragon. What Don John is now beginning to plot will amount to a resumption of his earlier insurrection.

    prove   verify, put to the proof. Compare I.i.259–65.

76   **wait . . . Lordship**   attend to your Lordship's wishes, await your orders. Compare line 17.

the greater that I am subdued; would the Cook
were a' my Mind. Shall we go prove what's to
be done?   75
BORACHIO   We'll wait upon your Lordship.   *Exeunt.*

II.i This scene takes place in a great hall in Leonato's house.

s.d. **Kinsman** probably Antonio's nephew (the 'Cousin' who appeared briefly in I.ii).

1 **Was . . . Supper?** Leonato's question implies that Don John and his companions arrived too late for the 'great Supper' referred to in the previous scene.

3 **tartly** bitterly, in a sour or acidic manner.

7 **He were** he would be. *Melancholy* (line 6) recalls I.iii.1–18.

8 **Mid-way** median (the Aristotelian mean between undesirable extremes). Compare I.i.26, I.iii.3–4, II.i.76.

9 **Image** still-life portrait (either a picture or a statue).

10–11 **my Lady's eldest Son** the spoiled child of an indulgent lady.

11 **evermore tattling** incessantly prattling (talking foolishly). Subsequent events will show 'Counte John' to be the tattler. Compare Beatrice's assessment of Benedick with what he has said of her in I.i.198–201, and what she has told him in I.i.120–21.

15 **With . . . Foot** along with an attractive, muscular physique. In *Troilus and Cressida*. I.ii.15–19, *Leg* alludes to a 'particular Addition' in a man who 'stands alone', and in *Henry V*, III.iv.54–63, *Foot* plays on the French verb for what a male member does with '*le Count*'.

17 **'a** he.

18 **get her good Will** win her favour. But Beatrice's phrasing is a reminder that *Will*, which can refer to erotic desire, is also a word with genital implications (as in Sonnets 135, 136). Compare I.i.245–46.

20 **shrewd** sharp, shrewish. Here *shrewd* means 'shrew'd', beshrewed or cursed.

22 **curst** 'shrew'd (cursed with a harsh, discordant disposition).

24 **lessen God's sending** diminish what God normally bestows [on shrews]. Here *lessen* plays on *lesson* (teach).

25 **God . . . Horns** Beatrice alludes to a proverb that God will not give a dangerous creature the means to do great harm. Her point in lines 25–26 is that an unruly woman ('curst Cow') who is 'too curst' (too shrewish) will not cuckold her husband, because no man will marry her and give her his 'horn' (member) in the first place.

ACT II

Scene 1

*Enter Leonato, his brother, his Wife, Hero his Daughter, and
Beatrice his Niece, and a Kinsman.*

LEONATO   Was not Counte John here at Supper?

BROTHER   I saw him not.

BEATRICE   How tartly that Gentleman looks, I
never can see him but I am Heart-burn'd an
Hour after.   5

HERO   He is of a very melancholy Disposition.

BEATRICE   He were an excellent Man that were
made just in the Mid-way between him and
Benedick: the one is too like an Image and
says nothing, and the other too like my Lady's   10
eldest Son, evermore tattling.

LEONATO   Then half Signior Benedick's Tongue in
Counte John's Mouth, and half Counte John's
Melancholy in Signior Benedick's Face.

BEATRICE   With a good Leg and a good Foot,   15
Uncle, and Money enough in his Purse, such a
Man would win any Woman in the World if 'a
could get her good Will.

LEONATO   By my troth, Niece, thou wilt never
get thee a Husband if thou be so shrewd of thy   20
Tongue.

BROTHER   In faith she's too curst.

BEATRICE   Too curst is more than curst; I shall
lessen God's sending that way, for it is said,
'God sends a curst Cow short Horns,' but a   25
Cow too curst he sends none.

29   **Just**   precisely, even so.

30   **at him**   before God (pestering him). *Blessing* echoes I.iii.68–70.

33   **in the Woollen**   between scratchy woollen blankets, without sheets.

34   **light**   alight. Used as an adjective, *light* can mean 'bawdy', 'wanton', or 'unchaste', and in this speech Leonato may be hinting that if Beatrice marries a man with 'no beard' (no masculine assertiveness) she may be 'light on' him and treat him like a docile calf.

37   **waiting**   attendant, serving a noble lady in her chamber.

43   **in . . . Berrord**   as a down payment from the bearward or bearherd (a man who maintains and trains bears and apes).

43–44 **lead . . . Hell**   Beatrice alludes to the fate proverbial for women who died as old maids. Katherina refers (with more evident anxiety) to the same superstition in *The Taming of the Shrew*, II.i.33–34.

46   **but**   only.

47   **like . . . Cuckold**   Beatrice refers to the resemblance between the Devil's horns and those associated with cuckolds.

51   **Saint Peter**   For the source of a gatekeeper's role for Peter, see Matthew 16:19.
     for   as for.

52   **the Bachelors**   all unmarried souls, including women (see Mark 12:25).

54   **Niece**   Antonio is addressing Hero.

57   **Cursy**   curtsy. *Father* echoes I.i.106–19.

62   **fitted**   matched, united. See the note to I.i.328.

64   **Metal**   material. Beatrice puns on *mettle*, substance, courage.

LEONATO   So, by being too curst, God will send
you no Horns.

BEATRICE   Just, if he send me no Husband, for
the which Blessing I am at him upon my Knees   30
every Morning and Evening: Lord, I could not
endure a Husband with a Beard on his Face, I
had rather lie in the Woollen!

LEONATO   You may light on a Husband that hath
no Beard.   35

BEATRICE   What should I do with him, dress him
in my Apparel and make him my waiting Gentle
woman? He that hath a Beard is more than a
Youth, and he that hath no Beard is less than
a Man: and he that is more than a Youth is not   40
for me, and he that is less than a Man I am not
for him, therefore I will even take Sixpence
in Earnest of the Berrord, and lead his Apes
into Hell.

LEONATO   Well then, go you into Hell.   45

BEATRICE   No, but to the Gate, and there will
the Divel meet me like an old Cuckold with
Horns on his Head, and say 'Get you to Heaven,
Beatrice, get you to Heaven, here's no place
for you Maids.' So deliver I up my Apes and   50
away to Saint Peter: for the Heavens, he shews
me where the Bachelors sit, and there live we
as merry as the Day is long.

BROTHER   — Well Niece, I trust you will be rul'd
by your Father.   55

BEATRICE   Yes faith, it is my Cousin's Duty to
make Cursy and say 'Father, as it please you.'
— But yet for all that, Cousin, let him be a
handsome Fellow, or else make another Cursy
and say 'Father, as it please me.'   60

LEONATO   Well Niece, I hope to see you one Day
fitted with a Husband.

BEATRICE   Not till God make Men of some other
Metal than Earth; would it not grieve a Woman

42

65   over-mast'red with   overcome and dominated by.

65–66 valiant Dust   Beatrice's satiric annihilation of male vanity is not
      unlike the Prince of Denmark's sarcasm about the pretensions
      of 'fine Dirt' (V.i.113) in the Graveyard Scene of *Hamlet*. The
      ultimate source for such reflections is Genesis 3:19, where
      God reminds the fallen Adam that 'dust thou art, and unto
      dust shalt thou return'.

66   make . . . Life   report on how she conducts her life.

67   wayward Marl   unruly clay; an allusion to Isaiah 29:16.

69   match . . . Kinred   marry one of my relatives. By *Brethren*
      Beatrice means 'equals', and one of her points is that she will
      never agree to obey, submit her will to, a creature she refuses
      to acknowledge as a superior.

71   solicit . . . kind   woo you in that manner [requesting your hand
      in marriage]. *Answer* (line 72) recalls I.ii.21–25; compare
      lines 74–77, 115–16, 179–80.

75   important   importunate; insistent on a quick response.

76   Measure   moderation, with wordplay on a dancing measure.
      See the note to line 8.

79   Cinquepace   a rapid capering, with five steps culminating in a
      leap. In lines 83–84 Beatrice implies that those with 'bad
      Legs' will sink apace (fade rapidly) as they approach death.
      first Suit   initial stage of wooing.

81   fantastical   fanciful, intricate and intriguing in its lively
      spontaneity.
      mannerly modest   decorous and solemn. Compare I.i.170.

82   State and Auncientry   stateliness and venerable dignity. *Legs*
      (line 84) recalls line 15.

86   apprehend passing shrewdly   observe with surpassing sharpness
      of vision. *Shrewdly* echoes lines 19–22.

87–88 see . . . Daylight   Beatrice's surface meaning is that it doesn't
      take a very acute eye to see something as large as a church in
      the full light of day. But since she is speaking about
      matrimony, her imagery is doubly apt: she can forecast the
      fate that awaits those who enter a church to marry.

to be over-mast'red with a piece of valiant   65
Dust? to make an Account of her life to a Clod
of wayward Marl? No, Uncle, I'll none: Adam's
Sons are my Brethren, and truly I hold it a
Sin to match in my Kinred.
LEONATO – Daughter, remember what I told you: 70
    if the Prince do solicit you in that kind, you
    know your Answer.
BEATRICE The Fault will be in the Music,
    Cousin, if you be not wooed in good time. If
    the Prince be too important, tell him there is   75
    Measure in every thing, and so daunce out the
    Answer. For hear me, Hero, Wooing, Wedding,
    and Repenting is as a Scotch Jig, a Measure,
    and a Cinquepace. The first Suit is hot and
    hasty like a Scotch Jig (and full as   80
    fantastical); the Wedding mannerly modest
    (as a Measure), full of State and Auncientry;
    and then comes Repentance, and with his bad
    Legs falls into the Cinquepace faster and
    faster, till he sink into his Grave.   85
LEONATO Cousin, you apprehend passing shrewdly.
BEATRICE I have a good Eye, Uncle, I can see a
    Church by Daylight.
LEONATO The Revellers are ent'ring, Brother,
    make good Room.   [*They all don their Masks.*] 90

Enter Prince, Claudio and Benedick,
and Balthaser, or Dumb John.
Maskers with a Drum.

S.D. **Balthaser, or Dumb John** This phrasing, from the stage
      direction in the Quarto printing, is puzzling. *Dumb*, which
      echoes I.i.218–19, may either be a misreading for *Don* or a
      reference to Don John's habitual silence. Compare *Dun John*
      in III.iii.117–18, and see the note to I.i.219. *Balthaser* (or
      Balthasar) is Don Pedro's musician (see II.iii). The *or* may
      indicate that the same actor played both Balthaser and Don
      John; in this scene that would require an exit after line 116
      and a re-entry at line 161.

91   **walk about** walk a bout (step to a dance measure). The music has begun.

93   **So** provided.

99   **Favour** (a) face ('the Lute'), as opposed to the 'Case' or 'Visor' (mask) that obscures it, and (b) attention, kind favours. *Lute* and *Case* are both erotically suggestive; see *Romeo and Juliet*, II.iii.49–108 (especially lines 56–62) and III.iii.84–90, for wordplay on *Case* as a term for the genitalia, particularly the female pudendum. *Case* recalls I.i.188–89.

101–2 **My . . . Jove** Don Pedro alludes to the classical myth about an occasion when Zeus and Hermes (Jove and Mercury) disguised themselves as mortals and visited the house of Philemon and Baucis, a peasant couple who received them with gracious hospitality. Don Pedro's implication is that behind his 'Case' is the person of a ruler.

103   **thatch'd** bearded (to resemble the thatched roofs of peasant cottages). Compare lines 29–44.

105   **did like me** were willing to entertain my suit. Many editions assign this line, and lines 108, 110, to Balthaser, who has the last two speeches (lines 113, 116) in what is usually construed as a single conversation. Other editions reassign all five of the male speeches to Borachio, who will have a significant exchange with Margaret later in the play. The Everyman edition retains the speech assignments that appear in the Quarto and First Folio texts.

107   **ill** bad, undesirable.

113   **Amen** As Balthaser speaks, he apparently replaces Benedick as Margaret's dance partner. *Match* (line 112) echoes lines 67–69.

115   **Clark** clerk, a church official who spoke the responses (including the *Amens*) during religious services. Margaret is asking him to say 'Amen' (so be it) to her latest prayer.

119   **At a word** in a word, in brief.

122   **so ill well** Ursula uses an oxymoron (a linking of opposites) to imply that to 'counterfeit' (imitate) Antonio 'well' requires a masker who can convey an 'ill' mannerism so convincingly that he seems 'ill' himself.

PEDRO   Lady, will you walk about with your
Friend?

HERO   So you walk softly, and look sweetly, and
say nothing, I am yours for the Walk, and
especially when I walk away.   95

PEDRO   With me in your company.

HERO   I may say so when I please.

PEDRO   And when please you to say so?

HERO   When I like your Favour: for God defend
the Lute should be like the Case.   100

PEDRO   My Visor is Philemon's Roof, within the
House is Jove.

HERO   Why then your Visor should be thatch'd.

PEDRO   Speak low if you speak Love.

BENEDICK   Well, I would you did like me.   105

MARGARET   So would not I for your own sake,
for I have many ill Qualities.

BENEDICK   Which is one?

MARGARET   I say my Prayers aloud.

BENEDICK   I love you the better: the Hearers may   110
cry Amen.

MARGARET   God match me with a good Dauncer.

BALTHASER   Amen.

MARGARET   And God keep him out of my Sight when
the Daunce is done: answer, Clark.   115

BALTHASER   No more Words, the Clark is answered.

URSULA   I know you well enough, you are Signior
Antonio.

ANTONIO   At a word I am not.

URSULA   I know you by the waggling of your Head.   120

ANTONIO   To tell you true, I counterfeit him.

URSULA   You could never do him so ill well
unless you were the very Man: here's his dry

124 **up and down** from top to bottom. Ursula may also mean that Antonio's hand is 'waggling' (line 120) in a palsied manner; and perhaps she is stroking or moving it 'up and down' in a way that hints at the erotic sense of 'Wit' (line 127) as a word that can refer both to wilful desire and to the genitalia (see the notes to I.i.72, 245). A 'dry Hand' was a conventional sign of age and impotence.

128 **Go to, mum** go on, no more words from you.

129 **appear ... End** make themselves known, and that's all there is to it. Compare I.i.320–21.

131 **you ... me** if you'll excuse me.

135 **'Hundred Merry Tales'** a popular collection of ribald stories, many of them coarse, first published in 1526. *Disdainful* (line 134) recalls I.i.122–26.

137 **What's** what man is. Normally *what* is used when the questioner is seeking information about the social position or function of a person; Beatrice provides such an answer in line 142. Compare I.i.35.

142 **Prince's Jester** Don Pedro's court 'Fool', line 143 (that is, a hired clown rather than a high-ranking gentleman and a soldier). Compare I.i.39–42.

143 **only his** either (a) his only, or (b) but his special.

144 **impossible** incredible; incapable of being true.
Libertines licentious, irresponsible people.

145 **the Commendation** the source of the 'delight' people take in him. *Wit* (line 146) echoes lines 126–27.

149 **boorded me** accosted me (literally, come alongside me with the intent of boarding in an attack). Beatrice uses a nautical term that accords with her description of the visiting maskers as a 'Fleet'.

152 **break a Comparison** attempt a joke (one that involves comparing Beatrice to someone or something else, in the way that she is doing when she describes Benedick as 'the Prince's Jester'). Beatrice's imagery implicitly likens Benedick to a tilter who fails to make a direct hit and ends up splintering his own lance, and striking himself or being struck (line 154), rather than injuring his adversary. See the notes to I.i.62–73, 150. *Break* anticipates line 162; *mark'd* (noticed, line 153) recalls I.i.220–23. And Beatrice's phrasing looks forward to II.iii.250–53.

Hand up and down, you are he, you are he.

ANTONIO   At a word, I am not.   125

URSULA   Come, come, do you think I do not know
you by your excellent Wit? can Virtue hide
it self? go to, mum, you are he, Graces will
appear, and there's an End.

BEATRICE   Will you not tell me who told you so?   130

BENEDICK   No, you shall pardon me.

BEATRICE   Nor will you not tell me who you are?

BENEDICK   Not now.

BEATRICE   That I was disdainful, and that I had
my good Wit out of the 'Hundred Merry Tales':   135
well, this was Signior Benedick that said so.

BENEDICK   What's he?

BEATRICE   I am sure you know him well enough.

BENEDICK   Not I, believe me.

BEATRICE   Did he never make you laugh?   140

BENEDICK   I pray you what is he?

BEATRICE   Why he is the Prince's Jester, a very
dull Fool, only his Gift is in devising
impossible Slaunders. None but Libertines
delight in him, and the Commendation is not   145
in his Wit, but in his Villainy, for he both
pleases Men and angers them, and then they
laugh at him, and beat him: I am sure he is in
the Fleet, I would he had boorded me.

BENEDICK   When I know the Gentleman, I'll tell   150
him what you say.

BEATRICE   Do, do, he'll but break a Comparison
or two on me, which peradventure, not mark'd,
or not laugh'd at, strikes him into Melancholy,
and then there's a Partridge Wing saved, for   155

48

156– **We . . . Leaders** Beatrice is reminding her partner that they
57   must keep up with the other dancers; evidently her remarks
       have stunned him into temporary paralysis.
160   **Turning** shift in direction. Benedick's wording echoes
       I.i.126–28. *Amorous on* (in love with), line 161, recalls
       I.i.330–38; *break* (line 162) recalls I.i.336, and echoes lines
       152–53.
       [*Manet Claudio.*] Claudio remains on stage. At this point Don
       John and Borachio step forward. If they have not entered
       earlier in the scene (see the note to the stage direction that
       follows line 90), they make their initial appearance as
       everyone but Claudio departs.
162– **break . . . it** disclose his affection for Hero and request
63   permission to woo her as his prospective bride. *Break* echoes
       line 152; compare I.i.319.
163   **but** only.
166   **Bearing** posture, manner. This word echoes I.i.69–71, 269–77.
169   **near my Brother** This remark indicates that Don John is not
       wearing a visor; he takes it for granted that Claudio
       recognizes him. Either he has removed his mask, then (if it
       was as a masked 'Dumb John' that the actor playing him
       entered at line 90), or he has exited and re-entered unmasked
       sometime before he begins speaking in line 160. The early
       texts indicate no entry for Borachio at all in this scene; as
       noted at line 105, most editors add him to the list of
       'Maskers' who appear after line 90. What would seem at least
       as likely is that Borachio emerges with Don John as all the
       Maskers but Claudio exit.
172   **his Birth** his noble blood. *Affection* (line 175) recalls I.i.306.
178   **Banquet** a dessert course of fruits, wine, and sweetmeats.
180   **ill News** evil tidings. *Ill* echoes lines 107, 122–23, 159–60.
182– **Friendship . . . Love** Earlier in his career, Shakespeare had
83   devoted an entire play to this theme: *The Two Gentlemen of
       Verona*. In view of the imagery Don Pedro has employed to
       describe his mission (see the note to I.i.335), it is not
       implausible that Claudio might think that 'the Prince was for
       himself' (line 181). In the Folio, line 181 reads 'the Prince
       woes for himselfe'. It will turn out that Don Pedro's wooing
       brings 'woes' not only to himself, but to a number of other
       characters in Messina.
183   **Office** duties (such as the one the Prince has volunteered to
       undertake on Claudio's behalf).

the Fool will eat no Supper that Night: we
must follow the Leaders.
BENEDICK   In every good thing.
BEATRICE   Nay, if they lead to any Ill, I will
leave them at the next Turning.   *Dance. Exeunt.*   160
                                      [*Manet Claudio.*]
JOHN   Sure my Brother is amorous on Hero, and
hath withdrawn her Father to break with him
about it: the Ladies follow her, and but one
Visor remains.
BORACHIO   And that is Claudio, I know him by his   165
Bearing.
JOHN   Are not you Signior Benedick?
CLAUDIO   You know me well, I am he.
JOHN   Signior, you are very near my Brother in
his Love, he is enamour'd on Hero; I pray you   170
dissuade him from her, she is no equal for
his Birth. You may do the part of an honest
Man in it.
CLAUDIO   How know you he loves her?
JOHN   I heard him swear his Affection.   175
BORACHIO   So did I too, and he swore he would
marry her to night.
JOHN   Come, let us to the Banquet.
                        Exeunt. Manet Claudio.
CLAUDIO   Thus answer I in name of Benedick,
But hear these ill News with the Ears of
        Claudio: 180
'Tis certain so, the Prince woos for himself.
Friendship is constant in all other things
Save in the Office and Affairs of Love:
Therefore all Hearts in Love use their own
        Tongues.
Let every Eye negotiate for it self,   185
And trust no Agent: for Beauty is a Witch,

187   **Faith** fidelity, truth to one's commitments.
        Blood uncontrolled passion. Compare I.i.135–36, 259–63.

188   **an Accident . . . Proof** an instance of the kind of inconstancy
        that is proven (demonstrated) anew every hour.

189   **mistrusted not** failed to anticipate and prevent. See the notes to
        I.i.254, I.iii.34. *Proof* recalls I.iii.74–75.

194–   **Even . . . of?** Benedick alludes to the custom whereby a
96   forsaken lover wove a garland out of willow leaves and wore
        it around his or her neck. Desdemona refers to the same
        custom in the Willow Song (IV.iii) of *Othello*, and it is hinted
        at in the Queen's description of Ophelia's death
        (IV.vii.162–79) in *Hamlet*. *County* echoes lines 1, 13.

198   **Scarf** the sash worn diagonally across the chest.
        one way in some fashion.

202   **Drovier** drover; a dealer of 'Bullocks' and other cattle.

203   **served you thus** treated you this way (with *served* used
        sarcastically to remind Claudio that the Prince had indeed
        promised to offer his services).

205   **strike . . . Blindman** swing out wildly in every direction, like a
        frustrated player in a game of blindman's buff. If Claudio is
        still wearing his visor (as he appears to be when Benedick
        seeks to verify his identity in line 190), the 'Blindman'
        reference is reinforced by what the audience is witnessing on
        the stage.

206–7   **'twas . . . Post** Benedick's remark applies to any situation in
        which the recipient of bad news directs his anger against the
        messenger rather than against the person who did the injury
        (compare *Antony and Cleopatra*, II.v and III.xiii). But it
        appears to allude in particular to a Spanish tale in which a
        boy steals a sausage from his blind master, is beaten for it,
        and then tricks his master into bumping his head on a stone
        post. *Meat* (punning on 'mate') recalls I.i.46–48, 98–99,
        124–26. The verb *beat* echoes what Beatrice has said in lines
        146–49. *Post* hints at the same implications as those noted for
        Stake in I.i.241.

209   **Fowl** bird (compare lines 230–43). The Quarto spelling, *foule*,
        hints at both 'foul' (reminding us that Claudio believes
        himself to be the victim of foul play) and 'fool'.

210   **Sedges** sawgrass, rushes, usually found alongside rivers.

216   **puts . . . Person** attributes to everyone the acrid personality she
        herself bears. *Merry* (line 213) echoes line 53.

Against whose Charms Faith melteth into Blood.
This is an Accident of hourly Proof,
Which I mistrusted not: farewell therefore,
  Hero.

Enter Benedick.

BENEDICK Count Claudio.   190
CLAUDIO Yea, the same.
BENEDICK Come, will you go with me?
CLAUDIO Whither?
BENEDICK Even to the next Willow, about your
  own Business, County. What Fashion will you   195
  wear the Garland of? about your Neck, like an
  Usurer's Chain? or under your Arm, like a
  Lieutenant's Scarf? You must wear it one way,
  for the Prince hath got your Hero.
CLAUDIO I wish him joy of her.   200
BENEDICK Why that's spoken like an honest
  Drovier, so they sell Bullocks: but did you
  think the Prince would have served you thus?
CLAUDIO I pray you leave me.
BENEDICK Ho now you strike like the Blindman: 205
  'twas the Boy that stole your Meat, and you'll
  beat the Post.
CLAUDIO If it will not be, I'll leave you.   *Exit.*
BENEDICK Alas poor hurt Fowl, now will he
  creep into Sedges. But that my Lady Beatrice   210
  should know me, and not know me: the Prince's
  Fool! Hah, it may be I go under that Title
  because I am merry. Yea, but so I am apt to
  do my self wrong: I am not so reputed, it is
  the base (though bitter) Disposition of   215
  Beatrice, that puts the World into her Person,

217   **gives me out**   describes me to others.

222   **Lady Fame**   Benedick likens himself to *Fama* in Book IV of Vergil's *Aeneid*, a personification of Rumour or Gossip.

223   **Lodge in a Warren**   lodging (burrow) in an enclosed area for the breeding of rabbits or other game. Rabbits were proverbially associated with *melancholy*, a word that echoes lines 6, 12–14, 154.

225   **Goodwill**   favour, consent. Compare lines 15–18.

227–   **bind ... Rod**   combine a number of strands to make himself a
28   whip. *Company* (line 226) recalls line 96.

230   **flat**   simple, downright.

231–   **Bird's Nest**   Benedick's schoolboy metaphor, which echoes lines
32   209–10, is an apt image for what he and Claudio believe Don Pedro to have stolen (compare *Romeo and Juliet*, II.iv.73–75).

233–   **Wilt ... Stealer**   Is Claudio guilty of a trespass simply because
34   of the trust he has placed in me? Don Pedro also means that the only 'sin' he himself has committed is to have carried out his 'Trust' (commission). But in view of what has just happened, and of what will happen later in the play, his words are pertinent in ways that neither he nor Benedick can now appreciate. Don John is the primary 'Stealer' here; but both Claudio and Benedick can be held accountable for at least some degree of 'Transgression' against the 'Trust' they owe their friend. *Trust* echoes lines 188–89.

238   **bestowed on you**   either (a) used to whip you for the injury you have done him, or (b) given you to whip him with. Compare I.i.10–12.

240   **them**   the birds in the nest.

242–   **If ... honestly**   If the kind of 'Singing' they do (for Claudio) is
43   in keeping with the import of your words, then you speak as a man who is both honest (true to your pledge to Claudio) and honourable. *Answer* echoes lines 179–80; see the note to line 71.

244   **hath ... you**   feels 'wrong'd by you' (line 246) and plans to seek a champion to challenge you to a duel unless you either account for your remarks or apologize for them.

247   **Indurance**   endurance.

248   **Block**   a lifeless (and hence unresponding) hunk of wood or stone. Compare I.i.76–78, II.i.205–7.

and so gives me out. Well, I'll be revenged as
I may.

Enter the Prince.

PEDRO   Now Signior, where's the Counte, did you
see him?   220
BENEDICK   Troth, my Lord, I have played the part
of Lady Fame, I found him here as melancholy
as a Lodge in a Warren. I told him, and I
think I told him true, that your Grace had not
the Goodwill of this yoong Lady, and I off'red   225
him my company to a Willow Tree, either to make
him a Garland, as being forsaken, or to bind
him up a Rod, as being worthy to be whipp'd.
PEDRO   To be whipp'd, what's his Fault?
BENEDICK   The flat Transgression of a School-boy,   230
who, being overjoyed with finding a Bird's
Nest, shews it his Companion, and he steals it.
PEDRO   Wilt thou make a Trust a Transgression?
the Transgression is in the Stealer.
BENEDICK   Yet it had not been amiss the Rod   235
had been made, and the Garland too, for the
Garland he might have worn himself, and the
Rod he might have bestowed on you, who (as I
take it) have stol'n his Bird's Nest.
PEDRO   I will but teach them to sing, and restore   240
them to the Owner.
BENEDICK   If their Singing answer your Saying,
by my faith you say honestly.
PEDRO   The Lady Beatrice hath a Quarrel to you,
the Gentleman that daunc'd with her told her   245
she is much wrong'd by you.
BENEDICK   O she misus'd me past the Indurance
of a Block; an Oak but with one green Leaf on
it would have answered her; my very Visor

250   **assume life**   become animate. The 'Life' that Benedick attributes
to his 'Visor' (mask) hints at the possibility that his 'cold
Blood' (I.i.135) might undergo 'a great Thaw' (line 253) in
other respects; see the notes to I.i.241, 245.

252–   **duller . . . Thaw**   more boring than melting ice. Benedick's
53   image may refer to a period when melting snow makes roads
impassable and keeps people at home.

253   **huddleing**   hurling and piling. The Quarto spelling suggests a
trisyllabic pronunciation.

254   **impossible Conveyance**   incredible rapidity and volume, as
distinguished from the 'impossible Conveyance' (impeded
travel) implied in lines 252–53. *Impossible* echoes I.iii.21–27,
II.i.142–44.

255   **at a Mark**   set up as a target, or standing next to a target. *Mark*
echoes line 153.

256   **Poinyards**   poniards, daggers.

258   **Terminations**   both (a) terms of derisory execution, and (b)
conclusions (see the notes to I.i.321, 335).

259–   **to the North Star**   all the way to the highest star in the heavens.
60

261   **Adam**   Benedick refers to the landowner who had the world all
to himself before he fell into sin and was banished from the
Garden of Eden; *transgress'd* (line 262) echoes lines 229–34.

262–   **She . . . spit**   Even worse than Omphale – the queen who
63   captured Hercules, decked him in women's clothes, and made
him spin thread among her maids – Beatrice would make him
turn the spit (or worse, turn on the spit).

263   **cleft**   split. In *Love's Labour's Lost*, I.ii.181–83, V.i.140–42,
V.ii.588–94, Hercules' 'Club' is treated as a figure for the
kind of attribute that earns the lusty Costard praise as
'Pompey the Huge' (V.ii.672). Borachio hints at the same
analogy in III.iii.146–48. *Fire* (line 264) recalls I.i.239–40.

265   **Atê**   a personification of the rash blindness that precipitates a
reckless act of audacity. Benedick is probably thinking of her
as the goddess who disrupted the Golden Age by introducing
the Golden Apple that Paris awarded to Aphrodite (Venus) on
an Eden-like Mount Ida in Greek myth. By offending two
other goddesses, Hera (Juno) and Athena (Minerva), Paris
sowed the cosmic discord that would end in the Trojan War.
Infernal continues the 'Fire' imagery of line 264 and prepares
the way for lines 267–70.

began to assume Life, and scold with her. She   250
told me, not thinking I had been my self, that
I was the Prince's Jester, that I was duller
than a great Thaw, huddleing Jest upon Jest,
with such impossible Conveyance upon me, that
I stood like a Man at a Mark, with a whole   255
Army shooting at me. She speaks Poinyards,
and every Word stabs. If her Breath were as
terrible as her Terminations, there were no
living near her, she would infect to the North
Star: I would not marry her though she were   260
endowed with all that Adam had left him before
he transgress'd. She would have made Hercules
have turn'd spit, yea, and have cleft his Club
to make the Fire too. Come, talk not of her:
you shall find her the infernal Atê in good   265
Apparel. I would to God some Scholar would
conjure her, for certainly while she is here
a Man may live as quiet in Hell as in a
Sanctuary, and People sin upon purpose,
because they would go thither. So indeed all   270
Disquiet, Horror, and Perturbation follows
her.

Enter Claudio, Beatrice, Leonato, Hero.

PEDRO   Look here she comes.
BENEDICK   Will your Grace command me any Service
to the World's End? I will go on the slightest   275

---

266   **Scholar**   a man (like Dr Faustus) learned in the magical arts.

268   **quiet**   peacefully, contentedly. See lines 270–72, and compare
I.iii.48–49. *Sanctuary* (a protected haven, such as a chapel)
suggests the Edenic state with which Adam was initially
'endowed'.

274   **command . . . Service**   order me on any kind of mission. *Service*
echoes line 203.

56

276 **Arrand** errand. Lines 274–83 recall I.i.82–84, 288–89.
the Antipodes the other side of the globe (literally, the place where people's feet stand opposite to our own).

277 **Tooth-picker** toothpick.

279 **Prester John** a legendary Christian priest-king of a Central Asian kingdom. *Prester* is a contraction of *Presbyter* (Greek for 'elder').

280 **great Cham** Khan (emperor) of the Mongols. *Beard* echoes lines 31–44.

281 **Pigmies** tiny inhabitants of India.

282 **Harpy** a foul, mythical creature with the face and body of a woman and the wings and claws of a bird of prey. *Conference* (discourse) recalls I.iii.61.

283 **Imployment** employment.

286 **indure** endure. Compare line 247.

290 **a double Heart** Beatrice's image may refer to the paired hearts of herself and Benedick, the doubled heart that resulted from his loan of his own heart to her. But what she hints at more strongly is that Benedick's own heart was 'double' (duplicitous, false), as distinguished from the 'single one' (true heart) she lent him in exchange. Just what she means by his having 'won' her heart with 'false Dice' (lines 291–92) is unexplained; but it is probably related to her earlier reference to his 'Jade's Trick' (I.i.150–51).

291 **mary** marry, truly. Compare I.iii.50, 55.

295 **put him down** conquered his unruly spirit (with a suggestion that she has figuratively rendered Benedick impotent).

296 **do me** put me down, achieve dominance over me, sexually and otherwise. Compare I.i.66–73, 117–19, II.i.61–69, III.ii.64–69. Beatrice's insistence on what she wouldn't want is an echo of Benedick's remarks about union with her in lines 260–62.

300–1 **wherefore . . . sad?** why do you look so melancholy?

306 **civil** both (a) stiffly correct, and (b) bitter (like oranges from Seville).

307 **something** somewhat.
jealous Beatrice plays on *yellow*, proverbially associated with jealousy. In line 308, *Complexion* means 'disposition'.

Arrand now to the Antipodes that you can devise
to send me on. I will fetch you a Tooth-picker
now from the furthest Inch of Asia, bring you
the length of Prester John's Foot, fetch you
a Hair off the great Cham's Beard, do you any   280
Embassage to the Pigmies, rather than hold
three words' Conference with this Harpy. You
have no Imployment for me?

PEDRO   None, but to desire your good Company.

BENEDICK   O God, Sir, here's a Dish I love not,   285
I cannot indure my Lady Tongue.   *Exit.*

PEDRO   Come, Lady, come, you have lost the Heart
of Signior Benedick.

BEATRICE   Indeed, my Lord, he lent it me awhile,
and I gave him use for it, a double Heart for   290
his single one; mary once before he won it
of me, with false Dice, therefore your Grace
may well say I have lost it.

PEDRO   You have put him down, Lady, you have
put him down.   295

BEATRICE   So I would not he should do me, my
Lord, lest I should prove the Mother of Fools.
I have brought Counte Claudio, whom you sent
me to seek.

PEDRO   Why how now, Counte, wherefore are you   300
sad?

CLAUDIO   Not sad, my Lord.

PEDRO   How then? sick?

CLAUDIO   Neither, my Lord.

BEATRICE   The Counte is neither sad, nor sick,   305
nor merry, nor well; but civil Counte, civil
as an Orange, and something of that jealous
Complexion.

309 **Blazon** description of him. In heraldry, a blazon is an enumeration of the symbolic details in a coat of arms. Here the word plays on *blaze*, and thus reinforces the imagery of lines 262–72.

311 **Conceit** concept, imagining.

312 **won** both (a) woon (wooed successfully), as in *Troilus and Cressida*, I.ii.307–8, and (b) won. *Good Will* (line 313) echoes lines 18, 225.

313 **broke ... Father** initiated matrimonial negotiations. Compare lines 162–63.

318 **all ... it** may everything in the world that is blessed with the grace of God say 'so be it'. Leonato's words echo lines 109–15. *Match* echoes line 112.

319 **Qu** cue, an Elizabethan actor's term that probably derives from an abbreviation of the Latin *quando*, when, or *qualis*, in what manner.

320 **Herault** herald, messenger.

321 **were** would be.

323 **dote upon** am beside myself with; am rendered dumb by.

325– **stop ... Kiss** Whether Hero takes her cue is not specified in the
26 early texts. But lines 330–32 suggest that she at least embraces her husband-to-be and whispers in his ear.

330 **on ... Care** on the windward side of Care (so as to avoid having its scent detected and thus becoming the prey of Care). Lines 329–30 define *merry* (line 328) as 'carefree'; compare I.i.63–64, I.iii.17–18, II.i.51–53, 134–35, 212–13, 305–6, 348–50, V.i.335–37.

333– **thus ... World** The idea that marrying is going to the world
34 may have derived from Luke 20:34, where Jesus says, 'The children of the world marry, and are given in marriage.' Being 'Sun-burnt' (dark, and thus conventionally unattractive), Beatrice says, she will avoid the fate of those who are 'Fair' (I.i.178).

339 **getting** begetting (with play on 'obtaining').
ne'er never, not. This idiom lies behind the colloquial 'nary'.

341 **come by them** obtain one of them. Beatrice's phrasing is probably meant to be coyly suggestive. Compare the use of *come* in II.iii.268–69 and V.ii.7–8.

PEDRO   I'faith, Lady, I think your Blazon to be
true, though I'll be sworn, if he be so, his   310
Conceit is false. – Here, Claudio, I have
wooed in thy Name, and fair Hero is won; I
have broke with her Father, and his good Will
obtained. Name the Day of Marriage, and God
give thee joy.   315

LEONATO   Counte, take of me my Daughter, and
with her my Fortunes. His Grace hath made the
Match, and all Grace say Amen to it.

BEATRICE   Speak, Counte, 'tis your Qu.

CLAUDIO   Silence is the perfectest Herault of   320
Joy. I were but little happy if I could say,
'how much?' – Lady, as you are mine, I am yours;
I give away my self for you, and dote upon the
Exchange.

BEATRICE   Speak, Cousin, or (if you cannot) stop   325
his Mouth with a Kiss, and let not him speak
neither.

PEDRO   In faith, Lady, you have a merry Heart.

BEATRICE   Yea, my Lord, I thank it, poor Fool,
it keeps on the windy side of Care. My Cousin   330
tells him in his Ear that he is in her Heart.

CLAUDIO   And so she doth, Coosin.

BEATRICE   Good Lord, for Alliance: thus goes
every one to the World but I, and I am Sun-
burnt, I may sit in a Corner and cry, 'Heigh ho   335
for a Husband.'

PEDRO   Lady Beatrice, I will get you one.

BEATRICE   I would rather have one of your
Father's getting: hath your Grace ne'er a
Brother like you? Your Father got excellent   340
Husbands if a Maid could come by them.

PRINCE   Will you have me? Lady.

BEATRICE   No, my Lord, unless I might have

344   **Working-days** everyday (as opposed to Sunday, when one donned one's finest apparel). Compare I.i.209–11. *Costly* (line 345) recalls I.i.90–92, 99–100; compare lines 389–90.

347   **Matter** substance (serious business). See I.i.288.

348   **Your . . . me** it is when you are not speaking that you need to ask my 'pardon' (line 346).

350   **borne** both (a) born (line 346), and (b) borne (carried as an infant). So also in line 353; compare I.ii.11.

351   **cried** suffered the pains of childbirth [like every other mother].

352   **daunc'd** danced [thereby disposing me to be merry].

356–   **By . . . pardon** After apologizing to her uncle for neglecting
57   whatever he asked her to attend to, Beatrice excuses herself by begging Don Pedro's pardon. The phrase *cry you mercy* ('beg your forgiveness') recalls I.i.26.

358   **pleasant spirited** This phrase hovers between 'pleasant, spirited' and 'pleasant-spirited'. *Pleasant* is roughly synonymous with *merry* (lines 328–30, 348–50), 'sportive'.

359–   **Melancholy Element** Earth, a dry and cold element, that was
60   also known as black bile. An excess of it in the system was thought to cause the condition or 'Complexion' (line 308) known as melancholy. Compare lines 222–23.

365   **indure** endure (as in line 286).

367–   **mocks . . . Suit** satirizes her suitors and thereby drives them off
68   in naked humiliation. Apparently Benedick is not the first man to have fled from Beatrice. Compare Katherina in *The Taming of the Shrew*.

369   **were** would be.

374–   **Time . . . Crutches** Time goes so slowly that it appears to be a
75   cripple. Claudio's phrasing recalls Beatrice's imagery in lines 73–85. Compare *The Tempest*, IV.i.23–31.

377   **a just Sevennight** exactly [and properly] a week.

378   **answer my Mind** accord with my concerns. *Answer* recalls I.i.221–22, I.ii.21–25, II.i.70–77, 114–16, 179–80, 242–49.

379   **shake the Head** look annoyed.

380   **Breathing** breathing-space, waiting period.
       warrant assure.

another for Working-days, your Grace is too
costly to wear every Day: but I beseech your   345
Grace pardon me, I was born to speak all
Mirth, and no Matter.

PRINCE   Your Silence most offends me, and to be
merry best becomes you, for out a' Question
you were borne in a merry Hour.   350

BEATRICE   No sure my Lord, my Mother cried,
but then there was a Star daunc'd, and under
that was I borne. – Cousins, God give you Joy.

LEONATO   Niece, will you look to those things I
told you of?   355

BEATRICE   I cry you mercy, Uncle. – By your
Grace's pardon.   *Exit.*

PRINCE   By my troth, a pleasant spirited Lady.

LEONATO   There's little of the Melancholy
Element in her, my Lord; she is never sad but   360
when she sleeps, and not ever sad then: for I
have heard my Daughter say, she hath often
dreampt of Unhappiness, and wak'd her self
with Laughing.

PEDRO   She cannot indure to hear tell of a   365
Husband.

LEONATO   O by no means, she mocks all her
Wooers out of Suit.

PRINCE   She were an excellent Wife for Benedick.

LEONATO   O Lord, my Lord, if they were but a   370
Week married, they would talk themselves mad.

PRINCE   County Claudio, when mean you to go to
Church?

CLAUDIO   To morrow, my Lord. Time goes on
Crutches till Love have all his Rites.   375

LEONATO   Not till Monday, my dear Son, which
is hence a just Sevennight, and a Time too
brief too, to have all things answer my Mind.

PRINCE   Come, you shake the Head at so long a
Breathing, but I warrant thee, Claudio, the   380
Time shall not go dully by us; I will in the

382 **one . . . Labours** a seemingly impossible task. To atone for murdering his wife and children in a fit of madness visited upon him by the goddess Hera, Hercules submitted his will to Eurystheus, King of Mycenae, who imposed twelve 'labours' upon him. Don Pedro will move two mountains (lines 383–85); see the note to line 384.

384 **Mountain of Affection** overwhelming infatuation. *Affection* echoes line 175. *Mountain* echoes Beatrice's first reference to 'Signior Mountanto' (I.i.31–32). It also alludes to the New Testament equivalent of a Herculean labour, the removal of a mountain by the exercise of the faith of 'a grain of mustard seed' (Matthew 17:20).

386 **fashion** achieve. Compare lines 195–96. *Match* echoes lines 316–18.

387 **minister** provide as willing servants.

390 **ten Nights' Watchings** ten nights without sleep.

393 **do . . . Office** perform any appropriate task.

395 **unhopefullest** unworthiest of being called 'a good Husband' (line 394). Don Pedro is as yet but dimly aware that Benedick is not 'the unhopefullest' candidate for husbandry in another sense. Whether he realizes it or not, Benedick is hopeful that his days as a bachelor are coming to an end.

397 **Strain** extraction, lineage.
    approved proven, attested, 'confirm'd' (line 398).

398 **Honesty** honourable character (as in lines 242–43).

399 **humour** play to the humour (ruling disposition, psychological proclivity) of and cajole. Compare I.iii.18.

401 **practise on** trick, manipulate. Compare I.i.338.

402 **in dispight of** in spite of. Compare I.i.243–44. *Wit* echoes lines 144–46.

403 **queasy** uneasy, nervous.

404–5 **Cupid . . . Archer** Cupid will no longer be known as the only power capable of instilling love with his arrows. *Cupid* echoes I.i.39–44, 259–68, 280–81; *onely* (line 406) recalls I.i.305 and plays on 'one-ly' in a way that parallels III.iv.76.

407 **Drift** plan (literally, 'drive').

II.ii This scene takes place somewhere in Leonato's house.

Interim undertake one of Hercules' Labours,
which is to bring Signior Benedick and the
Lady Beatrice into a Mountain of Affection,
th'one with th'other. I would fain have it   385
a Match, and I doubt not but to fashion it,
if you three will but minister such Assistance
as I shall give you Direction.

LEONATO   My Lord, I am for you, though it cost
me ten Nights' Watchings.   390

CLAUDIO   And I, my Lord.

PRINCE   And you too, gentle Hero?

HERO   I will do any modest Office, my Lord, to
help my Cousin to a good Husband.

PRINCE   And Benedick is not the unhopefullest   395
Husband that I know: thus far can I praise
him, he is of a noble Strain, of approved
Valour, and confirm'd Honesty. I will teach
you how to humour your Cousin, that she shall
fall in love with Benedick. – And I, with   400
your two Helps, will so pracatise on Benedick,
that in dispight of his quick Wit, and his
queasy Stomach, he shall fall in love with
Beatrice. If we can do this, Cupid is no
longer an Archer, his Glory shall be ours,   405
for we are the onely Love-Gods. Go in with
me, and I will tell you my Drift.   *Exeunt.*

Scene 2

Enter John and Borachio.

JOHN   It is so, the Counte Claudio shall marry
the Daughter of Leonato.

3   cross   thwart. This verb can refer to a lance's hitting the
       opponent athwart his breastplate (at a glancing angle) rather
       than straight on. See the note to II.i.152.

4   Bar   obstacle.
       Cross   hindrance, 'Impediment'. Compare lines 3, 7–8. In time
       the power associated with another 'Cross' will cross these
       doublecrossing villains.

5   med'cinable to me   a source of healing for my wounds. It is an
       indication of Don John's perversity that the one thing that can
       make him feel well is that which will bring pain to someone
       else. Compare I.iii.1–18. Sick echoes I.i.303–6.

7   Affection   desires (specifically, his inclination for Hero).
       Compare II.i.175, 379–85.
       ranges . . . mine   parallels mine exactly (or amounts to an equal
       sum on my side of the balance), since it is 'athwart his' (see
       the note to line 3).

9   covertly   stealthily (under cover). Honestly recalls II.i.398.

13   since   ago.

14   waiting   attendant, as in II.i.37.

16   unseasonable Instant   untimely, inappropriate moment.
       Compare IV.i.180.

17   appoint   arrange with, schedule.

19   Life   potency. Once again Don John's imagery is significant; for
       him the only value in any manifestation of life is its capacity
       to blight truth, beauty, love, and joy. See II.i.249–50.

22   temper   mix or blend (like an apothecary with a prescription),
       make. Another sense of temper, 'moderate' or 'bring to a
       proper or settled state or quality', will also prove pertinent,
       but only in a way that is compatible with Don John's twisted
       nature. Compare temporize, I.i.283.

25   Estimation   reputation.
       hold up   uphold, support, concern yourself with.

26   contaminated Stale   soiled piece of used merchandise. Compare
       Adriana's remarks in II.i.95–99 and II.ii.125–52 of The
       Comedy of Errors. Other meanings of Stale are (a) decoy,
       bait, (b) dupe or object of scorn, and (c) horse urine.

27   make of that   provide to substantiate that accusation. Proof
       echoes II.i.188–89.

BORACHIO   Yea, my Lord, but I can cross it.

JOHN   Any Bar, any Cross, any Impediment, will
be med'cinable to me: I am sick in Displeasure   5
to him, and whatsoever comes athwart his
Affection ranges evenly with mine. How canst
thou cross this Marriage?

BORACHIO   Not honestly, my Lord, but so covertly
that no Dishonesty shall appear in me.   10

JOHN   Show me briefly how.

BORACHIO   I think I told your Lordship a year
since how much I am in the favour of Margaret,
the waiting Gentlewoman to Hero.

JOHN   I remember.   15

BORACHIO   I can at any unseasonable Instant of
the Night appoint her to look out at her Lady's
Chamber Window.

JOHN   What life is in that to be the Death of
this Marriage?   20

BORACHIO   The Poison of that lies in you to
temper. Go you to the Prince your Brother,
spare not to tell him that he hath wronged his
Honour in marrying the renowned Claudio,
whose Estimation do you mightily hold up, to a   25
contaminated Stale, such a one as Hero.

JOHN   What Proof shall I make of that?

BORACHIO   Proof enough, to misuse the Prince, to
vex Claudio, to undo Hero, and kill Leonato;
look you for any other Issue?   30

---

29   **vex**   torment, shake, annoy.

30   **Issue**   result. Borachio uses a word normally associated with the
bearing of fruit (whether defined as children or as the harvest
of one's labours); in this case, the intended issue (outcome) is
to prevent issue (a prosperous marriage) by blighting a union
in the bud.

31   **dispight** spite, 'vex'. The Shakespearean spelling combines *dis-* (a prefix connoting negation, reversal, or separation) and *spight* (annoy, harm). Compare II.i.402; *onely* (only) recalls II.i.406.

33   **a meet Hour** a suitable time [here one for a meeting that will be the very opposite of *meet*, 'seasonable' or 'proper']. *Meet* recalls I.i.124–26, II.i.46–48, 205–7.

35   **intend** pretend.

36   **Zeal** earnest, watchful concern. The adjective *zealous* is the source of the related word *jealous*; compare II.i.305–8.

39   **cozen'd** deceived, cheated. *Match* (line 38) recalls II.i.379–88.

40   **semblance of a Maid** [more] appearance of a virgin.
       discovered dis-covered, disclosed. Compare I.ii.11–13.

42   **Trial** 'Proof', lines 28–29 (putting the accusation to the test to verify it).

43   **Likelihood** probability, plausibility, 'semblance' (line 40).

46   **intended** planned. Compare *intend*, line 35.

47–48 **so . . . matter** arrange things so.

50   **Disloyalty** infidelity.
       Jealousy unfounded suspicion. See the note to line 36.

51   **Assurance** certainty.
       all . . . overthrown all the wedding plans discarded.

52   **adverse Issue** negative outcome (literally, monstrous birth). Like Borachio in line 30, Don John describes his plans as a debasement of conception, pregnancy, and childbirth.

53   **put . . . Practice** set it in motion. Don John's phrasing recalls the 'Practice' agreed to in I.i.338. It also echoes the 'practise' plotted (II.i.401) in the immediately preceding scene. That one was designed to produce a far different 'Issue' by bringing together two 'adverse' personalities; this one is designed to break up an impending union between two personalities whose relationship is built on harmony.
       cunning both (a) knowing, skilful, and (b) deceitful. Compare line 55, and see the note to IV.i.36.

55   **constant** both (a) consistent, convincing, and (b) unswerving, steadfast. Once again the conspirators' language is a reminder of the values – in this case the constancy that is essential both to love and to true friendship (see II.i.182–83) – that they are hellbent to 'cross' (lines 3–8).

57   **presently** forthwith, as in I.i.316, 338.

JOHN   Onely to dispight them I will endeavour any
thing.

BORACHIO   Go then, find me a meet Hour, to draw
Don Pedro and the Counte Claudio alone; tell
them that you know that Hero loves me; intend   35
a kind of Zeal both to the Prince and Claudio
(as in love of your Brother's Honour who hath
made this Match) and his Friend's Reputation,
who is thus like to be cozen'd with the
semblance of a Maid, that you have discover'd   40
thus. They will scarcely believe this without
Trial: offer them Instances which shall bear
no less Likelihood than to see me at her
Chamber Window, hear me call Margaret Hero,
hear Margaret term me Claudio, and bring them   45
to see this the very Night before the intended
Wedding, for in the mean time I will so fashion
the matter that Hero shall be absent, and
there shall appear such seeming Truth of
Hero's Disloyalty that Jealousy shall be call'd   50
Assurance, and all the Preparation overthrown.

DON JOHN   Grow this to what adverse Issue it can, I
will put it in Practice: be cunning in the
working this, and thy Fee is a thousand Ducats.

BORACHIO   Be you constant in the Accusation,   55
and my Cunning shall not shame me.

JOHN   I will presently go learn their Day of
Marriage.   *Exeunt.*

II.iii   This scene takes place in Leonato's garden.

4   **bring . . . Orchard** Since the Boy never reappears, it would seem that the primary reason for this command is to let the audience know where Benedick is, or will be waiting. But Benedick's sending the Boy on an errand may also be intended to remind us of the speaker's own desire to be sent on an errand in II.i.274–83. The phrase *Chamber Window* (line 2) provides a link with the previous scene; see II.ii.16–18, 41–47.

5   **I . . . Sir** What the Boy means is that he'll be so fast that it will seem as if he never left. Benedick takes the Boy literally.

7   **wonder** marvel. Compare I.i.120–21, I.iii.10–14.

11   **Argument** theme, basis, object, example. Benedick's words recall what Don Pedro has said about him in I.i.264–65. They also remind us of Don Pedro's promise in II.i.337 to get Beatrice a husband.

14   **the Drum . . . Fife** instruments for military purposes.

15   **Tabor** small drum (like the 'Pipe', for social occasions).

17   **Armour** suit of armour.

18   **carving** devising, planning.

19   **Doublet** the close-fitting jacket worn by gentlemen.
        woont wont, accustomed.

19–20 **to the Purpose** directly, without circumlocution.

21   **turn'd Ortography** transformed into the very embodiment of linguistic flourishes and rhetorical elaboration in an exaggerated emphasis on speaking and writing with precise correctness.

22   **fantastical Banquet** assortment of exotic, fanciful delicacies.

23   **converted** turned around. Compare Benedick's self-assurance in I.i.126–32.

24–25 **be . . . Oyster** take a vow that Love will never degrade me to an oyster. An oyster is (a) dumb, (b) downtrodden, and (c) subject to being devoured. These are all traits Benedick has associated with husbands. He may also be alluding to the proverb 'Undone as you would undo an oyster'.

28   **well** uninfected; unaffected by her (not inclined to bestow my 'Grace' or favour).

30   **Graces** gifts of beauty, wisdom, and worthiness.

Scene 3

Enter Benedick alone.

BENEDICK Boy.

[*Enter Boy.*]

BOY Signior.
BENEDICK In my Chamber Window lies a Book,
   bring it hither to me in the Orchard.
BOY I am here already, Sir.   *Exit.*   5
BENEDICK I know that, but I would have thee
   hence and here again. – I do much wonder, that
   one man, seeing how much an other man is a
   Fool when he dedicates his Behaviours to Love,
   will, after he hath laugh'd at such shallow   10
   Follies in others, become the Argument of his
   own Scorn, by falling in Love. And such a man
   is Claudio. I have known when there was no
   Music with him but the Drum and the Fife, and
   now had he rather hear the Tabor and the Pipe.   15
   I have known when he would have walk'd ten Mile
   afoot to see a good Armour, and now will he lie
   ten Nights awake carving the Fashion of a new
   Doublet. He was woont to speak plain, and to the
   Purpose (like an honest Man and a Soldier),   20
   and now is he turn'd Ortography, his Words are
   a very fantastical Banquet, just so many strange
   Dishes. May I be so converted and see with these
   Eyes? I cannot tell, I think not: I will not be
   sworn but Love may transform me to an Oyster,   25
   but I'll take my Oath on it, till he have made
   an Oyster of me, he shall never make me such a
   Fool. One Woman is Fair, yet I am well; an
   other is Wise, yet I am well; an other Virtuous,
   yet I am well. But till all Graces be in one   30

31 **Grace** favour, acceptance. Compare I.iii.23, 28–29,
    II.i.316–18, 339–47. Here *come* hints at the sense noted in
    II.i.341.

33 **cheapen her** bargain for her.

35 **for an Angel** either (a) even if she were an angel, or (b) for a
    coin, the Angel, worth ten shillings. A *Noble* was worth
    two-thirds that amount.

36 **Discourse** ability to speak with eloquence.

37 **of . . . God** Benedick's concession on this point compromises
    his insistence that a woman be 'Fair' (line 34), echoing lines
    28–30.

S.D. **Music** This stage direction is probably an indication that music
    is to be heard within (behind the stage doors).

42 **As** as if.
    grace do honour to, complement. See the note to line 31.

45 **We'll . . . Pennyworth** we'll give the sly youngster a penny's
    worth of entertainment for his effort to outfox us. Claudio's
    imagery probably alludes to a game called 'Fox in the Hole',
    in which a boy designated as the 'hid fox' was beaten as he
    attempted to flee from his lair to another safe place; compare
    Beatrice's remarks in II.i.146–49. The bargain Claudio
    promises to 'fit' Benedick with echoes lines 32–37.

47 **tax** burden, task. Compare I.i.46–48.

48 **slaunder** slander, bear false witness against.

49 **Witness** testimony.
    still always.
    Excellency one who is excellent at what he does.

50 **To . . . Perfection** to mask his own skill (by declaring it to be
    other than what it is). In a play in which much is made of
    disguises, and in a scene in which everyone is feigning in some
    way, it is fitting that the Prince refers to Balthaser's pretended
    reluctance to sing as a 'strange [alien] face'. Compare
    II.i.31–33, 99–102, 179–80.

51 **woo** plead, attempt to persuade. Again, Don Pedro's phrasing
    is pertinent to the larger situation. *Woo* recalls II.i.311–12.

53–55 **Since . . . loves** Balthaser is still being coy. He is implying that,
    like a lover who is only in quest of momentary pleasure with a
    woman 'he thinks not worthy' of marriage, the Prince is
    merely feigning a real 'Suit' (solicitation, recalling II.i.367–68)
    for purposes of seduction. Compare I.i.283.

Woman, one Woman shall not come in my Grace.
Rich she shall be, that's certain; Wise, or
I'll none; Virtuous, or I'll never cheapen her;
Fair, or I'll never look on her; Mild, or come
not near me; Noble, or not I for an Angel; of   35
good Discourse, an excellent Musician, and her
Hair shall be of what Colour it please God. Hah!
the Prince and Monsieur Love, I will hide me
in the Arbour.

Enter Prince, Leonato,
Claudio, Music.

PRINCE   Come, shall we hear this Music?   40
CLAUDIO   Yea, my good Lord. How still the Evening
    is,
As hush'd on purpose to grace Harmony!
PRINCE   — See you where Benedick hath hid himself?
CLAUDIO   — O very well, my Lord: the Music ended,
    We'll fit the Kid-Fox with a Pennyworth.   45

Enter Balthaser with Music.

PRINCE   Come Balthaser, we'll hear that Song
    again.
BALTHASER   O good my Lord, tax not so bad a
    Voice,
To slander Music any more than once.
PRINCE   It is the Witness still of Excellency,
To put a strange Face on his own Perfection.   50
I pray thee sing, and let me woo no more.
BALTHASER   Because you talk of Wooing I will
    Sing,
Since many a Wooer doth commence his Suit
To her he thinks not worthy, yet he woos,
Yet will he swear he loves.
                            Nay pray thee come,   55

56 **hold longer Argument** argue against me any longer. Compare lines 7–12, and see the note to I.i.265.

57 **Notes** musical notes (and the monetary 'Notes' to be paid for them) or written messages on note paper.

59 **Crotchets** both (a) quarter notes, and (b) whims, eccentric word-fancies.

60 **Note . . . nothing** notes on notes, indeed, and thus nothing 'to the Purpose' (lines 19–20). Don Pedro probably means that instead of providing real music (melodic notes, including those termed 'Crotchets'), Balthaser is substituting empty verbal conceits: observations or 'Notes' about the musical notes his 'Ortography' (line 21) is preventing from being heard. The Prince's wordplay is a reminder that *nothing* sounded much like *noting* in Shakespeare's time. Don Pedro is probably punning on the shape of the whole note, whose figure (O) was identical with that for the number 'nothing'. Both could signify the female pudendum, which was jestingly referred to as 'an O-thing' or 'a no-thing'.

61 **Air** Benedick is probably punning on (a) a musical air (melody), (b) the movement of air involved in the making of music, and (c) the empty air (the nothing) of the dialogue he has just overheard. As Benedick speaks, Balthaser is no doubt playing an air on a stringed instrument.

62 **ravish'd** transported into an ecstasy.
Sheep's Guts the strings of a violin or lute.

63 **hale** haul, draw.

64 **Horn** Benedick probably means a hunting horn or a military bugle (compare I.i.249–52, and see lines 13–15). But this word can also refer to (a) the erect 'horn' of an aroused male, and (b) the horned brows of a cuckold. See II.i.25, 45–49.

70 **blithe and bonny** carefree and cheerful.

72 **hey nonny nonny** a refrain that appears to signify nothing but hints at the erotic joys of 'nothing' (see the note to line 60).
Converting (lines 71, 79) echoes lines 23–24.

73 **moe** more.

74 **Dumps** both (a) mournful moods, and (b) solemn tunes.

75 **Fraud** deception, inconstancy (as in lines 65–68).

PRINCE
  Or if thou wilt hold longer Argument,
  Do it in Notes.
BALTHASER   Note this before my Notes,
  There's not a Note of mine that's worth the
    noting.
PRINCE Why these are very Crotchets that he
  speaks,
  Note Notes forsooth, and nothing.   60
BENEDICK — Now divine Air, now is his Soul
  ravish'd. Is it not strange that Sheep's Guts
  should hale Souls out of men's Bodies? well
  a Horn for my Money when all's done.

THE SONG

    Sigh no more Ladies, sigh no more: 65
      Men were Deceivers ever,
    One Foot in Sea, and one on Shore,
      To one thing constant never,
    Then sigh not so, but let them go,
      And be you blithe and bonny,   70
    Converting all your Sounds of Woe
      Into hey nonny nonny.

    Sing no more Ditties, sing no moe
      Of Dumps so dull and heavy;
    The Fraud of Men was ever so   75
      Since Summer first was leavy.
    Then sigh not so, but let them go,
      And be you blithe and bonny,
    Converting all your Sounds of Woe
      Into hey nonny nonny.   80

---

76   **leavy**   leafy (adorning plants and trees with leaves), with play
      on *leavy* as a nonce-word to describe the infidelity of
      fraudulent 'Deceivers' (line 66) who promise to stay with their
      lovers forever but then leave as soon as summer's greenery
      begins to fade with the advent of autumn.

82   **ill**   bad, inept. Compare II.i.179–80.

83   **Faith**   in faith.

84   **for a Shift**   both (a) for a makeshift occasion (when no one
      better is available), and (b) for a trick. For another meaning of
      Shift, see the note to line 144.

85   **And**   if.

85–86 **should have**   had.

87   **bode**   portend, foreshadow.

88   **as live**   as lief, as soon.
      Night-Raven   a bird whose croak was thought to be a sign of
      impending doom. In *Hamlet* (III.ii.278–79), the raven is
      associated with revenge.

89   **Plague**   disease, affliction.

90   **mary**   marry, truly.
      hear Balthaser   Most editions insert a comma after *hear*; but
      Don Pedro may be speaking this line to someone other than
      Balthaser. *Chamber Window* (line 93) echoes line 2.

99   **stalk on**   keep moving in that direction. Claudio uses a hunting
      term.
      Foul   both (a) fowl, and (b) foul man. See the note to II.i.209.

100   **sits**   both (a) settles, like a bird in a bush, and (b) sits up to note
      what is being said.

102   **wonderful**   astonishing. Compare lines 7–12.

105   **abhor**   avoid with revulsion. *Behaviours* (line 104) echoes lines
      7–12.

106–7 **Sits . . . Corner?**   Does the wind blow from that direction? Can
      that really be what is happening?

110   **inraged Affection**   Leonato means 'uncontrollable passion'. But,
      in view of the bitterness Beatrice has expressed on several
      occasions (as in I.i.150–51 and II.i.289–93), the audience has
      probably begun to suspect that she does indeed respond to
      Benedick with a complex of emotions that can be described
      either as 'enraged affection' or as 'affection embedded in a
      state of rage'. *Affection* recalls II.i.381–85.

111   **infinite**   farthest reaches, infinity.

PRINCE   By my troth, a good Song.

BALTHASER   And an ill Singer, my Lord.

PRINCE   Ha, no no faith, thou singst well enough
for a Shift.

BENEDICK   — And he had been a Dog that should   85
have howl'd thus, they would have hang'd him,
and I pray God his bad Voice bode no Mischief;
I had as live have heard the Night-Raven, come
what Plague could have come after it.

PRINCE   Yea mary, doost thou hear Balthaser? I   90
pray thee get us some excellent Music. For
to morrow night we would have it at the Lady
Hero's Chamber Window.

BALTHASER   The best I can, my Lord.

PRINCE   Do so, farewell.   *Exit Balthaser.*   95
— Come hither, Leonato, what was it you told
me of to day, that your Niece Beatrice was in
love with Signior Benedick?

CLAUDIO   — O ay, stalk on, stalk on, the Foul
sits. — I did never think that Lady would have   100
loved any Man.

LEONATO   No nor I neither, but most wonderful,
that she should so dote on Signior Benedick,
whom she hath in all outward Behaviours seemed
ever to abhor.   105

BENEDICK   — Is't possible? Sits the Wind in that
Corner?

LEONATO   By my troth, my Lord, I cannot tell
what to think of it, but that she loves him
with an inraged Affection, it is past the   110
infinite of Thought.

112 **May . . . counterfeit** The premise of Don Pedro's supposition is that Beatrice may now be displaying a 'Passion' (line 115) that is meant to be taken (erroneously) as 'Affection' for Benedick. It would see more likely, however, that 'she doth but counterfeit' in the opposite way: in the 'outward Behaviours' (line 104) by which she endeavours to signify her *lack* of affection for Benedick. *Counterfeit* echoes II.i.121; compare *Romeo and Juliet*, II.iii.50–55, where Mercutio and Romeo play on the words *counter* and *fit* to depict a copulative 'encounter' (see the note to I.i.335).

113 **like** likely.

115 **Life** essence, core. Compare II.ii.19–20.

116 **discovers** discloses, reveals. See II.ii.39–41.

117 **shews** shows. Here the Quarto spelling permits ironic wordplay on the aphetic form of *eschews*, 'shuns'.

120 **sit** Leonato's verb echoes lines 99–100, 106–7, and anticipates lines 143–45.

123 **amaze me** bewilder me (have me wandering in a maze).

125 **invincible** impenetrable, invulnerable. *Affection* echoes line 110; compare lines 134–35.

128 **Gull** trick, counterfeit. It *is* a gull, of course. But one of the ironies of the situation is that what Benedick takes to be a genuine representation of Beatrice's condition is in fact that: on the most fundamental psychological level, it is not a counterfeit at all.

129 **the White-bearded Fellow** Leonato.

130 **sure** surely, certainly.

131 **Reverence** aged dignity. *Hide* echoes line 43.

132 **ta'en the Infection** caught the disease. Compare I.i.87–92, II.i.257–62.

133 **hold it up** keep up the deception.

140 **encount'red** combated with. Claudio employs a military metaphor; but, as noted at I.i.335, *encounter* is often used to describe another kind of engagement. *Scorn* echoes lines 7–12; compare lines 112, 192–95.

144 **Smock** chemise, undergarment, 'Shift' (line 84).

148 **pretty** charming, cute.

PRINCE   May be she doth but counterfeit.

CLAUDIO   Faith like enough.

LEONATO   O God! counterfeit? There was never
Counterfeit of Passion came so near the Life   115
of Passion as she discovers it.

PRINCE   Why what Effects of Passion shews she?

CLAUDIO   — Bait the Hook well, this Fish will
bite.

LEONATO   What Effects, my Lord? She will sit   120
you, you heard my Daughter tell you how.

CLAUDIO   She did indeed.

PRINCE   How how, I pray you! you amaze me,
I would have thought her Spirit had been
invincible against all Assaults of Affection.   125

LEONATO   I would have sworn it had, my Lord,
especially against Benedick.

BENEDICK   — I should think this is a Gull, but
that the White-bearded Fellow speaks it:
Knavery cannot sure hide himself in such   130
Reverence.

CLAUDIO   — He hath ta'en the Infection,
hold it up.

PRINCE   Hath she made her Affection known to
Benedick?   135

LEONATO   No, and swears she never will, that's
her Torment.

CLAUDIO   'Tis true indeed, so your Daughter
says. 'Shall I,' says she, 'that have so oft
encount'red him with Scorn, write to him that   140
I love him?'

LEONATO   This says she now when she is beginning
to write to him, for she'll be up twenty times
a Night, and there will she sit in her Smock,
till she have writ a Sheet of Paper: my   145
Daughter tells us all.

CLAUDIO   Now you talk of a Sheet of Paper, I
remember a pretty Jest your Daughter told us
of.

151– **Benedick ... Sheet** either (a) the two names in the fold of a
52   sheet of paper, or (b) the two names between two sheets of
        paper. Here *Sheet* carries a plural sense. Modern editions
        normally place the names in quotation marks; Elizabethan
        printers did not use quotation marks the way we do, however,
        and in this case the suggestiveness of the 'Jest' comes across
        better if the reader sees the words in a manner that approxi-
        mates the way Benedick is intended to overhear them. The
        allusion to bedsheets recalls II.i.31–33.

155   **Halfpence** pieces the size of halfpence coins. The currency
        amounts noted in this scene have become progressively
        smaller (see lines 35, 45 and 64).

156   **immodest** forward, unmaidenlike (with a hint of the kind of
        impudence implied in the 'pretty Jest'). Compare II.i.393–94.

157   **flout** mock, scorn. See I.i.297–99.

165   **Ecstasy** rapture; literally, a condition in which a person feels
        beside (indeed outside) herself.
        overborne overwhelmed.

166   **sometime afeard** sometimes afraid.

166– **a desperate out-rage** an act of self-destruction deriving from
67   her despair (hopeless condition). *Out-rage* echoes *outward*
        (line 104) and *inraged* (line 110).

168– **It ... it** The point of this 'Gull' (line 128), of course, is to
69   accomplish the objective Don Pedro states. *Discover* echoes
        lines 114–16.

170   **End** purpose. Compare I.i.150–51, 297–99, 320–21,
        II.i.128–29, 274–75.

172   **it ... Alms** it would be an act of charity.

173– **out of all Suspicion** beyond all doubt. *Out* echoes lines
74   166–67.

175   **exceeding** exceedingly, surpassingly. *Wise* echoes lines 28–29,
        32–33; compare lines 198–206.

177   **Wisdom** both (a) intelligence, and (b) prudence, self-control.
        Blood passion. Compare I.i.135–36, 259–63, I.iii.28–31,
        II.i.185–87.

178   **tender** young and delicate.
        we ... one experience shows that in ten out of eleven
        instances.

182– **I ... me** I wish she had devoted this madness to me. Don
83   Pedro is speaking the truth here (see II.i.333–45).

LEONATO   O when she had writ it, and was reading   150
it over, she found Benedick and Beatrice
between the Sheet.

CLAUDIO   That.

LEONATO   O she tore the Letter into a thousand
Halfpence, rail'd at her self, that she should   155
be so immodest to write to one that she knew
would flout her. 'I measure him,' says she,
'by my own Spirit, for I should flout him if
he writ to me, yea though I love him I should.'

CLAUDIO   Then down upon her Knees she falls,   160
weeps, sobs, beats her Heart, tears her Hair,
prays, curses, 'O sweet Benedick! God give me
Patience.'

LEONATO   She doth indeed, my Daughter says so,
and the Ecstasy hath so much overborne her that   165
my Daughter is sometime afeard she will do a
desperate Out-rage to her self, it is very true.

PRINCE   It were good that Benedick knew of it
by some other, if she will not discover it.

CLAUDIO   To what End: he would make but a   170
Sport of it, and torment the poor Lady worse.

PRINCE   And he should, it were an Alms to hang
him: she's an excellent sweet Lady, and (out
of all Suspicion) she is virtuous.

CLAUDIO   And she is exceeding wise.   175

PRINCE   In every thing but in loving Benedick.

LEONATO   O my Lord, Wisdom and Blood combating
in so tender a Body, we have ten Proofs to one
that Blood hath the Victory; I am sorry for
her, as I have just Cause, being her Uncle, and   180
her Guardian.

PRINCE   I would she had bestowed this Dotage on
me, I would have daff'd all other Respects

---

183   I . . . Respects   I would have set aside all other considerations.
Here *daff'd* is a variation on *doff'd*, the past tense of a verb
that means 'do off'.

184   **half my self** Don Pedro alludes to the commonplace (from Genesis 2:24) that a husband and his wife are 'one flesh'.

185   **'a** he.

191   **bate** abate; lessen or cease. *Bate* can also mean 'flutter' when it refers to the flapping wings of an excited falcon. And in the expression *with bated breath* it refers to a suspended state of inhalation that results from anticipation or anxiety. *Crossness* recalls II.ii.7–8.

192   **tender** offer. But *make tender of her Love* could also mean 'allow her heart to become tender enough to be receptive to love'. Compare line 178.

194– **a contemptible Spirit** a disposition that prompts him to show
95   contempt for others.

196   **proper** both (a) worthy, respectable, and (b) handsome (synonymous with 'outward Happiness', line 197, an echo of lines 104, 166–67).

202   **Hector** the champion of the Trojans.

203   **Quarrels** differences that might require him to uphold his honour in a duel. This speech will prove unintentionally ironic.

206   **Fear** caution, here defined as a prudence deriving from a pious desire to live in accordance with Christian precepts, including the admonition to turn the other cheek and leave vengeance to the Lord (Romans 12:17–21).

208   **keep Peace** probably an allusion to Matthew 5:9, 'Blessed are the peacemakers'.

208–9 **if . . . Trembling** if he starts a quarrel, he should approach the duel with a different kind of fear, the knowledge that he is making himself subject to God's wrath and will probably die and be damned.

212   **large Jests** seemingly audacious wisecracks.

215– **let . . . counsel** let her endure her passion and try to outlive it
16   with the help of a good spiritual adviser. *Impossible* (line 217) echoes line 106.

219   **by** through.

220   **the while** in the meantime.

and made her half my self: I pray you, tell
Benedick of it, and hear what 'a will say.   185
LEONATO   Were it good, think you?
CLAUDIO   Hero thinks surely she will die, for
  she says she will die if he love her not, and
  she will die ere she make her Love known, and
  she will die if he woo her rather than she will   190
  bate one Breath of her accustomed Crossness.
PRINCE   She doth well, if she should make tender
  of her Love, 'tis very possible he'll scorn
  it, for the Man (as you know all) hath a
  contemptible Spirit.   195
CLAUDIO   He is a very proper Man.
PRINCE   He hath indeed a good outward Happiness.
CLAUDIO   Before God, and in my Mind, very wise.
PRINCE   He doth indeed shew some Sparks that are
  like Wit.   200
CLAUDIO   And I take him to be valiant.
PRINCE   As Hector, I assure you, and in the
  managing of Quarrels you may say he is wise,
  for either he avoids them with great Discretion
  or undertakes them with a most Christian-like   205
  Fear.
LEONATO   If he do fear God, 'a must necessarily
  keep Peace; if he break the Peace, he ought to
  enter into a Quarrel with Fear and Trembling.
PRINCE   And so will he do, for the man doth fear   210
  God, howsoever it seems not in him by some
  large Jests he will make. Well, I am sorry for
  your Niece; shall we go seek Benedick and tell
  him of her Love?
CLAUDIO   Never tell him, my Lord; let her wear   215
  it out with good Counsel.
LEONATO   Nay that's impossible, she may wear her
  Heart out first.
PRINCE   Well, we will hear further of it by
  your Daughter, let it cool the while. I love   220
  Benedick well, and I could wish he would

222   **modestly** humbly. This word echoes line 156.

224   **Dinner** the main midday meal.

229   **carry** hold up (line 133), that is, the 'Net' referred to in line 227.

230   **Dotage** infatuation, love-madness. Compare lines 182–83.

231   **and . . . matter** without any basis for their 'Opinion'. Don Pedro appears to be unaware that there *is* 'such matter'. And that is what will make the 'Dumb Shew' that follows this gulling so different from the one that follows the gulling of Malvolio in *Twelfth Night*.

232   **merely . . . Shew** nothing more than a pantomime (here one in which each will be finding a significance in the other's silent behaviour that is not intended by the agent).

234   **Trick** deception. Compare I.i.150.

234–   **the . . . borne** the conferring was conducted in a way that was
35   both serious and sad (because of their concern for Beatrice). What Benedick doesn't know is that the conversation was only 'sadly *borne*' (carried, in the sense implied in line 229).

237   **have . . . Bent** are drawn to the utmost (like an archer's bow). *Affections* echoes lines 124–25, 134–35.

238   **requited** reciprocated, responded to in kind.

239   **censur'd** judged, criticized.

241   **Sign** 'outward Behaviours' (line 104) to indicate her true feelings.

242   **think** expect. So also in line 259.

243–   **happy . . . mending** blessed are those who are able to bear
44   criticism of their faults and reform their behaviour accordingly. Benedick's phrasing echoes such passages as Matthew 11:15, 'He that hath ears to hear, let him hear,' and it relates to one of the principal themes of Shakespeare's two *Henry IV* plays. What Benedick says is that he will note (attend to and act upon) what he has just noted (overheard). Compare lines 220–23.

245   **Fair** attractive (though not necessarily of the lightest complexion, if Beatrice is to be taken literally in II.i.333–35). See the note to line 37.

247   **reprove** refute, disprove.
       but except.

modestly examine himself, to see how much he
is unworthy so good a Lady.

LEONATO   My Lord, will you walk? Dinner is ready.

CLAUDIO   – If he do not dote on her upon this, I   225
will never trust my Expectation.

PRINCE   – Let there be the same Net spread for
her, and that must your Daughter and her
Gentlewomen carry. The Sport will be, when
they hold one an Opinion of an other's Dotage,   230
and no such matter: that's the Scene that I
would see, which will be merely a Dumb Shew.
Let us send her to call him in to Dinner.

> *Exeunt.* [*Manet Benedick.*]

BENEDICK   This can be no Trick: the Conference
was sadly borne, they must have the truth of   235
this from Hero, they seem to pity the Lady. It
seems her Affections have their full Bent: love
me? why it must be requited. I hear how I am
censur'd, they say I will bear my self proudly
if I perceive the Love come from her; they say   240
too that she will rather die than give any Sign
of Affection. I did never think to marry. I
must not seem proud, happy are they that hear
their Detractions, and can put them to mending.
They say the Lady is Fair: 'tis a Truth, I can   245
bear them Witness. And Virtuous: 'tis so, I
cannot reprove it. And Wise, but for loving me:
by my troth it is no addition to her Wit, nor
no great Argument of her Folly, for I will be
horribly in love with her. I may chaunce have   250

248–   **by . . . Folly**   In other Shakespearean contexts *addition* refers to
49   the male member; *Wit* and *Argument* can allude to the
           genitalia of either gender; and *Folly* can apply to wantonness
           and to a variety of sexual situations. See the notes to I.i.72,
           265, II.i.15. *Argument* echoes lines 7–12.

251 **Quirks** quibbles, gibes, 'Quips' (line 255). Benedick's jousting imagery (lines 250–52) echoes I.i.62–73, 150–51, II.i.152–57, 295–96. Here he implies that anyone who tries to penetrate his armour will merely break a lance in the process.

254 **Meat** solid food. Compare I.i.43–53, II.i.205–7.

255 **Sentences** *sententiae*, the Latin word for pithy proverbs.

257 **Career . . . Humour** course (full tilt) of his disposition.

262 **Marks** signs (line 241). Compare II.i.152–57, 255–56.

263 **Will** This is another word that frequently carries genital implications; see the note to I.i.245. Beatrice's phrasing provides subliminal support for the other 'Marks of Love' that the doting Benedick believes himself to spy in her 'Dumb Shew' (line 232).

268– **if . . . come** Beatrice's language unconsciously hints at the kind
69 of 'Pain' that might be translated into 'Pleasure' (line 270). See the second note to V.ii.14. Speed plays on *Pains* in I.i.115–36 of *The Two Gentlemen of Verona*; and *come* is a word that carries erotic implications in I.i.126–27, II.i.83–85, 126–27, 340–41, II.iii.30–31, and in *All's Well That Ends Well* (see II.iv.47–49 and IV.iii.67) and *Measure for Measure* (see II.i.126–30).

271– **Yea . . . withal** either (a) Yes, just as much pleasure as a person
72 may take from swallowing a knife's point and being choked like a jackdaw, or, more likely, (b) Yes, just as much pleasure as you may derive from a knife's point (my message), and I hope you choke on it like a daw (a sense that would illustrate Benedick's comment in II.i.256 that Beatrice 'speaks Poinyards'). Again Beatrice's imagery is erotically suggestive. See the note to I.i.245.

273 **you . . . well** if you have no appetite, sir, fare you well [I'll return and say I did what I was 'bid'].

275– **there's . . . that** Benedick is probably interpreting *Against* (line
76 263) to mean 'in anticipation of' or 'in keeping with'. It seems unlikely that he picks up on the physical sense that *Against my Will* could carry. Much of the humour in the situation derives, of course, from our awareness that, whatever the unconscious implications of what she says, Beatrice intends no 'double Meaning' of any sort.

281 **a Jew** that is, a person who refuses to be converted (a sense that recalls I.i.130–32 and II.iii.23–24, 242–44).

some odd Quirks and Remnants of Wit broken
on me, because I have railed so long against
Marriage: but doth not the Appetite alter? A
Man loves the Meat in his Youth that he cannot
indure in his Age. Shall Quips and Sentences,   255
and these paper Bullets of the Brain, awe a
Man from the Career of his Humour? No, the
World must be peopled. When I said I would
die a Bachelor, I did not think I should live
till I were married. Here comes Beatrice: by   260
this Day, she's a fair Lady, I do spy some
Marks of Love in her.

Enter Beatrice.

BEATRICE   Against my Will I am sent to bid you
come in to Dinner.
BENEDICK   Fair Beatrice, I thank you for your   265
Pains.
BEATRICE   I took no more Pains for those Thanks
than you take Pains to thank me; if it had
been painful I would not have come.
BENEDICK   You take Pleasure then in the Message.   270
BEATRICE   Yea, just so much as you may take
upon a Knive's Point, and choke a Daw withal:
you have no Stomach, Signior, fare you well.   *Exit.*
BENEDICK   Ha, 'against my Will I am sent to
bid you come to Dinner': there's a double   275
Meaning in that. 'I took no more Pains for
those Thanks than you took Pains to thank me':
that's as much as to say 'any Pains that I
take for you is as easy as Thanks'. If I do
not take Pity of her I am a Villain, if I do   280
not love her I am a Jew: I will go get her
Picture.   *Exit.*

III.i   We now proceed to a second gulling scene in Leonato's garden. Whereas the preceding scene was entirely in prose, this one is all in blank verse.

s.d.   **Ursley** Ursula.

3   **Proposing** conversing (literally, putting or holding forth). Compare line 12.

4   **Whisper** whisper into.

7   **pleached Bower** an arbour formed of intertwined branches. Compare I.ii.9–10.

10   **advaunce their Pride** assert (literally, uplift) themselves insolently. *Pride* is associated with various forms of haughtiness and aspiration in Elizabethan usage, including erotic 'ambitions', as in Sonnet 151, where 'Flesh' is said to be 'proud' of the 'Pride' that, 'rising at thy Name, doth point out thee / As his triumphant Prize'. In this instance Hero's imagery is a reminder of the 'advancement' that has occurred in the preceding scene, in no small part because Benedick, examining himself, has resolved to forswear pride; see II.iii.238–44.

12   **listen our Propose** overhear our conversation. Hero's wording is apt: she and her companions will set forward an interpretation of Benedick's condition as part of a plot to engineer another kind of proposal.
Office responsibility, assigned duty. Compare II.i.182–83, 393–94.

13   **Bear . . . it** carry it off well. Compare the phrasing in II.iii.133, 229.
leave us alone leave the rest to us.

14   **I'll make her come** Compare II.iii.268–69.

16   **trace this Alley** tread this pathway. Compare I.ii.8–11; *onely* (only), lines 17, 23, echoes II.ii.31.

18   **thy part** your role. Hero's words are a reminder that this is a plot with theatrical analogies. Compare II.i.221–22, and see line 31.

21   **sick in love** so deeply in love that it has made him sick.

23   **That . . . Hearsay** which enters only through the ears. *Cupid* (line 22) recalls II.i.404–6.

24   **Lapwing** a bird proverbial for its craft and stealthiness. Compare II.iii.99–100.

ACT III

Scene 1

Enter Hero and two Gentlewomen, Margaret and Ursley.

HERO   Good Margaret, run thee to the Parlour,
There shalt thou find my Cousin Beatrice,
Proposing with the Prince and Claudio.
Whisper her Ear and tell her I and Ursley
Walk in the Orchard, and our whole Discourse   5
Is all of her. Say that thou overheardst us,
And bid her steal into the pleached Bower
Where Honeysuckles, ripen'd by the Sun,
Forbid the Sun to enter: like Favourites
Made proud by Princes, that advaunce their
    Pride   10
Against the Power that bred it. There will she
    hide her,
To listen our Propose. This is thy Office,
Bear thee well in it, and leave us alone.

MARGARET   I'll make her come, I warrant you,
    presently.   [*Exit.*]

HERO   Now Ursula, when Beatrice doth come,   15
As we do trace this Alley up and down,
Our Talk must onely be of Benedick:
When I do name him, let it by thy part
To praise him more than ever man did merit.
My Talk to thee must be how Benedick   20
Is sick in love with Beatrice. Of this Matter
Is little Cupid's crafty Arrow made,
That onely wounds by Hearsay: now begin,
For look where Beatrice like a Lapwing runs

25 **Conference** conferring, conversation (as in II.iii.234).

26 **Angling** fishing (from the Anglo-Saxon word *angul*, fish-hook).
    Compare II.iii.118–19.

27 **Oars** fins.

28 **treacherous** both (a) traitorous, and (b) dangerous.

30 **couched** lowered into a crouching position.
    wood-bine Coverture bower formed by the honeysuckle.

31 **Fear you not** have no worries about. Compare line 13.

32 **loose** both (a) lose, and (b) set loose, fail to grasp.

33 **false sweet Bait** The 'Bait' that Hero and Ursula 'lay' (display
    as a lure) for Beatrice will be falsely sweet in the sense that it
    portrays Benedick in a way that they believe to be a
    misrepresentation of his genuinely sour disposition. What
    they don't yet know is that their 'false' portrait of him as
    sweet on Beatrice is actually a true one.

35–36 **as . . . Rock** as disdainful and ungovernable as wild female
    hawks.

37 **intirely** entirely.

38 **new trothed Lord** newly engaged husband-to-be.

42 **wrastle** wrestle. Hero hints at 'merry War' (I.i.63). *Affection*
    echoes II.iii.237 and anticipates line 55; *know of it* (line 43)
    plays on *acquaint*, line 40 (see the note to V.i.342), and hints
    at the kind of 'knowing' that comes from those who 'wrastle
    with Affection'.

45 **as full** fully.

46 **couch** recline (a reminder that Beatrice is now couching –
    crouching – nearby).

49 **Hart** heart. Here the spelling reinforces the notion that
    Beatrice's disdainful heart is made of the 'prouder Stuff' (line
    50) normally associated with males rather than with 'weaker
    vessels' (1 Peter 3:7). Beatrice's heart is likened to a stag deer
    that considers itself invulnerable to the Love God's arrow.
    Prouder echoes lines 9–11.

52 **Misprising** literally, mis-apprising; undervaluing, holding in
    contempt. Lines 51–52 suggest that 'Disdain' and 'Scorn' are
    haughty knights who enter the lists with nothing but
    contempt for the lances and armour of lesser tilters; see the
    note to II.iii.51.
    her Wit both (a) her sharp intelligence, and (b) her ability to
    discharge withering witticisms. See II.iii.248–49.

Close by the Ground, to hear our Conference.   25

Enter Beatrice.

URSULA   The pleasant'st Angling is to see the
    Fish
    Cut with her golden Oars the silver Stream,
    And greedily devour the treacherous Bait:
    So angle we for Beatrice, who even now
    Is couched in the wood-bine Coverture.   30
    Fear you not my part of the Dialogue.
HERO   Then go we near her that her Ear loose
    nothing
    Of the false sweet Bait that we lay for it.
    — No truly, Ursula, she is too disdainful,
    I know her Spirits are as coy and wild   35
    As Haggards of the Rock.
URSULA   But are you sure,
    That Benedick loves Beatrice so intirely?
HERO   So says the Prince, and my new trothed
    Lord.
URSULA   And did they bid you tell her of it,
    Madam?
HERO   They did intreat me to acquaint her of it,   40
    But I persuaded them, if they lov'd Benedick,
    To wish him wrastle with Affection,
    And never to let Beatrice know of it.
URSULA   Why did you so, dooth not the Gentleman
    Deserve as full as fortunate a Bed   45
    As ever Beatrice shall couch upon?
HERO   O God of Love! I know he doth deserve,
    As much as may be yielded to a Man:
    But Nature never fram'd a Woman's Hart
    Of prouder Stuff than that of Beatrice.   50
    Disdain and Scorn ride sparkling in her Eyes,
    Misprising what they look on, and her Wit
    Values it self so highly, that to her
    All Matter else seems weak: she cannot love,

55 **Nor ... Affection** nor be shaped by or receive any projection
of affection. Hero's phrasing is erotically suggestive. *Project*
means 'thrust forward', and Shakespeare uses it elsewhere
with phallic import (compare *Troilus and Cressida*,
II.ii.129–41). *Matter*, line 54, echoes line 21.

56 **self-indear'd** in love (endeared) with herself.

57 **were not** would not be.

61 **spell him backward** either (a) use perverse language, or spell
out words letter by letter (perhaps in a transverse manner), to
conjure up a negative image of him (sorcerers sometimes said
prayers backwards to summon demons), or (b) use spells to
drive him away (back from her) by portraying any virtues he
has as vices. Hero's phrase plays on *spill*, and it can also carry
an erotic sense that pertains to a 'backward' Beatrice, supine
'with her Face upward' (III.ii.69); compare V.ii.9–10.

62 **should ... Sister** was too pretty to be a real man. Lines 61–62
recall II.i.34–42.

63 **black** darkened by the sun (and thus the opposite of 'fair'). See
the note to II.i.333–34.
drawing ... Antique creating, or deriving Benedick's
appearance from, the image of a grotesque.

64 **Made ... Blot** erred and made a dark ink blot.
a Launce ill-headed a lance without a sharp or fitting head
(point).

65 **Agot** agate, here a stone set in a seal ring with a tiny figure of a
man cut in it.
vildly vilely, wretchedly.

66 **Vane** weathervane (with a hint of vanity: emptiness and
vainglory). The line recalls I.i.120–21, II.i.7–11.

67 **moved with none** unresponsive to any winds; *moved* is
disyllabic here. *Block* echoes II.i.247–48.

70 **Simpleness** innocence, honest virtue.
purchaseth deserve, have earned. Lines 68–70 recall
II.iii.19–28.

71 **commendable** attractive, worthy of her; pronounced
'cóm-men-dá-ble'.

72 **odd** at odds, obstinate.
from all Fashions in opposition to every type of man and every
form of human behaviour.

Nor take no Shape nor Project of Affection, 55
She is so self-indear'd.
URSULA   Sure I think so,
    And therefore certainly it were not good
    She knew his Love lest she'll make Sport at it.
HERO   Why you speak Truth, I never yet saw Man,
    How wise, how noble, young, how rarely
        featured, 60
    But she would spell him backward. If fair fac'd,
    She would swear the Gentleman should be her Sister;
    If black, why Nature, drawing of an Antique,
    Made a foul Blot; if tall, a Launce ill-headed;
    If low, an Agot very vildly cut; 65
    If speaking, why a Vane blown with all Winds;
    If silent, why a Block moved with none.
    So turns she every Man the Wrong Side out,
    And never gives to Truth and Virtue that
    Which Simpleness and Merit purchaseth. 70
URSULA   Sure, sure, such Carping is not
        commendable.
HERO   No, not to be so odd, and from all
        Fashions,
    As Beatrice is, cannot be commendable,
    But who dare tell her so? If I should speak,
    She would mock me into Air; O she would laugh me 75
    Out of my self, press me to death with Wit.
    Therefore let Benedick, like cover'd Fire,
    Consume away in Sighs, waste inwardly:
    It were a better Death than die with Mocks,

---

75   **mock . . . Air**   reduce me to nothing with her scorn.

76   **press . . . Death**   a torture for accused prisoners who refused to
        enter a plea when confronted with a criminal charge. *Wit*
        echoes line 52, and anticipates line 89.

77   **cover'd Fire**   a fire covered to make it burn slowly or die.
        Compare I.i.238–44, II.i.262–64, III.i.30.

80   **Tickling**   here trisyllabic. Compare II.i.253. Hero is describing
      another form of torture, but in other contexts *die* and *tickling*
      have sexual implications (see *Troilus and Cressida*,
      III.i.120–34, IV.v.61, and V.ii.45–46). Compare III.iv.74–77.

83   **counsaile**   counsel, advise. See also in line 102.

84   **honest**   honourable; truthful (*truly*), but not actually damaging
      to her reputation or slanderous to her character.

86   **ill**   both (a) evil, malicious, and (b) unhealthy (a sense that
      coheres with *impoison*).

92   **onely**   only; foremost. Here as elsewhere, the Renaissance
      spelling plays suggestively on *one*, a word linked to phallic
      assertion in *The Two Gentlemen of Verona*, II.v.18–38,
      Romeo and Juliet, II.iii.72–73, *Julius Caesar*, I.ii.153–54,
      III.i.69–71, and *Macbeth*, I.vii.72–74. Compare line 17, and
      see the note to II.i.404–5.

93   **excepted**   with the exception of. Compare Benedick's comment
      in I.i.197–201.

96   **Shape**   physical attributes. Compare line 55 and II.i.15–18.
      bearing Argument   manliness and eloquence in upholding his
      dignity and honour. Compare II.iii.56, 201–9, 248–49, and
      Romeo and Juliet, II.iii.105–8; *bearing* echoes line 13.

97   **Report**   reputation. The word *foremost* hints at a virile 'Project
      of Affection' (line 55).
      through   both (a) throughout, and (b) penetrating.

100   **When . . . married**   what time are you to be wed?

101   **every day to morrow**   for the rest of my days beginning
      tomorrow. Here as occasionally elsewhere (see *Macbeth*,
      V.v.19–23), *to morrow* can mean more than the modern
      word *tomorrow*; compare line 103, and see I.i.330.

102   **Attires**   apparel I'm considering for the occasion.
      Counsaile   counsel, advice.

104   **limed**   snared in sticky birdlime like a woodcock.

105   **Haps**   chance occurrences (here the coincidence that Beatrice
      just happens to have overheard this conversation). *Cupid* (line
      106) echoes lines 21–23.

109   **Contempt, farewell**   Compare Benedick's repentance and
      conversion from pride and contempt in II.iii.242–44.
      adew   adieu (French for 'farewell', 'to God'). Compare *Hamlet*,
      I.v.90, 109–10, where *Adew* resolves itself into 'a Dew'
      (I.ii.129–30) of tearful anguish.

Which is as bad as die with Tickling.   80
URSULA   Yet tell her of it, her what she will
    say.
HERO   No rather I will go to Benedick,
    And counsaile him to fight against his Passion,
    And truly I'll devise some honest Slaunders,
    To stain my Cousin with; one doth not know   85
    How much an ill Word may impoison Liking.
URSULA   O do not do your Cousin such a Wrong,
    She cannot be so much without true Judgement,
    Having so swift and excellent a Wit
    As she is priz'd to have, as to refuse   90
    So rare a Gentleman as Signior Benedick.
HERO   He is the onely Man of Italy,
    Always excepted my dear Claudio.
URSULA   I pray you be not angry with me, Madam,
    Speaking my Fancy: Signior Benedick,   95
    For Shape, for bearing Argument and Valour,
    Goes foremost in Report through Italy.
HERO   Indeed he hath an excellent good Name.
URSULA   His Excellence did earn it, ere he had it.
    When are you married, Madam?   100
HERO   Why every day to morrow: come go in,
    I'll shew thee some Attires, and have thy
        Counsaile,
    Which is the best to furnish me to morrow.
URSULA   — She's limed, I warrant you: we have
        caught her, Madam.
HERO   — If it prove so, then Loving goes by Haps,   105
    Some Cupid kills with Arrows, some with Traps,
                            Exeunt. [*Manet Beatrice.*]
BEATRICE   What Fire is in mine Ears? Can this
        be true?
    Stand I condemn'd for Pride and Scorn so much?
    — Contempt, farewell, and maiden Pride, adew,

110   **No . . . such**   No honourable words are spoken behind the backs of those who are too proud.

111   **requite thee**   reciprocate your love. Compare II.iii.238.

112   **Taming . . . Hand**   a continuation of the 'Hart' imagery in lines 49–50.

116   **better then reportingly**   both (a) on the basis of more than report, and (b) better then, having heard it reported in a way that 'can be no Trick' (II.iii.234).

III.ii   This scene takes place elsewhere at Leonato's house.

2   **consummate**   solemnized in a public ceremony, concluded.

3   **bring**   accompany, escort.

4   **vouchsafe**   condescend to permit.

8   **only . . . with**   only take the liberty of imposing on.

11   **cut Cupid's Bowstring**   impaired the Love God's ability to shoot (and thus prevented himself from being infected with love's melancholy). Don Pedro is explaining why Benedick is 'all Mirth' (line 10). He may be suggesting that even when Benedick appears to have been hit by Cupid's arrow, he evades the commitment that true love normally implies; compare what Beatrice has said about Benedick's unreliability in I.i.73–74, 150–51, II.i.287–97. The reference to Cupid echoes III.i.106.

12   **Hangman**   executioner. Don Pedro is probably punning on other senses of *Hangman*: (a) bawd (one who serves as a go-between for men who desire to 'hang' themselves in houses of the sort referred to in I.i.262–63), and (b) cuckolder (one who induces a man to 'hang' his 'Bugle in an invisible Baldrick', a pudendum, and then hangs horns on his forehead, as described in I.i.249–52). The bawd Pompey alludes to the first type of hangman in his conversation with the executioner in IV.ii.33–56 of *Measure for Measure*.

13   **sound**   whole (unbroken), healthy. Don Pedro puns on the sound a bell makes.

14   **Clapper**   Like *Tongue* and *Heart* (which is here equivalent to Will), this image suggests a male 'Bugle' to sound a female 'Baldrick' (see the note to line 12).

No Glory lives behind the Back of such.   110
— And Benedick, love on, I will requite thee,
Taming my wild Heart to thy loving Hand:
If thou dost love, my Kindness shall incite
   thee
To bind our Loves up in a holy Band.
For others say thou dost deserve, and I   115
Believe it better then reportingly.   *Exit.*

Scene 2

Enter Prince, Claudio, Benedick, and Leonato.

PRINCE   I do but stay till your Marriage be
consummate, and then go I toward Aragon.
CLAUDIO   I'll bring you thither, my Lord, if
you'll vouchsafe me.
PRINCE   Nay that would be as great a Soil in the   5
new Gloss of your Marriage as to shew a Child
his new Coat and forbid him wear it. I will
only be bold with Benedick for his Company,
for from the Crown of his Head to the Sole of
his Foot, he is all Mirth; he hath twice or   10
thrice cut Cupid's Bowstring, and the little
Hangman dare not shoot at him; he hath a
Heart as sound as a Bell, and his Tongue
is the Clapper, for what his Heart thinks,
his Tongue speaks.   15
BENEDICK   Gallants, I am not as I have been.
LEONATO   So say I, me thinks you are sadder.
CLAUDIO   I hope he be in love.

19   **Truant**   ne'er-do-well, villain.

20   **Blood**   both (a) nobility (as in I.iii.29), and (b) affection,
      passion (as in I.i.135–36). Compare II.iii.177–79.

21   **if . . . Money**   if he's down in the dumps, it's because he lacks
      the wealth he wishes he had.

23   **Draw it**   pull it (but with a suggestion that Benedick's real
      'ache' is in the kind of sword-like 'Colt's Tooth' that Lord
      Sandys calls 'a Stump' in *Henry VIII*, I.iii.47–49). For later
      references to 'tooth-aches' and to the copulative H-figure they
      suggest, see III.iv.53–57 and V.i.26, 34–38.

24   **Hang it**   Benedick means something like 'confound it!' But he is
      also alluding to the practice of hanging and then drawing
      (disembowelling) and quartering criminals.

25   **draw it**   In addition to the wordplay noted above, Claudio is
      probably picking up on the bawdy sense of *hang* in line 24;
      among other things, *draw it* can also mean (a) drain it off,
      and (b) withdraw it.

28   **Where . . . Worm**   Which is caused by nothing more than a
      humour (an imbalance or improper mixture of fluids in the
      system) or a burrowing worm. Leonato is probably
      continuing the metaphorical play on *Tooth-ache* with a
      suggestion that Benedick is actually suffering from a swollen
      'Worm'.

30   **but**   but only.

32   **Fancy**   infatuation, lovesickness. In lines 33, 38, the word
      means 'proclivity' or 'taste'.

36   **Germaine**   German.
      Waste   wordplay on (a) *waist* and (b) *wasteland*, bogs or 'Slops'
      (line 37). *Shape* (line 35) echoes III.i.96.

37   **Slops**   loose and baggy breeches of the kind worn by Germans.

38   **no Doublet**   that is, a waist-length cape instead of a tight-fitting
      laced jacket.

43   **old Signs**   traditional indications of lovesickness.

47–48 **the . . . Balls**   his beard is now stuffing for tennis balls.

51   **Civet**   a fashionable musky perfume extracted from scent
      glands of the civet cat. *Beard* (line 50) recalls II.i.277–82.

55   **Note**   sign, mark. Compare II.iii.56–60.

56   **woont**   wont, accustomed.

PRINCE   Hang him Truant, there's no true Drop
of Blood in him to be truly touch'd with Love;   20
if he be sad, he wants Money.
BENEDICK   I have the Tooth-ache.
PRINCE   Draw it.
BENEDICK   Hang it.
CLAUDIO   You must hang it first, and draw it   25
afterwards.
PRINCE   What? sigh for the Tooth-ache.
LEONATO   Where is but a Humour or a Worm.
BENEDICK   Well, every one cannot master a Grief,
but he that has it.   30
CLAUDIO   Yet say I, he is in love.
PRINCE   There is no appearance of Fancy in him,
unless it be a Fancy that he hath to strange
Disguises, as to be a Dutchman to day, a
Frenchman to morrow, or in the Shape of two   35
Countries at once, as a Germaine from the Waste
downward, all Slops, and a Spaniard from the
Hip upward, no Doublet; unless he have a Fancy
to this Foolery, as it appears he hath, he is
no Fool for Fancy, as you would have it appear   40
he is.
CLAUDIO   If he be not in love with some Woman,
there is no believing old Signs. 'A brushes
his Hat 'a Mornings: what should that bode?
PRINCE   Hath any man seen him at the Barber's?   45
CLAUDIO   No, but the Barber's Man hath been seen
with him, and the old Ornament of his Cheek
hath already stuff'd Tennis Balls.
LEONATO   Indeed he looks younger than he did, by
the loss of a Beard.   50
PRINCE   Nay 'a rubs himself with Civet, can you
smell him out by that?
CLAUDIO   That's as much as to say, the sweet
Youth's in love.
PRINCE   The greatest Note of it is his Melancholy.   55
CLAUDIO   And when was he woont to wash his Face?

57   **paint himself**   'wash his Face' (line 56) with cosmetics. Don
        Pedro alludes to what Benedick has said in I.i.271–77.

60   **crept . . . Lute-string**   declined into the kind of spirit that is
        more inclined to love-songs. Compare II.i.99–100,
        II.iii.13–15.

60–61 **govern'd by Stops**   both (a) controlled by the frets (small bars
        of wood or wire) on the finger-board of a lute, and (b) subject
        to the palpitations and shortness of breath associated with
        seizures of emotion.

62   **tells . . . him**   discloses that he is suffering from 'Melancholy'
        (line 55), in this case the solemn moods of a lover. Here *heavy*
        (sad) may play on 'heave' (shiver from amorous fever); and
        the phrase *heavy Tale* can also refer to a blood-engorged male
        'tail' (see the note to I.i.335), as in *Romeo and Juliet*,
        II.iii.105–8, a sense that will permit *tells* to mean 'tolls' and
        thus echo the 'Clapper' image of lines 12–15. Compare *A
        Midsummer Night's Dream*, V.i.367: 'The iron Tongue of
        Midnight hath told Twelve'.

65   **I warrant**   I'll wager.

66   **knows him not**   both (a) doesn't know what kind of fellow he
        really is, and (b) doesn't yet know him carnally.

67   **ill Conditions**   faults, bad qualities.

68   **dispight**   spite. Compare II.ii.31.

69   **buried . . . upwards**   Don Pedro plays on the orgasmic sense of
        dies in line 68 and the copulative sense of *knows* in line 66.
        Shakespeare gives *buried* the same implication when Bertram
        refers to himself as having 'buried a Wife' (but not in the way
        he thinks) in IV.iii.102–3 of *All's Well That Ends Well*. See
        the notes to III.i.42, 61.

70   **Charm**   magical cure.

73   **these Hobby-horses**   Benedick compares Don Pedro and
        Claudio to the clowns who impersonated erotically aggressive
        men on horseback in morris dances (performed in costume on
        May Day).

78   **then**   thus, therefore. *Break* (broach the subject of matrimony),
        line 74, recalls II.i.161–63, II.iii.208–9, 250–53; *parts* (line
        77) echoes III.i.31.

81   **Good den**   good evening (a salutation appropriate any time
        after noon).

PRINCE   Yea, or to paint himself? for the which
I hear what they say of him.

CLAUDIO   Nay but his jesting Spirit, which is
now crept into a Lute-string, and now govern'd   60
by Stops.

PRINCE   Indeed that tells a heavy Tale for him:
conclude, conclude, he is in love.

CLAUDIO   Nay but I know who loves him.

PRINCE   That would I know too, I warrant one that   65
knows him not.

CLAUDIO   Yes, and his ill Conditions, and in
dispight of all, dies for him.

PRINCE   She shall be buried with her Face upwards.

BENEDICK   Yet is this no Charm for the Tooth-   70
ache. – Old Signior, walk aside with me, I have
studied eight or nine wise Words to speak to
you, which these Hobby-horses must not hear.
                              [*Exit with Leonato.*]

PRINCE   For my Life, to break with him about
Beatrice.   75

CLAUDIO   'Tis even so: Hero and Margaret have
by this played their parts with Beatrice, and
then the two Bears will not bite one another
when they meet.

Enter John the Bastard.

BASTARD   My Lord and Brother, God save you.   80

PRINCE   Good den, Brother.

BASTARD   If your Leisure serv'd, I would speak
with you.

PRINCE   In private?

BASTARD   If it please you, yet Count Claudio may   85
hear, for what I would speak of concerns him.

87   **What's the matter?**   both (a) what's wrong? and (b) what is the
      subject matter that you 'would speak of' (line 86)?

93   **Impediment**   obstacle, reason not to marry. Claudio echoes a
      phrase from the marriage service in the Book of Common
      Prayer (1549). Compare IV.i.12–14.

94   **discover**   disclose. Compare II.iii.168–69.

96   **aim . . . me**   draw a more accurate bead on my character. In
      due course, Claudio and Don Pedro will 'aim better' at Don
      John as a result of what he manifests here.

99   **holp**   helped.

100   **Suit all spent**   wooing poorly invested. *Ill* echoes line 67.
      bestowed   provided.

103   **Circumstances short'ned**   to make a long story short, to
      abbreviate all the circumstances involved in the conclusion I
      have to report to you.

104   **disloyal**   both (a) unfaithful to you, and (b) disloyal to her
      betrothal vows. Compare line 108 and II.ii.50.

109   **paint out**   portray the full extent of. *Paint* echoes lines 56–57.

111– **fit . . . it**   make her conform to it [by what I tell you about her
12   character]. Don John's verb is graphically apt. Lavatch and
      the Countess play on a related sense of *fit* in II.ii.15–35 of
      All's Well That Ends Well. Compare I.i.328–29, II.iii.44–45.

112   **Warrant**   assurance, warranty [of the truth of my testimony].

113   **to night**   tonight (compare III.i.101). Here Don John's words
      are a reminder that he plans to conduct his victims 'to night'
      in both a literal and a metaphorical sense.

114   **Window ent'red**   Don John's phrasing is designed to suggest an
      erotic sense that coheres with the literal sense. His phrasing
      recalls II.iii.91–93.

116   **fit your Honour**   suit your reputation and standing as a
      gentleman. See the note to lines 111–12.

124   **why**   to show why.

PRINCE   What's the matter?

BASTARD   — Means your Lordship to be married
to morrow?

PRINCE   You know he does.   90

BASTARD   I know not that when he knows what I
know.

CLAUDIO   If there be any Impediment, I pray you
discover it.

BASTARD   You may think I love you not: let that   95
appear hereafter, and aim better at me by that
I now will manifest. For my Brother (I think he
holds you well, and in dearness of Heart) hath
holp to effect your ensuing Marriage: surely
Suit ill spent, and Labour ill bestowed.   100

PRINCE   Why what's the matter?

BASTARD   I come hither to tell you, and
Circumstances short'ned (for she has been too
long a' talking of), the Lady is disloyal.

CLAUDIO   Who, Hero?   105

BASTARD   Even she, Leonato's Hero, your Hero,
every man's Hero.

CLAUDIO   Disloyal?

BASTARD   The Word is too good to paint out her
Wickedness. I could say she were worse: think   110
you of a worse Title, and I will fit her to
it. Wonder not till further Warrant. Go but
with me to night, you shall see her Chamber
Window ent'red, even the Night before her
Wedding Day. If you love her, then to morrow   115
wed her: but it would better fit your Honour
to change your Mind.

CLAUDIO   May this be so?

PRINCE   I will not think it.

BASTARD   If you dare not trust that you see,   120
confess not that you know: if you will follow
me, I will shew you enough, and when you have
seen more, and heard more, proceed accordingly.

CLAUDIO   If I see any thing to night, why I should

128   **disgrace** both (a) 'shame' (line 126), and (b) cast into disfavour, condemn.

130   **you . . . Witnesses** you too have witnessed the truth of what I have just told you.

      bear it coldly reserve your own judgement; be calm and rational. Compare III.i.13, 95–97. Don John knows that the suspicion he has just planted will so impassion Claudio that he'll proceed with anything but 'cold Considerance' (2 *Henry IV*, V.ii.97). Borachio will later describe Claudio and Don Pedro as 'possess'd' (III.iii.168–70) by Don John's villainy. *Coldly* recalls I.i.135–36, where Beatrice expresses thanks for her 'cold Blood', her ability to govern her passions with what Duke Theseus calls 'cool Reason' in V.i.6 of *A Midsummer Night's Dream*. *Issue* (line 131), 'outcome', echoes II.ii.52–53; *shew* (show) hints at an aphetic form of *eschew*, as in I.i.23.

132   **untowardly turned** perverted into the opposite of what it had been till now. A scene that began with jests about Benedick's conversion from a confirmed bachelor into a soon-to-be-married man concludes with ominous indications that Claudio is about to be converted from a soon-to-be-married man into an embittered bachelor.

133   **strangely** both (a) incredibly, and (b) perversely.

III.iii   This scene takes place on a street in Messina.

S.D.   **Dogberry** The head constable's name alludes to the fruit of the wild dogwood. *Verges* derives from 'verjuice', the juice of an unripe fruit. But the name of Dogberry's deputy may also relate to the role he plays as a man who verges on competence as an officer of the law; see III.v.34–36, where he is on the brink of disclosing some important information before the condescending head constable stifles him.

      Compartner co-partner.

      Watch volunteer night-watchmen.

1   **good . . . true** honest, law-abiding citizens.

3   **Salvation** Verges probably means 'damnation' or 'perdition'.

5   **Allegiance** Dogberry apparently means 'treason'.

7   **Charge** commission, assignments. Compare I.i.217, and lines 25, 81, 97, 177.

10   **desartless** The artless Dogberry means 'desertful' or 'deserving'.

      Constable leader of the force.

not marry her to morrow in the Congregation,   125
where I should wed, there will I shame her.
PRINCE   And as I wooed for thee to obtain her,
I will join with thee to disgrace her.
BASTARD   I will disparage her no farther till
you are my Witnesses; bear it coldly but till   130
Midnight, and let the Issue shew it self.
PRINCE   O Day untowardly turned!
CLAUDIO   O Mischief strangely thwarting!
BASTARD   O Plague right well prevented! so will
you say, when you have seen the Sequel.   *Exeunt.*   135

Scene 3

*Enter Dogberry and his Compartner
with the Watch.*

DOGBERRY   Are you good Men and true?
VERGES   Yea, or else it were pity but they should
suffer Salvation Body and Soul.
DOGBERRY   Nay, that were a Punishment too good
for them, if they should have any Allegiance   5
in them, being chosen for the Prince's Watch.
VERGES   Well, give them their Charge, Neighbour
Dogberry.
DOGBERRY   First, who think you the most
desartless Man to be Constable?   10
WATCH 1   Hugh Ote-cake, Sir, or George Sea-cole,
for they can write and read.
DOGBERRY   Come hither, Neighbour Sea-cole, God

14   **good Name**   Sea-cole's name derives from the high-quality coal
      shipped by sea from Newcastle to the south of England in
      Shakespeare's day. Ote-cake's name suggests that he raises
      oats when he is not serving as a member of the Watch.

15   **well-favoured**   both (a) 'bless'd', and (b) handsome.
      Characteristically, Dogberry attributes to 'Fortune' what is
      actually a 'Gift' of 'Nature'. Another potential meaning for
      well-favoured is 'kindly treated', well-liked.

17   **Maister**   a word halfway between *master* and the more modern
      mister, both of which derive from the Latin *magister*.
      Compare line 179, IV.ii.8, and V.i.232.

19   **for**   as for. So also in line 20.
      Favour   both (a) grace (see the note to line 15), and (b) facial
      appearance, pleasing countenance.

22   **Vanity**   empty pretension. But Dogberry probably means
      'virtue'.

23   **senseless**   Dogberry means 'sensible'.
      fit   suitable. Compare III.ii.111–17.

25   **Lanthorn**   lantern (so spelled because in the Elizabethan period
      its sides were made of thin, translucent horn).

26   **comprehend . . . Men**   Dogberry means 'apprehend [arrest] all
      vagrant men'. But *comprehend* (seize hold of) is just as apt a
      term, given the vagabonds (wandering, unattached men) the
      Watch will be looking for.

27   **stand**   stand still; stay. But see the note to line 178.

29   **Note**   [further] notice. Dogberry's advice, if heeded, would
      mean that those whose duty is to 'note' would fail to do so.
      Compare III.ii.55.

30   **presently**   immediately, as in III.i.14.

35   **meddle**   mingle, associate. It doesn't occur to Dogberry that the
      Watch *should* meddle with the Prince's enemies in another
      sense: arrest those who are meddling. For another sense of
      meddle, see *Troilus and Cressida*, I.i.87–88, and *Measure for
      Measure*, V.i.127.

38   **tolerable**   Dogberry means 'intolerable'.

40   WATCH   It is not clear which watchman utters this line; as with
      the speeches commencing at lines 48, 53, 59, 74, 97, 106,
      116, and 135, it is simply designated 'WATCH' in the Quarto
      and Folio texts. Most of today's editions assign all nine
      speeches to the Second Watchman.

hath bless'd you with a good Name. To be a
well-favoured Man is the Gift of Fortune, but   15
to write and read comes by Nature.

WATCH 2   Both which, Maister Constable.

DOGBERRY   You have: I knew it would be your
Answer. Well, for your Favour, Sir, why give
God thanks, and make no Boast of it; and for   20
your Writing and Reading, let that appear when
there is no need of such Vanity. You are
thought here to be the most senseless and fit
Man for the Constable of the Watch: therefore
bear you the Lanthorn. This is your Charge,   25
you shall comprehend all vagrom Men; you are
to bid any Man stand, in the Prince's name.

WATCH 2   How if 'a will not stand?

DOGBERRY   Why then take no Note of him, but
let him go, and presently call the rest of the   30
Watch together, and thank God you are rid of a
Knave.

VERGES   If he will not stand when he is bidden,
he is none of the Prince's Subjects.

DOGBERRY   True, and they are to meddle with none   35
but the Prince's Subjects. — You shall also
make no Noise in the Streets: for, for the
Watch to babble and to talk, is most tolerable,
and not to be indured.

WATCH   We will rather sleep than talk, we know   40
what belongs to a Watch.

DOGBERRY   Why you speak like an ancient and most
quiet Watchman, for I cannot see how Sleeping
should offend: onely have a care that your Bills
be not stol'n. Well, you are to call at all the   45

---

42   **ancient** Dogberry means 'old, experienced'. But *ancient* can
        also mean 'ensign' (standard-bearer), Iago's rank in *Othello*.

44   **Bills** halberds (spears with hooked battle-axes affixed to their
        blades). *Onely* (only) echoes III.i.92.

51–52 **not . . . for** Dogberry means 'not the good men and true you
assumed them to be'. But they will in the process prove
themselves to be precisely 'the Men you took them for'
(drunks) earlier when you didn't take (apprehend) them.

55   **true Man** non-thief, law-abiding citizen, as in line 1. *Office*
(position) recalls III.i.12.

57   **make** have to do. The phrase *meddle or make* was a cliché. See
the note to line 35.

57–58 **the . . . Honesty** you demonstrate and safeguard your virtue
with increasing vigour.

62   **they . . . defil'd** Dogberry's squeamishness derives from the
Apocryphal book Ecclesiasticus: 'he that toucheth pitch shall
be defiled' (13:1). *Pitch* is tar.

64   **shew . . . is** prove true to his nature.

65   **steal . . . Company** sneak away from you. But of course the
consequence is that the thief will steal out of (away from) the
Watch's company in the sense which pertains most directly to
the thief's vocation, and in which he will not 'shew himself'
for 'what he is'.

68–69 **hang . . . Will** Dogberry means 'willingly hang a dog'. But his
phrasing comically echoes a common Elizabethan joke
whereby the phrase 'thereby hangs a tale' is linked to a man's
hanging 'tail' or 'Will'. See the notes to III.ii.62 and I.i.245,
II.iii.263, and compare *As You Like It*, II.vii.28.

77   **Ewe** mother sheep.

78   **baes** cries 'baa'.

79   **a Calf** that is, an infant that is not its own. As might be
expected, the proverb Dogberry recites is an implicit argument
for precisely the opposite of the course he recommends to the
Watch. See the note on *Calf* at II.i.25.

81   **end** conclusion. But the context suggests that another sense of
end (purpose) would be at least equally appropriate. Compare
II.iii.170.
Charge instructions for your post. See the note to line 7.

Alehouses, and bid those that are drunk get
them to Bed.

WATCH   How if they will not?

DOGBERRY   Why then let them alone till they are
sober; if they make you not then the better   50
Answer, you may say they are not the Men you
took them for.

WATCH   Well, Sir.

DOGBERRY   If you meet a Thief, you may suspect
him, by virtue of your Office, to be no true Man: 55
and for such kind of Men, the less you meddle
or make with them, why the more is for your
Honesty.

WATCH   If we know him to be a Thief, shall we not
lay Hands on him?   60

DOGBERRY   Truly by your Office you may, but I
think they that touch Pitch will be defil'd:
the most peaceable way for you, if you do take
a Thief, is to let him shew himself what he is,
and steal out of your Company.   65

VERGES   You have been always called a merciful
Man, Partner.

DOGBERRY   Truly I would not hang a Dog by my
Will, much more a Man who hath any Honesty
in him.   70

VERGES   If you hear a Child cry in the Night,
you must call to the Nurse and bid her still
it.

WATCH   How if the Nurse be asleep and will not
hear us.   75

DOGBERRY   Why then depart in peace, and let the
Child wake her with crying, for the Ewe that
will not hear her Lamb when it baes will never
answer a Calf when he bleats.

VERGES   'Tis very true.   80

DOGBERRY   This is the end of the Charge: you,

82   **present**   represent, stand in the place of. But Dogberry's next sentence suggests that he means 'apprehend' or 'prevent'.

84   **stay**   arrest. *Stay* derives from the same Latin word (*stare*) as *stand*.

85   **birlady**   by our Lady (a reference to the Virgin Mary).

87   **Statues**   Dogberry means 'statutes', of course; but in his confusion about what it means to 'present the Prince's own Person', this malapropism is amusingly apt. Dogberry's practice would have the effect of turning the Prince himself into a statue (an imitation of the 'Person' who arrests him). *Statues* derives from the First Folio text; the Quarto reads *statutes*. Since the Folio text of this play is generally derivative, there is doubt about whether it provides an authoritative reading here; *Statues* accords so perfectly with Dogberry's other blunders, however, that it seems more than plausible.

88   **without . . . willing**   unless the Prince is willing [to be stayed]. *Mary* (truly), line 87, recalls II.iii.90.

94   **and**   if. So also in line 109.

95–96 **keep . . . own**   Dogberry varies the oath of confidentiality administered to a person being sworn in to serve on a grand jury. *Charge* (commission), line 97, echoes line 81.

103   **Coil**   swirl of activity.
      vigitant   Dogberry combines 'vigilant' (watchful) and 'visitant'; as is usually the case, his error is so fitting as to seem inspired.

108   **at thy Elbow**   a variation of the proverbial ' "At your side," said the pickpocket.' Compare *I Henry IV*, II.i.53.

109   **Mass**   by the Mass.

110   **Scab**   both (a) crusted sore, and (b) rogue or scoundrel. Here as in line 94, *and* means 'if'.

111   **I . . . Answer**   I'll get even with you. *Answer* echoes lines 50–52, 67–69; *Tale* evokes lines 68–69.

114   **Penthouse**   overhang, sloping roof.

115   **utter all**   spill out everything. The proverbial phrase 'like a true drunkard' (a variation on the Latin *in vino veritas*, 'in wine truth') alludes to the speaker's name, which derives from the Spanish word *borracho*, 'drunkard'. Borachio may not be a 'good Man', but he will eventually prove 'true' (line 1) in more than one sense.

Constable, are to present the Prince's own
Person. If you meet the Prince in the Night,
you may stay him.

VERGES   Nay birlady, that I think 'a cannot.   85

DOGBERRY   Five Shillings to one on't with any
man that knows the Statues, he may stay him;
mary not without the Prince be willing, for
indeed the Watch ought to offend no Man, and
it is an Offence to stay a Man against his   90
Will.

VERGES   Birlady I think it be so.

DOGBERRY   Ha ha ha, well, Masters, good night;
and there be any Matter of Weight chaunces,
call up me; keep your Fellows' Counsailes, and   95
your own, and good night. – Come, Neighbour.

WATCH   Well, Masters, we hear our charge; let us
go sit here upon the Church Bench till two,
and then all to Bed.

DOGBERRY   One Word more, honest Neighbours: 100
I pray you watch about Signior Leonato's Door,
for the Wedding being there to morrow, there is
a great Coil to night. Adieu, be vigitant, I
beseech you.   *Exeunt* [*Dogberry and Verges*].

Enter Borachio and Conrade.

BORACHIO   What, Conrade?   105

WATCH   – Peace, stir not.

BORACHIO   Conrade, I say.

CONRADE   Here, Man, I am at thy Elbow.

BORACHIO   Mass, and my elbow itch'd, I thought
there would a Scab follow.   110

CONRADE   I will owe thee an Answer for that, and
now forward with thy Tale.

BORACHIO   Stand thee close then under this
Penthouse, for it drizzles Rain, and I will,
like a true Drunkard, utter all to thee.   115

WATCH   – Some Treason, Masters, yet stand close.

117 **Dun** a variation on *Don* (a Spanish title for gentlemen), and here one that plays on *dun* as a word that means (a) 'dark', 'dull', or 'dingy' in colour, (b) 'gloomy' in mood or atmosphere, (c) horse-like (from the game 'Dun in the Mire', in which a log representing a mired horse was to be lifted and extricated by the assembled party), and (d) 'silent' or 'done' (from the saying 'Dun's the Mouse'). See the reference to *Dumb John* in the stage direction at II.i.90.

120 **so dear** so expensive, worth so much to the purchaser. Conrade's phrasing, which echoes I.i.121–22, 133–35, provides a reminder of the endearment that Don John's 'Villainy' is designed to nullify.

122 **so rich** so well endowed to pay. Here *rich* plays on the sense that means 'exquisite, precious'.

124 **make** earn, demand.

125 **wonder** marvel. Compare III.ii.112.

126 **unconfirm'd** inexperienced; not yet brought into full communion (adulthood) in the congregation of thieves. Compare II.i.396–98.

128 **is . . . Man** is nothing with respect to, or in comparison with, a man (different from the man himself). Borachio varies the proverb that the cowl does not make the monk. Feste alludes to the same commonplace in I.v.61 of *Twelfth Night*. *Fashion* (style) 126–53, recalls III.i.72.

133– **what . . . is** how Fashion steals away men's true forms
34 (natures), and deforms them, by the apparel it seduces them into donning. Compare Beatrice's remarks in I.i.76–78.

136 **this seven year** for the last seven years.
goes . . . down walks about.

137 **gentle Man** both (a) gentleman in social rank, and (b) 'true Man' (line 55).

139 **Vane** weathervane. In the following speech Borachio describes 'Fashion' as if it were a wind that 'turns about' such a device. Compare III.i.66.

141 **giddily** dizzyingly (in such a way as to cause men to lose their bearings, indeed their very sense of identity). *Turns* echoes III.ii.132.

142 **Hot-bloods** passionate (hot-headed) gallants.

BORACHIO   Therefore know, I have earned of Dun
   John a thousand Ducats.
CONRADE   Is it possible that any Villainy should
   be so dear?   120
BORACHIO   Thou shouldst rather ask if it were
   possible any Villainy should be so rich? for
   when rich Villains have need of poor ones,
   poor ones may make what Price they will.
CONRADE   I wonder at it.   125
BORACHIO   That shews thou art unconfirm'd: thou
   knowest that the Fashion of a Doublet, or a
   Hat, or a Cloak, is nothing to a Man.
CONRADE   Yes, it is Apparel.
BORACHIO   I mean the Fashion.   130
CONRADE   Yes, the Fashion is the Fashion.
BORACHIO   Tush, I may as well say the Fool's
   the Fool; but seest thou not what a deformed
   Thief this Fashion is?
WATCH   — I know that Deformed, 'a has been a vile   135
   Thief, this seven year, 'a goes up and down like
   a gentle Man: I remember his Name.
BORACHIO   Didst thou not hear some body?
CONRADE   No, 'twas the Vane on the House.
BORACHIO   Seest thou not, I say, what a deformed   140
   Thief this Fashion is, how giddily 'a turns
   about all the Hot-bloods between fourteen and
   five and thirty, sometimes fashioning them like
   Pharaoh's Soldiers in the rechy Painting,

---

143   **fashioning them**   both (a) dressing them, and (b) remaking
      them.

143–   **like . . . Painting**   like the depictions of Pharaoh's armies in
44   grimy old paintings of the Israelites' exodus from Egypt.
           Rechy (*rechie* in both the Quarto and Folio texts) is usually
           spelled 'reechy' in modern editions; here it means both 'reeky'
           (smoky) and 'wretched' (squalid). Compare III.ii.109–10.

145   **God Bel's Priests** the priests of Bel (the pagan god Baal) in the Book of Daniel. After Daniel proved that these priests served a false god, King Cyrus of Persia executed them. Borachio refers to a stained-glass picture of the episode.

146– **shaven Hercules** Borachio is probably combining the stories of
47   two strongmen who were frequently likened to each other: (a) Hercules, a victim of Queen Omphale, who dressed him as a woman and forced him to become one of her spinning maids (see II.i.262–63), and (b) Samson, who was defeated by the Philistines after he allowed Delilah to shave off the long hair that was the source of his might (Judges 16). Compare II.i.379–85 and IV.i.320–25.

147   **smirch'd** soiled.

148   **Codpiece** the baggy flap at the front of a man's breeches to house his private 'Club'. See the note on Hercules' 'massy' (massive) appendage at II.i.263.

149– **the . . . Man** Fashion causes a man to go through many
50   changes of apparel. Here as in III.i.116 *then* can mean either 'then' or 'than' (the usual rendering of the word in this passage).

155   **to night** both (a) tonight, and (b) to night (here symbolic of the darkness that signifies ignorance, error, and evil). Compare III.ii.113.

156   **by . . . Hero** pretending that she was really Hero. The phrase *leans me*, an example of what grammarians term the ethical dative, means 'leans for me'. *Chamber Window* echoes III.ii.112–15.

159   **vildly** vilely, in a disorderly fashion.

163   **Incounter** encounter. Compare I.i.100, 335, II.iii.140.

168   **possess'd them** took possession of them (like 'the Divel', line 166). Compare lines 160–61, and see I.i.199.

170   **confirm** validate, prove (or seem to prove) true. Compare line 126.

171   **enrag'd** in a mad fury. See the note to II.iii.110.

sometime like God Bel's Priests in the old   145
Church Window, sometime like the shaven
Hercules in the smirch'd Worm-eaten Tapestry,
where his Codpiece seems as massy as his Club.
CONRADE   All this I see, and I see that the
Fashion wears out more Apparel then the Man,   150
but art not thou thy self giddy with the
Fashion too, that thou hast shifted out of
thy Tale into telling me of the Fashion?
BORACHIO   Not so neither, but know that I have
to night wooed Margaret, the Lady Hero's   155
Gentlewoman, by the name of Hero; she leans
me out at her Mistress' Chamber Window, bids
me a thousand times good night. I tell this
Tale vildly: I should first tell thee how the
Prince, Claudio, and my Master, planted, and   160
placed, and possessed, by my Master Don John,
saw afar off in the Orchard this amiable
Incounter.
CONRADE   And thought they Margaret was Hero?
BORACHIO   Two of them did, the Prince and   165
Claudio, but the Divel my Master knew she
was Margaret, and partly by his Oaths, which
first possess'd them, partly by the dark Night
which did deceive them, but chiefly by my
Villainy, which did confirm any Slander that   170
Don John had made, away went Claudio enrag'd,
swore he would meet her as he was appointed
next Morning at the Temple, and there before
the whole Congregation shame her with what he
saw o'er night, and send her home again without   175
a Husband.

177 **charge**   command (but here with a hint of another sense, 'accuse'). Compare lines 81, 97. *Shame* (another variation on 'accuse'), line 174, echoes III.ii.124–26. Modern editions usually reassign this speech and the one commencing at line 183 to the Second Watchman; at the same time they reassign to the First Watchman the speeches here attributed to 'WATCH 2' (lines 179, 186).

178 **stand**   stand still (for an arrest). Lines 180–82 activate another (erotic) sense. Compare lines 26–27, 33–34, 83–91, 113–14.

179 **right Maister**   true head. *Maister* echoes line 17.

180 **recover'd**   The Watchman means 'discovered'.

181 **Lechery**   The Watchman means 'treachery' (treason). In this case it pertains to the supposed lechery of Hero. Meanwhile it reinforces the inadvertent reminders of 'Lechery' in such passages as line 179, where *Call up* and *right* (which can refer to the upright bearing of a Constable's 'Club', line 148) cohere with several references to standing firm against those who meddle with the peace.

184 **Lock**   a lock of hair (presumably from a woman with whom he has engaged in lechery). Such love-locks were often adorned with favours (ribbons and the like) from the lover's lady.

186 **You'll . . . forth**   you'll be forced to produce Deformed as one of your accomplices.

189 **obey**   The word the context requires is 'charge'. Most editors attribute this line to one of the Watchmen, but both the Quarto and the Folio assign it to Conrade. It may be that Conrade is responding to the Watchmen's ludicrous remarks about 'Deformed' with a parody of their malapropisms: if so, he transposes *charge* and *obey*, assuming that these bumpkins will understand him to mean 'Masters, say no more, we obey you; let us charge [entreat] you to go with us [to jail].'

191 **taken up**   (a) hooked (see the note to line 44) or cut and dug up (see the note to line 192), and (b) arrested (compare lines 51–52), and (c) received on credit.

192 **Bills**   Borachio puns on (a) implements for pruning or digging, (b) the kinds of bills (spiked weapons) the Watchmen are wielding, and (c) the promissory notes (bonds) that purchasers provide as security for a 'Commodity' (article or set of goods, including agricultural products) obtained on credit. Compare I.i.39–40.

WATCH 1   We charge you in the Prince's name,
stand.

WATCH 2   – Call up the right Maister Constable,
we have here recover'd the most dangerous piece   180
of Lechery, that ever was known in the Common-
wealth.

WATCH 1   And one Deformed is one of them, I know
him, 'a wears a Lock.

CONRADE   Masters, Masters.   185

WATCH 2   You'll be made bring Deformed forth, I
warrant you.

CONRADE   Masters, never speak, we charge you,
let us obey you to go with us.

BORACHIO   We are like to prove a goodly   190
Commodity, being taken up of these men's
Bills.

CONRADE   A Commodity in Question, I warrant you.
– Come, we'll obey you.   *Exeunt.*

Scene 4

Enter Hero, and Margaret, and Ursula.

HERO   Good Ursula, wake my Cousin Beatrice,
and desire her to rise.

URSULA   I will, Lady.

HERO   And bid her come hither.

URSULA   Well.   [*Exit.*]   5

---

193   **in Question**   both (a) subject to questioning (criminal
investigation), and (b) of dubious worth. *Obey* (line 194)
echoes lines 188–89.

III.iv   This scene occurs in one of Hero's rooms.

2   **desire**   request.

5   **Well.**   Yes, even so.

6   **Rebato**   stiff collar or ruff.

7   **were**   would be.

9   **troth's**   troth (faith) it's. So also in line 18.

9–10   **I warrant**   I assure you.

13   **Tire**   headdress (complete with false hair and ornaments).

14   **a Thought**   a small amount.

15   **Fashion**   exquisitely designed piece of apparel. Compare line 23
     and III.iii.126–53.

16   **Millaine's**   Milan's.

17   **exceeds they say**   either (a) excels, they say, or (b) exceeds
     anything they say [about it].

19   **respect of**   comparison to.
     Cloth a' Gold   cloth woven from gold thread.
     Cuts   slashes to expose the material underneath.

20   **lac'd**   adorned.

20–21 **down Sleeves**   tight-fitting sleeves from the shoulders to the
     wrists.

21   **side Sleeves**   open, ornamental sleeves suspended from the
     shoulders.

21–22 **round Underborne**   trimmed along the bottom.

22   **blewish**   blueish. This spelling form, common in the early
     printings of Shakespeare, permits possible wordplay on the
     past tense of *blow*.

23   **queint**   quaint, pleasing. *Fashion*, echoing line 15, recalls
     III.iii.126–53.

26   **heavy**   weighted with anxiety (an inexplicable foreboding).
     Compare III.ii.62.

31   **in a Beggar**   'in all', even a beggar (Hebrews 13:4). Compare
     IV.i.130.

33   **saving your Reverence**   a formula (here used satirically) to beg
     the listener's pardon before saying something indelicate.

34   **And bad Thinking**   if evil imaginations (a dirty mind).
     wrest   both (a) twist, seize, and (b) arrest, suspend. This
     sentence is a reminder of the 'bad Thinking' (foolish
     instructions and inept procedures) that have wrested 'true
     Speaking' (open discourse) by Borachio and Conrade in the
     preceding scene; see the note to III.iii.115.

MARGARET   Troth, I think your other Rebato
were better.

HERO   No pray thee, good Meg, I'll wear this.

MARGARET   By my troth's not so good, and I
warrant your Cousin will say so.   10

HERO   My Cousin's a Fool, and thou art another,
I'll wear none but this.

MARGARET   I like the new Tire within excellently,
if the Hair were a Thought browner: and your
Gown's a most rare Fashion i'faith, I saw the   15
Duchess of Millaine's Gown that they praise so.

HERO   O that exceeds they say.

MARGARET   By my troth's but a Night-gown in
respect of yours, Cloth a' Gold and Cuts, and
lac'd with Silver, set with Pearls, down   20
Sleeves, side Sleeves and Skirts, round
Underborne with a blewish Tinsel, but for a
fine queint graceful and excellent Fashion,
yours is worth ten on't.

HERO   God give me joy to wear it, for my Heart   25
is exceeding heavy.

MARGARET   'Twill be heavier soon by the weight
of a Man.

HERO   Fie upon thee, art not ashamed?

MARGARET   Of what, Lady? of speaking honourably?   30
Is not Marriage honourable in a Beggar? is not
your Lord honourable without Marriage? I think
you would have me say, saving your Reverence,
a Husband. And bad Thinking do not wrest
true Speaking, I'll offend no body. Is there any   35

36 **Harm** offence, transgression.

37 **and** provided. Lines 37–38 play on two senses of *right*: (a) upright (see the note to III.iii.181), and (b) correct, proper, authorized.

38 **light** wanton (as opposed to *heavy*, grave, legitimate). See the note on *light* at II.i.34, and compare lines 47–49.

40 **Coze** Coz (cousin).

42 **in . . . Tune** in the 'melody' of one who is not feeling well.

44 **Clap's** clap us; let us thrust ourselves.
    'Light a' Love' a song referred to with similar ribaldry in I.ii.82–84 of *The Two Gentlemen of Verona*.

45 **Burden** a pun on (a) a bass (heavy) undertune, and (b) a burdensome (heavy, serious) theme, with wordplay on (c) a man's weight (lines 27–28).

47 **Ye . . . Heels** (a) you dance 'Light of Love' with your heels, (b) you kick your heels up (literally) in a lighthearted manner, and (c) you alight on Love as you 'daunce it'. See the note to line 38.

48 **Stables** both (a) 'Barns' (endowments), and (b) 'standing' (from the Latin *stare*, to stand, from which *stabulum* derives).

49 **Barns** Beatrice puns on *bairns*, children.

50 **Construction** construing, with play on 'building' and on 'erection'. Compare *Twelfth Night*, III.i.119–30, especially line 123, and see the note to II.iv.95 of *Measure for Measure*.

50–51 **I . . . Heels** I turn my back on that and spurn it with the dust I kick as I exit in disgust. Compare Jesus' command to his disciples in Matthew 10:12–15.

56–57 **For . . . H** By *For* Beatrice probably means 'because of'; but the word can also mean 'out of a desire for'. Beatrice's wordplay on *H* derives from the fact that *ache* could be pronounced 'aitch'. Meanwhile she hints at an itch to form a reclining letter *H* with a man who has 'Stables enough' to produce 'Barns' (lines 48–49). Compare III.ii.22–27, V.i.26, 36. *Ill* (line 54) recalls III.ii.100.

58–59 **and . . . Star** if you haven't been converted into a heretic (having renounced your 'religion' against love), then sea pilots no longer navigate by the North Star. Compare III.iii.140–43 (for a previous reference to turning), II.iii.280–81 (for an earlier comment on conversion), and II.i.257–60 (for an allusion to the North Star).

Harm in 'the heavier for a Husband'? None, I
think, and it be the right Husband, and the
right Wife; otherwise 'tis light and not heavy.
Ask my Lady Beatrice else, here she comes.

Enter Beatrice.

HERO   Good morrow, Coze.   40
BEATRICE   Good morrow, sweet Hero.
HERO   Why how now? do you speak in the sick Tune?
BEATRICE   I am out of all other Tune, me thinks.
MARGARET   Clap's into 'Light a' Love', that goes
without a Burden, do you sing it, and I'll   45
daunce it.
BEATRICE   Ye light a' Love with your Heels, then
if your Husband have Stables enough you'll
see he shall lack no Barns.
MARGARET   O illegitimate Construction! I scorn   50
that with my Heels.
BEATRICE   'Tis almost five a' clock, Cousin,
'tis time you were ready. By my troth, I am
exceeding ill, hey ho.
MARGARET   For a Hawk, a Horse, or a Husband?   55
BEATRICE   For the Letter that begins them all,
H.
MARGARET   Well, and you be not turn'd Turk,
there's no more sailing by the Star.
BEATRICE   What means the Fool, trow?   60
MARGARET   Nothing I, but God send every one
their Heart's Desire.

---

60   **trow**   I wonder.

61   **God send**   may God send. In this speech and in line 75 *Heart*
probably has the meanings elsewhere associated with *Will* (see
II.iii.263); compare I.i.130–32, 331–35, III.i.111–12,
III.ii.10–15. And *Nothing* plays bawdily on 'no thing'; see the
note to III.ii.60. In this sentence *I* can be construed to mean
either 'I' (the first-person pronoun) or 'Ay' (yes).

65   **stuff'd** congested. Margaret picks up on the copulative sense
         that relates to Beatrice's 'Catching' (seizing hold of) the 'cold
         Blood' (I.i.135) of a 'Benedick'. Compare I.i.57–61, 90–92.

69   **profess'd Apprehension** made a profession of this kind of witty
         'catching' (based on the Latin sense of *apprehension*, 'taking
         hold').

70   **left it** ceased being adept at 'Apprehension' (now referring to
         'understanding', 'perception' and 'conception', both in the
         sense that pertains to thought and in the sense that results in
         pregnancy). *Wit* (line 71), which here relates to desire and to
         the genitalia as well as to mental quickness (see the note to
         II.i.124), echoes III.ii.52, 76, 89.

75   **Carduus Benedictus** the 'holy Thistle' that was thought to be a
         panacea. *Sick* (line 73) echoes line 42.

76   **onely thing** Here the Elizabethan spelling for *only* contains a
         pun on another 'Letter' (*1* or *I*), in this case one whose
         upright form relates to the 'pricking' (line 77) that is 'the
         onely thing for a Qualm' (faintness, with play on *come*).

81   **plain holy Thistle** an unadorned (naked) male 'Thistle' that is
         'whole-ly' devoted to being 'the one-ly thing' for the 'Calm'
         (as the Hostess pronounces *Qualm*, 'nausea', in *2 Henry IV*,
         II.iv.39–40) that will issue from a 'come' (see the note
         II.iii.268–69). While Margaret pretends to be giving a 'plain'
         (single-level) response, she delivers a 'double Meaning'
         (II.iii.275–76) whose 'Moral' (figurative sense) is not what the
         prudish Hero (see line 29) would consider a 'moral Meaning'.

83   **birlady** by our Lady. Compare III.iii.85.

84   **list** both (a) wish, and (b) enumerate, as Margaret has done in
         the preceding exchanges about the 'Moral in this *Benedictus*'
         (line 79). The second *list* in this line can mean 'lean' or 'tilt' to
         one side.

88–89 **such another** both (a) another who swore he would never fall
         in love, and (b) 'something else' (a slang sense that Pandarus
         uses in reference to his wanton niece in I.ii.291 of *Troilus and
         Cressida*).

89   **a Man** an ordinary man, a mere 'Mortal' (see I.i.54–61), who
         now admits that something other than 'cold Blood' may flow
         in his 'hard Heart' (I.i.131, 135). Compare I.i.109–14.

90   **in dispight of** in defiance or contempt of, despite. Compare
         III.ii.68.

HERO   These Gloves the Counte sent me, they are
an excellent Perfume.

BEATRICE   I am stuff'd, Cousin, I cannot smell.   65

MARGARET   A Maid and stuff'd! there's goodly
catching of Cold.

BEATRICE   O God help me, God help me, how long
have you profess'd Apprehension?

MARGARET   Ever since you left it, doth not my   70
Wit become me rarely?

BEATRICE   It is not seen enough, you should wear
it in your Cap. By my troth, I am sick.

MARGARET   Get you some of this distill'd
Carduus Benedictus, and lay it to your Heart,   75
it is the onely thing for a Qualm.

HERO   There thou prickst her with a Thistle.

BEATRICE   *Benedictus*, why *Benedictus*? you have
some Moral in this *Benedictus*.

MARGARET   Moral? No by my troth, I have no moral   80
Meaning, I meant plain holy Thistle. You may
think perchaunce that I think you are in love;
nay birlady I am not such a Fool to think
what I list, nor I list not to think what I
can, nor indeed I can not think, if I would   85
think my Heart out of Thinking, that you are
in love, or that you will be in love, or that
you can be in love. Yet Benedick was such
another, and now he is become a Man: he swore
he would never marry, and yet now in dispight   90
of his Heart he eats his Meat without grudging.

---

91   **he ... grudging**   he partakes of the food that is set before him
without complaining about it (an echo of I.i.43–53, 124–27,
and II.iii.253–55). Margaret may be punning on *Mate*, which
was then a homonym; for similar wordplay see I.i.47, and
compare I.ii.68–69 of *The Two Gentlemen of Verona*.

92 **converted** This word echoes I.i.124–32, II.iii.23–28, 243–44, and III.i.109.

93 **your Eyes** Margaret alludes to the organs of sight; but *Eyes* could also refer to the female genialia (see *Troilus and Cressida*, II.i.87 and V.ii.96–101, *Henry V*, II.i.34–38), and to the male 'I' (see *The Two Gentlemen of Verona*, I.i.115–22 and II.v.20–38) that makes all 'one' between a man and a woman. *Nothing I* may play on the same senses in line 61. Margaret's implicaton in lines 92–94 is that, despite her claim to be above the frailties that afflict women who lack her 'cold Blood' (I.i.135), Beatrice is just as susceptible to the promptings of erotic desire as are those who openly acknowledge that they are 'Hot-bloods' (III.iii.142).

97 **Not . . . Gallop** Margaret's point is that her 'Pace' (line 95) is not the forced canter a horseman employs for a brief burst of speed, but a sustainable gallop. Compare II.iii.250–57.

III.v This scene takes place in Leonato's house. Judging from the reference to the time in III.iv.52, it is still early in the morning, a few hours after the events dramatized in III.iii.

S.D. **Headborough** parish constable.

3 **Mary** truly. Compare III.iii.88. Dogberry's use of a word that echoes *marry*, both here and in line 7, is a reminder of the occasion that makes this a 'busy Time' (line 6) for Leonato.

4 **Confidence** Dogberry probably means 'conference' (private conversation). *Confidence* can convey the same idea, and here it also reminds us that this is a Constable in whom one reposes little confidence.
   decerns Dogberry means 'concerns'. In time, however, it will emerge that what the Watch 'decerns', however dimly, is more than the graver members of this aristocratic society are able to discern. It will turn out that Dogberry is not totally wrong to assert that his 'Confidence' (his secure complacency) 'decerns' (sees and reflects) the Governor 'nearly'.

10 **Goodman** Like 'honest Neighbour' (lines 1–2), a term of respect for an ordinary yeoman (ranked below a gentleman).

12 **blunt** Dogberry means 'sharp'. What he unwittingly reveals is that his own 'Wits' are at least as 'blunt' as the 'Goodman' he describes so condescendingly. Compare V.ii.11–14.

And how you may be converted I know not, but
me thinks you look with your Eyes as other
Women do.

BEATRICE   What Pace is this that thy Tongue   95
keeps?

MARGARET   Not a false Gallop.

Enter Ursula.

URSULA   Madam, withdraw, the Prince, the Count,
Signior Benedick, Don John, and all the
Gallants of the Town are come to fetch you   100
to Church.

HERO   Help to dress me, good Coze, good Meg,
good Ursula.   [*Exeunt.*]

Scene 5

*Enter Leonato, and the Constable, and
the Headborough.*

LEONATO   What would you with me, honest
Neighbour?

DOGBERRY   Mary Sir, I would have some
Confidence with you, that decerns you nearly.

LEONATO   Brief, I pray you, for you see it is a   5
busy Time with me.

DOGBERRY   Mary this it is, Sir.

VERGES   Yee in truth it is, Sir.

LEONATO   What is it, my good Friends?

DOGBERRY   Goodman Verges, Sir, speaks a little   10
of the Matter, an Old Man, Sir, and his Wits
are not so blunt, as God help I would desire

18 **odorous** Dogberry means 'odious' (detestable). A similar
malapropism occurs in III.i.83–84 of *Midsummer Night's
Dream*.
Palabras words; an abbreviation of the Spanish *pocas
palabras*, few words.

20 **tedious** long-winded, wearying. Dogberry believes that
Leonato is complimenting him.

22 **the . . . Officers** Dogberry's placement of *poor* (lowly, humble)
unwittingly returns the poor (pitiable) Duke's compliment.

24 **of** on. So also in line 41. *Part* (line 23) recalls III.i.18, 31.

28 **Exclamation on** Dogberry means 'acclamation of'. One
meaning of *Exclamation* is 'accusation' or 'vociferous
complaint', and *on* can mean 'on the part of'. Dogberry's
words will prove prophetic. *Pound*, which Dogberry uses as a
unit of currency, can also be a unit of weight (see lines 24–26)
and a word for a physical blow; see I.i.90–92.

33 **fain** gladly.

34–35 **excepting . . . presence** Verges varies the formula 'saving your
Reverence' (see III.iv.33), apologizing for using such an
offensive epithet as 'arrant Knaves' (line 36).

37–38 **he . . . talking** he does go on and on. In fact, Verges is finally
getting to the point, and Dogberry's interruption prevents the
'Old Man' from imparting a piece of information that would
make a great deal of difference to Leonato. See the headnote
to III.iii.

38–39 **when . . . out** Dogberry varies (probably because he
misunderstands) the proverb that 'when ale is in, wit is out'.
Here as elsewhere, his phrasing hints unwittingly at the
genital sense *Wit* can carry in other contexts (see the note to
III.iv.70). Leonato's response in lines 46–47 reinforces that
implication.

46–47 **he . . . you** Leonato ironically agrees with Dogberry. He
affirms (a) that Verges is behind Dogberry when he reaches
his destination (*comes*); but what he means is (b) that Verges
is much less tedious than Dogberry. The horse imagery echoes
III.iv.95–97.

48 **Gifts . . . give** Dogberry's smug pseudo-humility recalls
III.iii.14–16.

they were, but in faith honest, as the Skin
between his Brows.

VERGES   Yes I thank God, I am as honest as any   15
Man living, that is an Old Man, and no honester
than I.

DOGBERRY   Comparisons are odorous, Palabras,
Neighbour Verges.

LEONATO   Neighbours, you arc tedious.   20

DOGBERRY   It pleases your Worship to say so, but
we are the poor Duke's Officers; but truly for
mine own part, if I were as tedious as a King
I could find in my Heart to bestow it all of
your Worship.   25

LEONATO   All thy Tediousness on me, ah?

DOGBERRY   Yea, and't 'twere a thousand Pound more
than 'tis, for I hear as good Exclamation on
your Worship as of any Man in the City, and
though I be but a Poor Man, I am glad to hear   30
it.

VERGES   And so am I.

LEONATO   I would fain know what you have to say.

VERGES   Mary Sir, our Watch to night, excepting
your Worship's presence, ha' ta'en a couple of   35
as arrant Knaves as any in Messina.

DOGBERRY   A good Old Man, Sir, he will be
talking as they say; when the Age is in, the
Wit is out, God help us, it is a World to see.
— Well said, i' faith, Neighbour Verges, well,   40
God's a good Man, and two Men ride of a Horse,
one must ride behind. — An honest Soul,
i' faith, Sir, by my troth he is, as ever broke
Bread. — But God is to be worshipp'd, all Men
are not alike, alas good Neighbour.   45

LEONATO   Indeed, Neighbour, he comes too short
of you.

DOGBERRY   Gifts that God gives.

LEONATO   I must leave you.

51   **comprehended** Dogberry means 'apprehended'. How much the Watch 'comprehended' is another matter. Compare III.iv.68–69.

       aspitious Dogberry means 'suspicious'. The word he uses suggests 'auspicious' and 'ass-specious' and anticipates later developments.

54–55 **Take . . . me** Conduct the interrogation yourself and bring the results to me. *Take* echoes III.iii.50–52, 190–92.

57   **It . . . suffigance** Dogberry means that 'it shall be done as you say'. By *suffigance* he probably means 'sufficient'. But the word also sounds enough like *suffering* to suggest to the audience that what will ensue from this combination of Leonato's 'great Haste' (line 55) and Dogberry's incompetence is some pain that might have been forestalled.

62   **wait upon them** do them the service you refer to. Compare I.iii.16–17.

64   **Sea-cole** a member of the Watch who can 'write and read' (III.iii.12).

65   **Gaol** 'Jail' (line 71).

       examination examine, question. Compare II.iii.220–23, 243–44.

66   **wisely** Verges means 'intelligently and responsibly'.

69   **Noncome** a condition of bewilderment. Dogberry probably means *non plus* (Latin for 'perplexity'); his phrasing is an abbreviation of *non compos mentis*, Latin for 'not of a composed [sound] mind'. *Wit* (line 67) echoes lines 38–39.

       the learned Writer Dogberry's high-sounding phrase refers to Sea-cole's rudimentary literacy.

70   **Excommunication** Appropriately, Dogberry's phrasing suggests the negation of a 'communication'. What he means, of course, is 'examination' (line 65), here one that will result in a condemnation. Dogberry's malapropism is a reminder that matters of communication and community are very much to the point in the case to be 'set down' (lines 69–70). More than one form of excommunication (censure, exclusion from communion) will result from Dogberry's failure to conduct his business effectively and 'wisely' (line 66).

DOGBERRY   One Word, Sir, our Watch, Sir, have   50
indeed comprehended two aspitious Persons, and
we would have them this Morning examined before
your Worship.

LEONATO   Take their Examination your self and
bring it me: I am now in great Haste, as it   55
may appear unto you.

DOGBERRY   It shall be suffigance.

LEONATO   Drink some Wine ere you go: fare you
well.

[*Enter Messenger.*]

MESSENGER   My Lord, they stay for you, to give   60
your Daughter to her Husband.

LEONATO   I'll wait upon them, I am ready.

DOGBERRY   Go, good Partner, go get you to Francis
Sea-cole, bid him bring his Pen and Inkhorn to
the Gaol: we are now to examination these Men.   65

VERGES   And we must do it wisely.

DOGBERRY   We will spare for no Wit, I warrant
you: here's that shall drive some of them to a
Noncome. Only get the learned Writer to set
down our Excommunication, and meet me at the   70
Jail.   [*Exeunt.*]

IV.i   This scene takes place in a church, possibly a chapel attached to Leonato's household.

1   **be brief**   Leonato's demand for brevity is probably related to his having just come from the conversation with Dogberry. The last thing Leonato wants now is to have to listen to a loquacious Friar. *Onely* (only) recalls III.iv.44.

2   **the . . . Marriage**   the simplest version of the marriage ceremony.

3   **recount . . . Duties**   instruct them in the Church's teachings about the obligations a husband and wife owe to each other. Here as elsewhere, *particular* can play on *part* (see the note to I.i.145) to draw attention to those aspects of marriage that involve conjugal union. Compare V.i.171–72.

7–8   **To . . . her**   It never occurs to Leonato that Claudio may not merely be quibbling over an 'illegitimate Construction' (III.iv.50) of the phrase 'marry this Lady'. He has no idea that Claudio is being 'plain' here, and is not facetiously pretending to disavow the inapplicable sense of a statement that can be construed with 'double Meaning' (II.iii.275–76).

12   **inward Impediment**   secret impurity or other obstacle. See the note to III.ii.93.

13   **charge**   command.

14   **on your Souls**   at peril of your souls [if you withhold it]. *Utter* recalls III.iii.113–15.

18   **I . . . none**   Leonato's interjection smacks not only of impatience but of hubris (overweening confidence). Compare line 18 with I.i.213–23.

20   **what . . . do!**   Claudio refers to Leonato, with the implication that Hero's father, knowing that his daughter is not free of 'Impediment', believes that he can pass her off as chaste. Claudio's echo of 'Father, forgive them, for they know not what they do' (Luke 23:34) reminds us that his words unwittingly apply to himself more than to Leonato. Claudio, too, is being blinded by the pride he invests in the maintenance of his honour. For a similarly ironic echo of Jesus' words from the cross, see *Julius Caesar*, III.i.233.

21–22   **why . . . Laughing**   well then, let some of them be the kinds of interjections (words expressing passion, such as 'ah, ha, he') that signify mirth. Benedick's phrasing parodies William Lily's 1549 Latin grammar.

ACT IV

Scene 1

Enter Prince, Bastard,
Leonato, Friar, Claudio, Benedick, Hero,
and Beatrice.

LEONATO Come, Friar Francis, be brief, onely to
the plain Form of Marriage, and you shall
recount their particular Duties afterwards.

FRANCIS — You come hither, my Lord, to marry
this Lady.   5

CLAUDIO No.

LEONATO To be married to her. — Friar, you come
to marry her.

FRANCIS Lady, you come hither to be married to
this Counte.   10

HERO I do.

FRIAR If either of you know any inward Impediment
why you should not be conjoined, I charge you
on your Souls to utter it.

CLAUDIO Know you any, Hero?   15

HERO None, my Lord.

FRIAR Know you any, Counte?

LEONATO I dare make his Answer, None.

CLAUDIO O what Men dare do! what Men may do!
what Men daily do, not knowing what they do!   20

BENEDICK How now, Interjections? why then,
some be of Laughing, as ah, ha, he.

23 **Stand . . . by** step to the side.

27 **Woorth** worth. *Gift* (line 28) echoes III.v.48.

28 **counterpoise** balance on the scales.

29 **render** both (a) give, and (b) surrender, return.
    again both (a) a second time, and (b) back to the original giver.

30 **learn** teach.

33 **Sign** This word echoes III.ii.43. *Semblance* can mean either (a) specious imitation, or (b) genuine likeness, true image.

36 **cunning** both (a) knowing, and (b) crafty. Claudio's accusation is all the more stunning for its echo of the Latin word *cunnus*; see the note to I.i.335. In line 35, as in II.iii.117, III.ii.131, *Shew* (show) hints at an apheticform of *eschew*.
    withal with.

38 **witness** bear witness to, testify in behalf of. Compare II.iii.49, 245–46, III.ii.129–30.

41 **luxurious** lecherous, lascivious. *Modesty* (line 42), echoing line 37, recalls II.iii.220–23.

43 **What do you mean** Leonato means 'what are you talking about?' In his reply Claudio shifts the sense of *mean* to 'intend'. Compare III.ii.88–89, III.iv.60.

44 **approved** both (a) proven, and (b) [falsely] commended. Compare II.i.396–98.

45 **Deer** Here as in I.i.122, 133, 153, *deer* (*deere* in the Quarto) can be construed to mean both (a) deer (referring to a stag), and (b) dear (precious, worthy).

45–47 **if . . . Virginity** if you yourself have overcome her maidenly resistance by your demands for prenuptial gratification. Here *Proof* means 'trial', a temptation to test her.

49 **imbrace** embrace.

50 **extenuate . . . Sin** excuse the sin of not waiting.

51 **with . . . large** with any suggestion that she do anything at variance with what the strictest chastity demanded. Here *large* has the connotations now associated with *broad*; compare II.iii.212, where Benedick is excused for 'large Jests' that challenge the limits of modesty and propriety.

53 **comely Love** chaste affection. Claudio's analogy calls to mind the counsel Laertes gives his sister in *Hamlet*, I.iii.1–85.

CLAUDIO — Stand thee by, Friar. — Father, by
    your leave,
  Will you with free and unconstrained Soul
  Give me this Maid your Daughter?   25
LEONATO As freely, Son, as God did give her me.
CLAUDIO And what have I to give you back whose
    Woorth
  May counterpoise this rich and precious Gift?
PRINCE Nothing, unless you render her again.
CLAUDIO Sweet Prince, you learn me noble
    Thankfulness.   30
  — There, Leonato, take her back again,
  Give not this rotten Orange to your Friend,
  She's but the Sign and Semblance of her Honour:
  Behold how like a Maid she blushes here!
  O what Authority and Shew of Truth   35
  Can cunning Sin cover it self withal!
  Comes not that Blood as modest Evidence
  To witness simple Virtue? — Would you not
    swear,
  All you that see her, that she were a Maid,
  By these exterior Shews? But she is none;   40
  She knows the Heat of a luxurious Bed;
  Her Blush is Guiltiness, not Modesty.
LEONATO What do you mean, my Lord?
CLAUDIO   Not to be married,
  Not to knit my Soul to an approved Wanton.
LEONATO Deer my Lord, if you in your own Proof   45
  Have vanquish'd the Resistance of her Youth,
  And made defeat of her Virginity.
CLAUDIO I know what you would say: if I have
    known her,
  You will say, she did imbrace me as a Husband,
  And so extenuate the forehand Sin. No, Leonato,   50
  I never tempted her with Word too large,
  But as a Brother to his Sister, shewed
  Bashful Sincerity, and comely Love.
HERO And seem'd I ever otherwise to you?

55   **Out ... it** Be done with your pretence of maiden innocence, you deceiver: I will denounce your crimes in public proclamations. Claudio's words echo what Jesus says to the Devil in Matthew 4:10.

56   **Diane in her orb** The Goddess of Chastity in her lunar orb.

57   **be blown** achieve full bloom. Claudio hints at the kinds of 'blows' (and resultant fruit-bearing) a more guileful woman alludes to in I.ii.287–90 of *Troilus and Cressida*.

58   **intemperate ... Blood** unrestrained in your lust. *Blood* echoes lines 37–38.

59   **Venus** Goddess of Love.
      pamp'red overly indulged, their appetites catered for at every turn.

60   **rage** go wild in uncontrollable frenzy.

61   **wide** both (a) wide of the mark, and (b) with wild abandon. Compare Claudio's use of *large* in line 51.

63   **gone about** gone to all the effort.

64   **Stale** used piece of merchandise, 'rotten Orange' (line 32). Compare II.ii.22–26.

65   **Are ... dream?** Can I really be awake? Leonato's imagery echoes I.ii.21–22.

70   **are ... own?** Claudio speaks with sarcastic self-assurance, not realizing that his question is a pertinent one. *Eyes* recalls I.i.195–96, 259–62, 306–15, II.i.87–88, 185–87, II.iii.23–24, III.i.51–56, III.iv.92–94.

72   **move** pose.

73   **kindly Power** the kind of authority a father has.

74   **in her** over her. *Answer* echoes line 18; *charge* (command), line 19, recalls line 13.

76   **beset** besieged, attacked from every direction.

77   **Catechizing** close questioning (as if I were a child who is yet to be confirmed for membership in an adult communion). See the note to III.iii.126.

CLAUDIO   Out on thee seeming, I will write
  against it,   55
  You seem to me as Diane in her Orb,
  As chaste as is the Bud ere it be blown:
  But you are more intemperate in your Blood
  Than Venus, or those pamp'red Animals
  That rage in savage Sensuality.   60
HERO   Is my Lord well that he doth speak so
  wide?
LEONATO   – Sweet Prince, why speak not you?
PRINCE   What should I speak?
  I stand dishonour'd that have gone about
  To link my dear Friend to a common Stale.
LEONATO   Are these things spoken, or do I but
  dream?   65
BASTARD   Sir, they are spoken, and these things
  are true.
BENEDICK   This looks not like a Nuptial.
HERO   True, O God!
CLAUDIO   Leonato, stand I here?
  Is this the Prince? is this the Prince's
  Brother?
  Is this Face Hero's? are our Eyes our Own?   70
LEONATO   All this is so, but what of this, my
  Lord?
CLAUDIO   Let me but move one Question to your
  Daughter,
  And by that fatherly and kindly Power
  That you have in her, bid her answer truly.
LEONATO   – I charge thee do so, as thou art my
  Child.   75
HERO   – O God defend me how am I beset.
  – What kind of Catechizing call you this?

78   **To ... Name**   [Its purpose is] to make you (a) supply an honest
      reply to every query addressed to you, and (b) give a true
      answer to the question of your identity (in this case one whose
      'Name' derives from a mythical symbol of fidelity, the Hero
      for whom Leander drowned while swimming the Hellespont).
      Claudio's comment combines (a) the kind of elementary
      question with which religious catechisms begin, and (b) the
      kind of interrogation with which criminal proceedings
      concern themselves as they seek to prove a person's guilt or
      innocence.

79   **blot**   obliterate with ink. Compare lines 55, 81, 120, and see
      III.i.63–64.

81   **Hero**   the name Hero. *Mary*, line 80, echoes III.v.34.

82   **he**   he that.
      yesternight   last night.

85   **that Hour**   Hero's reply indicates that she regards the time in
      question as shockingly 'unseasonable' (II.ii.16), almost so
      much so as to be unthinkable.

86   **Why ... Maiden**   Don Pedro probably means 'you are a liar'
      (since from his point of view it is already established that
      Hero talked with some man). What he may also be implying,
      however, is 'you are even worse than we thought [since you
      didn't even bother with such preliminaries as talking]; you
      had already fallen so far from true maidenhood that you
      didn't even feign the coyness that suggested a need to woo
      you.'

88   **grieved**   aggrieved; grievously wronged.

90   **Ruffian**   a 'rough one' (a coarse man, far below her gentle
      birth).

91   **liberal**   licentious, unrestrained. Compare II.i.144–45.

92   **Encounters**   Like *Cunning* (line 36), this word plays on a 'vile'
      term to literalize 'secret' acts too abhorrent 'to be named'
      (lines 93–94). See the note to I.i.335, and compare
      III.iii.158–63.

97   **much Misgovernment**   gross misdeeds (literally, lack of
      self-control). Lines 96–97 spell out what remains implicit in
      III.iv.33 and III.v.34–35.

98   **what ... been**   Claudio alludes to the proverbial fidelity of the
      classical heroine after whom Hero has been named.

CLAUDIO   To make you answer truly to your Name.
HERO   Is it not Hero, who can blot that Name
  With any just Reproach?
CLAUDIO   Mary that can Hero,   80
  Hero it self can blot out Hero's Virtue.
  What Man was he talk'd with you yesternight,
  Out at your Window betwixt twelve and one?
  Now if you are Maid, answer to this.
HERO   I talk'd with no Man at that Hour, my Lord.   85
PRINCE   Why then are you no Maiden. – Leonato,
  I am sorry you must hear: upon mine Honour,
  My self, my Brother, and this grieved Counte
  Did see her, hear her, at that Hour last Night,
  Talk with a Ruffian at her Chamber Window,   90
  Who hath indeed most like a liberal Villain
  Confess'd the vile Encounters they have had
  A thousand times in secret.
JOHN   Fie, fie, they are
  Not to be named, my Lord, not to be spoke of,
  There is not Chastity enough in Language   95
  Without Offence to utter them. – Thus, pretty
    Lady,
  I am sorry for thy much Misgovernment.
CLAUDIO   O Hero! what a Hero hadst thou been
  If half thy outward Graces had been placed
  About thy Thoughts and Counsailes of thy Heart?   100
  But fare thee well, most Foul, most Fair,
    farewell.
  Thou pure Impiety, and impious Purity,

---

100   **About**   around (so as to protect, like an unbreachable fortress).

102   **pure Impiety**   unadulterated instance of prenuptial adultery.
        Claudio uses oxymorons (self-cancelling descriptions) to
        convey the stark discrepancy between what Hero appears to
        be and what he is calling her.

103 **all . . . Love** every means by which love might gain entrance to my heart. Claudio implicitly compares himself to a besieged tower.

104 **Conjecture** suspicion [of infidelity].

105 **Thoughts of Harm** fear of the dishonour that comes to the man whose lover harms him and his reputation by being unfaithful. Compare Benedick's anxieties about cuckoldry in I.i.247–55.

107 **Hath . . . me** Is there no one here who will stab me and terminate my misery? Compare II.i.255–57.

108 **wherefore** why. So also in line 117.

109 **come** having come.

114 **Cover** Now that Hero's flame (synonymous with her 'Shame') is almost smothered, Leonato would have 'Fate' snuff it out completely. Compare III.i.77–80.

117 **look up** cast your impudent eyes towards Heaven (as if in pious prayer). As the King expires in V.iii of *King Lear*, Edgar tells him, 'Look up, my Lord.'

120 **printed . . . Blood** proclaimed in the blood that rushes to her cheeks. Compare lines 55, 79, 81, 137–38. *Blood* echoes lines 58–60.

123 **Thought I** if I thought.

124 **on . . . Reproaches** after all the rebukes you have deservedly received. *Rearward* reminds us how much has happened since Leonato's reference to a 'forehand Sin' (line 50).

125 **I I** I that I.

126 **Chid . . . Frame?** Did I chide Nature for being so frugal (stingy) in her bounty as to give me only a single child? Old Capulet speaks in much the same way in III.v.165–69 of *Romeo and Juliet*.

130 **a Beggar's Issue** a child abandoned by a beggar. Here, as in III.iv.31, *Beggar* probably refers to the kind of diseased hag a whore becomes after her beauty fails her. According to Robert Henryson's sequel to Chaucer's *Troilus and Criseyde*, this was the fate of Cressida.

For thee I'll lock up all the Gates of Love,
And on my Eyelids shall Conjecture hang,
To turn all Beauty into Thoughts of Harm,   105
And never shall it more be gracious.

LEONATO Hath no man's Dagger here a Point for
    me.   [*Hero swoons.*]

BEATRICE Why how now, Cousin, wherefore sink
    you down?

BASTARD Come let us go: these things come thus
    to Light,
Smother her Spirits up.   110
            [*Exeunt Don Pedro, Don John, and Claudio.*]

BENEDICK How doth the Lady?

BEATRICE   Dead, I think. – Help, Uncle.
    – Hero, why Hero. – Uncle. – Signior Benedick.
    – Friar.

LEONATO O Fate! take not away thy heavy Hand,
Death is the fairest Cover for her Shame
That may be wish'd for.   115

BEATRICE How now, Cousin Hero?

FRIAR   Have Comfort, Lady.

LEONATO Dost thou look up?

FRIAR   Yea, wherefore should she not?

LEONATO Wherefore? why doth not every earthly
    thing
Cry Shame upon her? Could she here deny
The Story that is printed in her Blood?   120
– Do not live, Hero, do not ope thine Eyes:
For did I think thou wouldst not quickly die,
Thought I thy Spirits were stronger than thy
    Shames,
My self would on the rearward of Reproaches
Strike at thy Life. Grieved I I had but one?   125
Chid I for that at frugal Nature's Frame?
O one too much by thee: why had I one?
Why ever wast thou lovely in my Eyes?
Why had I not with charitable Hand
Took up a Beggar's Issue at my Gates,   130

131   **smirched** soiled.
       Infamy shame, reproach. *Part* (line 132) echoes III.v.21–25; compare lines 142–43.

135   **on** of.

137   **Valuing of her** since I had measured my own self-worth by the price I placed on her. Compare III.iii.119–25.

138   **Pit of Ink** a variation on the 'Pitch' referred to in III.iii.62.

140   **Season** both (a) flavour, and (b) preservative (here restorative). Leonato's imagery is itself seasoned by a syntactically non-functional but thematically relevant meaning of *Salt*: lustful, lewd. Meanwhile the Governor's reference to washing off his daughter's sin (line 139) evokes such biblical passages as Psalm 51:2, Isaiah 1:15–18, and Matthew 27:24.

142   **attired in Wonder** shrouded in amazement.

144   **belied** the victim of a lie; falsely accused.

147   **this Twelvemonth** for every other night of the last year.

148   **Confirm'd** that proves it. Leonato fails to note that Beatrice's testimony actually refutes the charge levelled at Hero in lines 91–93. Compare III.iii.169–70.
       stronger made made even more secure (certain).

149   **Which . . . Iron** which was already locked tight in a prison cell. Compare III.v.63–71.

152   **Wash'd** he washed. See the note to line 140.

156   **By . . . Lady** because I have been observing the lady with close scrutiny. While everyone else has been 'noting' Hero's behaviour superficially, the Friar has been paying careful attention to her with a properly trained eye. What he has noted, he goes on to say, contains nothing to support the accusation that her cheeks have flushed with guilty shame.

157   **blushing Apparitions** illusory manifestations of guilt.

158   **innocent Shames** pallors of true innocence, the kinds of reactions that appear at the mere thought of shameful deeds. *Shames* echoes lines 119, 123, 133.

160   **a Fire** a radiance of righteous indignation. The Friar picks up on the fireplace imagery of lines 109–10 and 114–15. Instead of referring to Hero's embers as smothered, however, he describes them as a newly kindled flame. Like the Phoenix, he implies, a new Hero will rise from the ashes of the old to burn away the heresies ('Errors') of the 'Princes' who have brought her to the stake as an infidel. Compare I.i.238–44.

Who, smirched thus, and mired with Infamy,
I might have said 'No Part of it is mine,
This Shame derives it self from unknown Loins.'
But mine and mine I loved, and mine I prais'd,
And mine that I was proud on mine so much,   135
That I my self was to my self not mine:
Valuing of her, why she, O she is fall'n,
Into a Pit of Ink, that the wide Sea
Hath Drops too few to wash her clean again,
And Salt too little which may Season give   140
To her foul tainted Flesh.
BENEDICK   Sir, Sir, be patient.
For my part I am so attired in Wonder,
I know not what to say.
BEATRICE   O on my Soul
My Cousin is belied.
BENEDICK   Lady, were you her Bedfellow last
    Night?   145
BEATRICE   No truly, not, although until last
    Night
I have this Twelvemonth been her Bedfellow.
LEONATO   Confirm'd, confirm'd, O that is stronger
    made,
Which was before barr'd up with Ribs of Iron.
Would the two Princes lie, and Claudio lie,   150
Who loved her so, that speaking of her
    Foulness,
Wash'd it with Tears! Hence from her, let her
    die.
FRIAR   Hear me a little,
For I have only been silent so long,
And given way unto this course of Fortune,   155
By noting of the Lady; I have mark'd
A thousand blushing Apparitions
To start into her Face, a thousand innocent
    Shames,
In Angel Whiteness beat away those Blushes,
And in her Eye there hath appear'd a Fire   160

162   **maiden Truth**   both (a) true virginity, and (b) unblemished
        honesty. Compare lines 176–78.

163   **Reading**   both (a) noting, interpretation of what I see, and (b)
        learning, wisdom. Compare III.v.63–71.

164– **with . . . Book**   with the seal (warranty, authenticity) of
65   experience validates the tenor (contents or 'holding') of my
        story and my credentials as a man whose education befits his
        'Calling' (profession as an exponent and interpreter of
        'Divinity', holiness).

169   **Grace**   inbred 'Divinity' (see the note to lines 164–65). *Grace*
        echoes lines 99, 103–6 and II.iii.30–31.

171   **Perjury**   lying under oath when asked about the crime she is
        charged with.

172   **cover with Excuse**   cover over with a denial of guilt. Here
        Excuse refers not to obtaining pardon or extenuation for an
        offence, but to proving that no offence occurred in the first
        place. Compare lines 114, 142.

173   **in proper Nakedness**   'plain' (III.iv.81), in its own true image
        (with no improper attempt to hide or deny it).

174   **of**   of having seen illicitly.

176   **know more**   have any more physical knowledge. See the notes
        to III.ii.66, 69.

177   **warrant**   permit, authorize.

178   **lack Mercy**   be held against me; be forever unforgiven.

179   **Prove you**   if you prove. *Convers'd* means both (a) talked, and
        (b) engaged in intimate relations.

180   **Hours unmeet**   inappropriate times for a maiden to meet with a
        man. Compare line 85.

181   **Maintain'd . . . of**   permitted the exchange of; exchanged.

182   **Refuse me**   disinherit (refuse to acknowledge) me.

183   **Misprision**   'Misprising' (see III.ii.52), misevaluation;
        'illegitimate Construction' (III.iv.50).

184   **have . . . Honour**   are perfect instances of honour's shape (here
        likened to a bow pulled to its full bent) and inclination.

185   **Wisdoms**   sound judgements, discernments. Compare
        II.iii.177–79.

To burn the Errors that these Princes hold
Against her maiden Truth. Call me a Fool,
Trust not my Reading, nor my Observations,
Which with experimental Seal doth warrant
The tenure of my Book: trust not my Age,   165
My Reverence, Calling, nor Divinity,
If this sweet Lady be not Guiltless here,
Under some biting Error.
LEONATO   Friar, it cannot be,
Thou seest that all the Grace that she hath
    left
Is that she will not add to her Damnation   170
A Sin of Perjury, she not denies it:
Why seekst thou then to cover with Excuse
That which appears in proper Nakedness?
FRIAR   Lady, what Man is he you are accus'd of?
HERO   They know that do accuse me, I know none;   175
If I know more of any Man alive
Than that which maiden Modesty doth warrant,
Let all my Sins lack Mercy. – O my Father,
Prove you that any Man with me convers'd,
At Hours unmeet, or that I yesternight   180
Maintain'd the change of Words with any
    Creature,
Refuse me, hate me, torture me to Death.
FRIAR   There is some strange Misprision in the
    Princes.
BENEDICK   Two of them have the very bent of
    Honour,
And if their Wisdoms be misled in this,   185

186 **Practice of** intrigue (deception) behind; devising of. Compare II.ii.52–53.

187 **frame** the framing, devising. *Frame* echoes line 126.

192 **eat . . . Invention** eaten away my power to conceive [a proper revenge]. *Blood* (line 191) echoes line 37.

193 **made . . . Means** laid waste my power to effect what I set out to do.

194 **reft** bereft, robbed.

195 **they** 'The proudest of them' (line 190). **kind** manner. Compare II.i.71.

196 **Policy of Mind** ability to devise a suitable retaliation.

198 **To . . . throughly** to be thoroughly even with them. *Means* (lines 193, 197) echoes line 43.

199 **Counsel** spiritual guidance.

201 **secretly kept in** kept concealed (indoors). What the Friar suggests is that a counterfeit 'Death is the fairest Cover for her Shame / That may be wish'd for' (lines 114–15).

202 **publish it** announce publicly. Compare line 55.

203 **a mourning Ostentation** all the appearance of mourning. *Maintain* echoes lines 180–81.

204 **Monument** burial vault.

208 **well carried** carried out in a convincing manner. Compare II.iii.228–29, III.i.13, III.ii.130–31.

211 **Travail** labour (here that which precedes delivery). Compare the imagery in V.i.398–404 of *The Comedy of Errors*, a passage that also relates to V.i.188–89.

212 **maintain'd** 'carried' (line 208). Compare lines 180–81, 203, and I.i.243–46. *Excus'd* (line 214) echoes lines 172–73.

216 **prize . . . Worth** hold in lower esteem than its true worth merits. See *Antony and Cleopatra* I.ii.118–23.

218 **rack** either (a) take stock of (by inventorying our racks or shelves), or (b) stretch out to the full (as on the torturing rack). *Value* echoes lines 136–37.

The Practice of it lives in John the Bastard,
Whose Spirits toil in frame of Villainies.
LEONATO   I know not, if they speak but Truth of
    her,
These Hands shall tear her; if they wrong her
    Honour.
The proudest of them shall well hear of it.   190
Time hath not yet so dried this Blood of mine,
Nor Age so eat up my Invention,
Nor Fortune made such Havoc of my Means,
Nor my bad Life reft me so much of Friends,
But they shall find awak'd in such a kind   195
Both Strength of Limb and Policy of Mind,
Ability in Means, and Choice of Friends,
To quit me of them throughly.
FRIAR   Pause awhile,
And let my Counsel sway you in this case.
Your Daughter here, the Princess (left for Dead),   200
Let her awhile be secretly kept in,
And publish it that she is dead indeed;
Maintain a mourning Ostentation,
And on your Family's old Monument
Hang mournful Epitaphs, and do all Rites,   205
That appertain unto a Burial.
LEONATO   What shall become of this? what will
    this do?
FRIAR   Mary this well carried shall on her behalf
Change Slander to Remorse, that is some good,
But not for that dream I on this strange
    Course,   210
But on this Travail look for greater Birth.
She dying, as it must be so maintain'd,
Upon the Instant that she was accus'd,
Shall be lamented, pitied, and excus'd
Of every Hearer: for it so falls out   215
That what we have we prize not to the Worth
Whiles we enjoy it, but being lack'd and lost,
Why then we rack the Value, then we find

220   **fare**   happen (so that Hero will become 'fair' again).

221   **upon his Words**   Here the phrasing suggests an analogy with 'upon his sword' (an image that echoes II.i.256–57 and II.iii.271–72).

223   **Study of Imagination**   reveries, imaginative musings.

224– **And . . . Habit**   Here *Organ* probably means 'portion'. But it
25   will be most important that the 'Organ' at the focus of Claudio's accusation (see the note to line 36) 'come apparell'd in more precious Habit' (clothing or appearance). Compare line 172.

226   **moving delicate**   movingly delightful in its delicacy.

227   **Prospect**   view, vision; literally, forward looking. *Eye* echoes line 160.

229   **interest . . . Liver**   any claim upon the promptings of his affection. The liver was often depicted as a seat of passion.

232   **Success**   what ensues. *Fashion* (line 233) recalls III.iv.23.

234   **lay . . . Likelihood**   map it out in probabilities.

235   **levell'd false**   misdirected, off target.

237   **quench . . . Infamy**   extinguish the shock of his discovery of her shame. *Wonder* echoes lines 142–43.

238   **it . . . well**   things fail to turn out as we would wish.

240   **religious Life**   life in a convent. *Life* echoes lines 124–25, 194, 224–26.

243   **Inwardness**   deep friendship, intimacy. Compare lines 12–14.

246   **secretly**   confidentially. See lines 200–2.

247   **Being . . . Grief**   since I am virtually afloat on, and adrift within, my griefs.

249   **presently away**   let us proceed with our plans at once.

250   **For . . . Cure**   for to extreme or unusual maladies physicians apply extreme or unusual remedies. Here *strain* can mean (a) press or force (constrain), (b) extend, or (c) filter. Compare II.i.396–98, V.i.12.

252   **prolong'd**   postponed. As the Friar leads the wedding party away, the dramatic medium shifts from verse to prose.

The Virtue that Possession would not shew us
Whiles it was ours. So will it fare with Claudio: 220
When he shall hear she died upon his Words,
Th' Idea of her Life shall sweetly creep
Into his Study of Imagination,
And every lovely Organ of her Life
Shall come apparell'd in more precious Habit,   225
More moving delicate, and full of Life,
Into the Eye and Prospect of his Soul
Than when she liv'd indeed; then shall he mourn,
If ever Love had interest in his Liver,
And wish he had not so accused her,   230
No, though he thought his Accusation true.
Let this be so, and doubt not but Success
Will fashion the Event in better Shape
Then I can lay it down in Likelihood.
But if all Aim but this be levell'd false,   235
The Supposition of the Lady's Death
Will quench the Wonder of her Infamy.
And if it sort not well, you may conceal her,
As best befits her wounded Reputation,
In some reclusive and religious Life,   240
Out of all Eyes, Tongues, Minds, and Injuries.
BENEDICK   Signior Leonato, let the Friar advise
    you,
And though you know my Inwardness and Love
Is very much unto the Prince and Claudio,
Yet, by mine Honour, I will deal in this,   245
As secretly and justly as your Soul
Should with your Body.
LEONATO   Being that I flow in Grief,
    The smallest Twine may lead me.
FRIAR   'Tis well consented, presently away,
    For to strange Sores strangely they strain the
        Cure.   250
    — Come, Lady, die to live, this Wedding Day
    Perhaps is but prolong'd; have Patience and
        endure.   *Exeunt [all but Benedick and Beatrice].*

257   **freely** both (a) of my own volition, and (b) volubly (as in line 247).

261   **right her** restore justice to her.

264   **even** both (a) straightforward, just, level, and (b) easy. What Beatrice is hinting at will involve a third sense of *even*: (c) getting even.

266   **Office** job, duty. Compare III.iii.55, 61.

268   **strange** extraordinary. Compare lines 183, 210, 249, 270, and see I.ii.4–6, II.iii.21–23, 62–63, III.ii.32–34, V.iv.49.

269   **the . . . not** something that is a complete mystery to me (the thing of which I have no knowledge at all). Here *thing* and *know* are both sexually suggestive in a way that anticipates the ambiguities of *nothing* (which often means 'no thing', alludes to the female genitalia, and refers to naughtiness) in the enigmatic clauses that follow. See the notes to III.ii.60, III.iv.61, 76, IV.i.76, and compare line 289. Beatrice is imitating the unintentional equivocation in the first sentence of Benedick's preceding speech, which is so awkwardly phrased that it can yield (a) I love you more than anything in the world, or (b) I love nothing in the world just as much as I love you [that is, I love you and nothing with equal ardour], or (c) I love nothing just as well as you love nothing.

275   **Do . . . it** Do not make a vow that you will later be forced to eat (forswear). Compare lines 192, 221.

280– **devised to it** prepared and applied to it to make it palatable.
81   *Protest* means 'declare', 'vow'.

284   **stayed me** (a) arrested (detained) me, (b) forestalled me. Compare III.iii.84, IV.i.23. Here *a happy Hour* can mean either (a) an opportune moment, one that involves a strange coincidence, or (b) a joyous time. *Hour* echoes lines 85–90.

287– **I . . . protest** Beatrice's phrasing remains equivocal: she implies
88   that she loves Benedick, but she also says that her heart is empty of that which would allow it to swear love to anyone.

BENEDICK   Lady Beatrice, have you wept all this
while?
BEATRICE   Yea, and I will weep a while longer.   255
BENEDICK   I will not desire that.
BEATRICE   You have no Reason, I do it freely.
BENEDICK   Surely I do believe your fair Cousin is
wronged.
BEATRICE   Ah, how much might the Man deserve   260
of me that would right her!
BENEDICK   Is there any way to shew such
Friendship?
BEATRICE   A very even way, but no such Friend.
BENEDICK   May a Man do it?   265
BEATRICE   It is a Man's Office, but not yours.
BENEDICK   I do love nothing in the World so
well as you. Is not that strange?
BEATRICE   As strange as the thing I know not;
it were as possible for me to say I loved   270
nothing so well as you. But believe me not,
and yet I lie not; I confess nothing, nor I
deny nothing. I am sorry for my Coosin.
BENEDICK   By my Sword, Beatrice, thou lovest me.
BEATRICE   Do not swear and eat it.   275
BENEDICK   I will swear by it that you love me,
and I will make him eat it that says I love
not you.
BEATRICE   Will you not eat your Word?
BENEDICK   With no Sauce that can be devised to   280
it, I protest I love thee.
BEATRICE   Why then God forgive me.
BENEDICK   What Offence, sweet Beatrice?
BEATRICE   You have stayed me in a happy Hour,
I was about to protest I loved you.   285
BENEDICK   And do it with all thy Heart.
BEATRICE   I love you with so much of my Heart
that none is left to protest.
BENEDICK   Come bid me do any thing for thee.
BEATRICE   Kill Claudio.   290

292   **deny it** both (a) refuse it, and (b) forswear your vow not to 'eat your Word' (line 279).

295   **let me go** Evidently Benedick has seized hold of Beatrice to keep her from leaving. Fittingly, the first embrace of these merry warriors (I.i.63) is occasioned by a conflict. Beatrice's phrasing in line 294 is an oblique echo of the Boy's expression in II.iii.5.

298   **be Friends** become reconciled. *Friends* echoes lines 194–98.

302   **approved . . . height** proven to the utmost. *Approved* echoes lines 43–47, 178–82.

305   **bear . . . hand** lead her on, deceive her with false expectations.

307   **uncover'd** [suddenly] disclosed. Beatrice's phrasing depicts Claudio as a villain who had decided in advance to slander Hero (accuse her in a crime of which he knew her to be innocent), and who came to the church with an image of 'Slaunder' that he was planning to disrobe in a dramatic gesture. Her choice of words recalls line 172.

309   **eat . . . Marketplace** cut out his heart and eat it in public. Compare lines 275–81.

312   **proper Saying** fine remark. Compare II.i.242–43.

316   **Beat?** either (a) beaten? or, more likely, (b) Beat– ? Here Benedick appears to be cut off halfway through his sweetheart's name. Compare lines 310, 313.

317   **Counties** counts.

319   **Comfect** sweetmeat, comfit (confection), 'sweet Gallant'.

321   **would . . . Man** who would do the job of a true man (compare line 266), indeed the duties of a decent serving man (another sense of 'Man').

322   **melted into Cursies** dissolved into curtsies (like sweet candy). Compare the title character's contempt for cur-like 'Low-crooked Curtsies, and base Spaniel Fawning' in *Julius Caesar*, III.i.35–46.
       Complement compliant compliment; appeasement and flattery.

323   **turn'd into Tongue** both (a) reduced to words only, with no deeds to back them up, and (b) transformed into hypocritical dogs who lick villains as if they were candy (rather than eating out their hearts). *Turn'd* recalls III.iii.140–48.
       trim both (a) slender (like a long tongue), and (b) trimming (flattering, temporizing).

BENEDICK   Ha, not for the wide World.

BEATRICE   You kill me to deny it, farewell.

BENEDICK   Tarry, sweet Beatrice.

BEATRICE   I am gone, though I am here; there is
no Love in you, nay I pray you let me go.   295

BENEDICK   Beatrice.

BEATRICE   In faith I will go.

BENEDICK   We'll be Friends first.

BEATRICE   You dare easier be Friends with me
than fight with mine Enemy.   300

BENEDICK   Is Claudio thine Enemy?

BEATRICE   Is 'a not approved in the height
a Villain, that hath slaundered, scorned,
dishonoured my Kinswoman? O that I were
a Man! What, bear her in hand; until they   305
come to take Hands, and then with public
Accusation uncover'd Slaunder, unmitigated
Rancour? O God that I were a Man! I would
eat his Heart in the Marketplace.

BEATRICE   Hear me, Beatrice.   310

BEATRICE   Talk with a Man out at a Window, a
proper Saying.

BENEDICK   Nay but Beatrice.

BEATRICE   Sweet Hero, she is wrong'd, she is
slaund'red, she is undone.   315

BENEDICK   Beat?

BEATRICE   Princes and Counties! surely a
princely Testimony, a goodly Counte, Counte
Comfect, a sweet Gallant, surely. O that I
were a Man for his sake! or that I had any   320
Friend would be a Man for my sake! But Manhood
is melted into Cursies, Valour into Complement,
and Men are only turn'd into Tongue, and trim

324–   **He . . . it**   A man who does no more than utter a falsehood and
25   swear that it is the truth is now considered the epitome of
    valour. *Hercules* echoes III.iii.146–47.

327   **Grieving**   both (a) aggrieving, venting my complaints about the
    injustices I cannot redress, and (b) mourning. Compare lines
    88, 125, 247–48, and see I.i.322–23, III.ii.29–30, and
    V.i.8–32.

336   **engag'd**   committed to serve you.

338–   **render . . . Account**   both (a) pay me a high price, and (b) be
39   brought to a severe accounting (reckoning) for his misdeed.
    Render echoes line 29. Here as in line 45, *deer* can be
    construed to mean both (a) deer, and (b) dear (costly).
    Compare line 65 (*deare* in the Quarto) and V.i.179.

339   **As . . . me**   Judge me by what you hear I have done.

IV.ii   This scene takes place in a room at the local jailhouse.

S.D.   **Cleark**   clerk (but pronounced 'clark'). It may be that this
    officer doubles as the sexton (custodian of the parish church,
    responsible for bellringing and gravedigging); he is identified
    as such throughout IV.ii. In this scene the Quarto's speech
    designations are highly irregular, in most cases referring to the
    characters by the names (Kemp, Cowley) or types (Andrew,
    meaning 'Clown') of the actors who were to play the roles.
    in Gowns   all wearing the official robes of their offices.

1   **Dissembly**   Dogberry's malapropism suggests that this assembly
    is likely to be just as disorganized (dis-assembled) as the
    Constable's previous attempts to bring to justice the two
    dissemblers (liars, tricksters) the Watch has arrested.

2   **Cushion**   It is not clear whether the cushion is for the Clerk to
    sit on or for him to use as a writing table. In the bust of
    Shakespeare in Stratford's Holy Trinity Church, the poet is
    shown with a cushion under the paper he is writing upon.

3   **Malefactors**   evildoers. In line 4 Dogberry shows that he thinks
    that this high-sounding term applies to the two Constables. In
    a sense, he is right, at least about himself. See the notes to
    III.v.37–38, 57, 70.

4   **Mary**   in the name of the Virgin. Compare IV.i.80, 208, and see
    lines 10, 27, 39, 52.

5   **the Exhibition**   Verges may mean 'commission' (authority); but
    it is more likely that he means either 'offenders' or 'evidence'.
    In fact, these 'Offenders' *are* guilty of an 'Exhibition', a
    'Dissembly' (line 1).

ones too: he is now as valiant as Hercules,
that only tells a Lie, and swears it. I cannot   325
be a Man with Wishing, therefore I will die a
Woman with Grieving.

BENEDICK   Tarry, good Beatrice, by this Hand I
love thee.

BEATRICE   Use it for my Love some other way than   330
swearing by it.

BENEDICK   Think you in your Soul that Count
Claudio hath wrong'd Hero?

BEATRICE   Yea, as sure as I have a Thought, or a
Soul.   335

BENEDICK   Enough, I am engag'd, I will challenge
him, I will kiss your Hand, and so I leave you:
by this Hand, Claudio shall render me a deer
Account. As you hear of me, so think of me:
go comfort your Coosin, I must say she is dead,   340
and so farewell.   [*Fxeunt*.]

Scene 2

Enter the Constables, Borachio, and the Town Cleark
in Gowns.

DOGBERRY   Is our whole Dissembly appear'd?

VERGES   O a Stool and a Cushion for the Sexton.

SEXTON   Which be the Malefactors?

DOGBERRY   Mary that am I, and my Partner.

VERGES   Nay that's certain, we have the Exhibition   5
to examine.

SEXTON   But which are the Offenders? that are to
be examined. Let them come before Maister
Constable.

DOGBERRY   Yea, mary, let them come before me.   10
— What is your name, Friend?

BORACHIO   Borachio.

13 **write down Borachio** inscribe the name 'Borachio'. Dogberry's
    phrasing could also mean 'proclaim Borachio an offender'.
    Note what Claudio says in IV.i.55, and compare IV.i.119–20,
    137–38, 163–68, IV.ii.17, 20–21, 34–35, 45, 83–84, 94–95;
    also see I.i.259–77, II.iii.138–59, III.iii.9–22.

15 **Gentleman** Conrade is telling Dogberry that he will not answer
    to 'Sirrah' (a condescending mode of address for a child, a
    servingman, or another person of lowly station).

21–22 **God defend . . . Villains** God forbid that God should not
    precede such villains. Most editions place in quotation marks
    the words and phrases that Dogberry instructs the Sexton to
    record. But Dogberry's inability to make sophisticated
    discriminations between '*God*' *should go before* and *God
    should go before* comes across more readily if the dialogue is
    presented as it occurs in the original texts.

24 **False Knaves** Dogberry's phrase is unintentionally equivocal: it
    can mean 'not knaves', the opposite of 'true [genuine] knaves'.
    Borachio's reply that 'we are none' (line 27) can thus be taken
    as a true statement, and one with analogies to the ambiguities
    in Beatrice's reply to Benedick's declaration of love in the
    preceding scene (IV.i.269–73).

28 **witty** Dogberry probably means 'crafty'. Compare III.v.67–68.

29 **go . . . him** follow his trail, no matter how roundabout.

30 **a Word . . . Ear** This expression normally introduces a
    statement to be whispered confidentially. As such, it implies a
    degree of intimacy that would be ludicrous here.

33 **stand aside** step to the side. Compare III.ii.71, IV.i.23, 63–64,
    68.

34 **both in a Tale** in agreement on their story. Up to this point
    neither malefactor has had a chance to get into a 'Tale' (much
    less the kind of 'tail' that would befit their 'Lechery',
    III.iii.181). Compare III.iii.68–70, 158–59.

39 **eftest** With his usual aplomb, Dogberry combines 'eptest'
    (aptest) and 'deftest'.

41 **charge** order. Dogberry's command echoes IV.i.12–14, 75.

46 **Perjury** lying under oath. What Dogberry probably means is
    'slander'. There is a sense, however, in which he is right to
    object to calling a prince's brother 'Villain'; originally *Villain*
    meant 'peasant'. It is beyond Dogberry's imagining that a
    prince's brother could be a villain in the usual Renaissance
    (and modern) sense.

DOGBERRY   Pray write down Borachio. – Yours,
Sirrah.

CONRADE   I am a Gentleman, Sir, and my name is   15
Conrade.

DOGBERRY   Write down Maister Gentleman Conrade.
– Maisters, do you serve God?

BOTH   Yea Sir, we hope.

DOGBERRY   Write down, that they hope they serve   20
God: and write God first, for God defend but
God should go before such Villains. – Maisters,
it is proved already that you are little better
than false Knaves, and it will go near to be
thought so shortly; how answer you for your   25
selves?

CONRADE   Mary Sir, we say, we are none.

DOGBERRY   – A marvellous witty Fellow, I assure
you, but I will go about with him. – Come you
hither, Sirrah, a Word in your Ear, Sir, I say   30
to you, it is thought you are false Knaves.

BORACHIO   Sir, I say to you, we are none.

DOGBERRY   Well, stand aside. – 'Fore God, they
are both in a Tale: have you writ down, that
they are none?   35

SEXTON   Master Constable, you go not the way to
examine, you must call foorth the Watch that
are their Accusers.

DOGBERRY   Yea mary, that's the eftest Way,
let the Watch come forth. – Masters, I   40
charge you in the Prince's name, accuse these
Men.

WATCH 1   This Man said, Sir, that Don John the
Prince's Brother was a Villain.

DOGBERRY   – Write down, Prince John a Villain.   45
– Why this is flat Perjury, to call a Prince's
Brother Villain.

BORACHIO   Maister Constable.

50   **promise** Dogberry probably means 'warn' or 'warrant'. His
      phrasing keeps us aware of the wedding 'promise' that was
      not vowed in IV.i.

51   **else** besides that; in addition.

53   **of** from.

55   **Burglary** The word Dogberry wants is 'Perjury'. But *Burglary*
      may be the 'eftest Way' (line 39) for Shakespeare to remind
      the audience that the consequence of Don John's 'accusing the
      Lady Hero wrongfully' was to steal away her husband and (as
      far as anyone present knows) both her inheritance and her
      life: 'Flat [absolute] Burglary' indeed. *Flat* recalls II.i.230.

58   **mean** intend. Compare IV.i.43–44. *Assembly* (line 60) echoes
      line 1. In the process it reminds us that the dissembling of
      Don John and his cohorts brought 'disgrace' not only to Hero
      (compare III.ii.127–28) but to her accusers and to those who
      initially refused to believe in her innocence; in short, its effect
      was to 'trans-shape' (V.i.172) an 'Assembly' into a
      'Dissembly', and a true 'Semblance' (see IV.i.33) into a false
      one.

62   **Redemption** Dogberry means 'perdition' (damnation). In due
      course his prophecy will prove less ludicrous than one might
      expect. Compare lines 1, 3 and see *Measure for Measure*,
      II.i.46–57, V.i.432–34, for comments that hint at the same
      paradoxes as those mangled by the 'wise Officer' (II.i.58–59)
      of Messina.

65   **then** than. But here as in III.iii.150, the usual modern sense of
      'then' is also pertinent.

67   **stol'n away** This phrase offers yet another variation on 'flat
      Burglary' (line 55). It echoes III.iii.63–65, and it serves as a
      reminder that in more than one sense Don John has stolen out
      of the company of those with whom he came to Messina.

68   **refus'd** rejected and denounced. The Sexton's rhyme with
      'accus'd' makes the point with maximum effectiveness.

70   **bound** confined and shackled; bound over for trial.

73   **opinion'd** Dogberry probably means 'pinioned' (have their
      hands tied behind their backs). But *opinion'd* is amusingly
      pertinent: these men are to be registered in public 'Opinion'
      because of the 'Opinions' they have affected and effected.

74   **Coxcomb** fool (from the cap worn by a jester). Compare
      Conrade's sarcasm in III.iii.188–89, 193–94.

DOGBERRY   Pray thee, Fellow, peace, I do not
like thy Look, I promise thee.   50
SEXTON   What heard you him say else?
WATCH 2   Mary that he had received a thousand
Ducats of Don John, for accusing the Lady Hero
wrongfully.
DOGBERRY   Flat Burglary as ever was committed.   55
VERGES   Yea by Mass, that it is.
SEXTON   What else, Fellow?
WATCH 1   And that Counte Claudio did mean upon
his Words, to disgrace Hero before the whole
Assembly, and not marry her.   60
DOGBERRY   O Villain! thou wilt be condemn'd into
everlasting Redemption for this.
SEXTON   What else?
WATCH   This is all.
SEXTON   And this is more, Masters, then you can   65
deny. Prince John is this Morning secretly
stol'n away; Hero was in this manner accus'd,
in this very manner refus'd, and upon the
Grief of this suddenly died. – Maister
Constable, let these Men be bound, and brought   70
to Leonato's: I will go before and shew him
their Examination.   [*Exit.*]
DOGBERRY   Come, let them be opinion'd.
CONRADE   Let them be in the Hands of Coxcomb.
DOGBERRY   God's my Life, where's the Sexton?   75
Let him write down the Prince's Officer
Coxcomb. – Come, bind them, thou naughty
Varlet.
CONRADE   Away, you are an Ass, you are an Ass.

80   **suspect my Place**   Dogberry means 'respect my position'. But
      Conrade does 'suspect' his credentials for his 'Place'. Compare
      II.i.49–50.

81   **Years**   both (a) venerable age, and (b) long experience. Lines
      80–81 echo the Priest's remarks in IV.i.162–68, and
      Leonato's in IV.i.188–98.

84   **written down**   preserved in ink. See the note to line 13.

85   **Piety**   Dogberry probably means 'impiety', irreverence.

86   **prov'd upon thee**   demonstrated by the evidence presented
      against you. Compare IV.i.179, 302.

89   **as . . . Flesh**   as handsome a man. In *Romeo and Juliet*,
      I.i.31–32, 'pretty piece of Flesh' has a genital sense; see the
      Sonnet passage quoted in the note to III.i.10. Dogberry is
      totally unaware that his phrasing might lead anyone to
      'suspect' his 'Place' (line 80) and think him to be boasting of
      his attributes as a 'naughty Varlet' (lines 77–78) with 'every
      thing hansome about him' (lines 93–94).

91   **go to**   This phrase is normally an expression of dismissal or
      disapproval (comparable to 'come on!'); Dogberry appears to
      be using it as an intensifier ('indeed').

92   **Losses**   Dogberry may mean 'leases' or [successful] 'lawsuits'.
      Or he may be boasting that he has risen above reversals that
      would have defeated a less 'rich Fellow'. But *Losses* can also
      mean 'seminal emissions'.

94–95 **O . . . Ass!**   Through this scene, of course, Dogberry *has* been
      'writ down an Ass' and 'opinion'd' forever. See the second
      note to III.v.51.

DOGBERRY   Doost thou not suspect my Place? doost   80
thou not suspect my Years? – O that he were
here to write me down an Ass! But Maisters,
remember that I am an Ass; though it be not
written down, yet forget not that I am an Ass.
– No, thou Villain, thou art full of Piety as   85
shall be prov'd upon thee by good Witness. I
am a wise Fellow, and which is more, an
Officer, and which is more, a Householder,
and which is more, as pretty a piece of Flesh
as any is in Messina; and one that knows the   90
Law, go to, and a rich Fellow enough, go to,
and a Fellow that hath had Losses, and one
that hath two Gowns, and every thing hansome
about him. – Bring him away. O that I had been
writ down an Ass!   *Exeunt.*   95

V.i   This scene takes place in or near Leonato's house.

2   **second** back, ally with (like a second in a duel, a man who assists with the arrangements).

4   **profitless** uselessly, unavailingly. *Counsaile* (counsel, advice), lines 3, 5, recalls IV.i.100; compare lines 21, 23, 31.

5   **Sieve** a sifter or strainer that will hold no water.

7   **do . . . mine** are in accord with my own.

9   **over-whelm'd** defeated, overthrown.

12   **answer** equal, accord with. Compare IV.ii.25–26.
        Strain (a) emotion, (b) stress, and (c) musical passage or tune. See II.i.397–98, IV.i.250.
        for Strain with a corresponding strain.

13   **thus** instance [of suffering].
        Grief both (a) grievance (wrong, injustice), and (b) sorrow. Compare lines 2, 17, 21, 32.
        for such for such griefs as I suffer.

14   **Lineament, Branch** line (feature), limb.

16   **sorrow, wag** feel sad, shake his head. Compare II.i.120–24, III.i.16–17, III.iii.135–37, and see line 119. Most of today's editions emend the first part of this line to read *Bid sorrow wag* ('Tell sorrow to go away').
        cry hem either (a) say 'down the hatch' (an expression that refers to downing a full container of liquor in one gulp, as in *1 Henry IV*, II.iv.16–19), or (b) clear his throat before a lengthy speech (as in *Troilus and Cressida*, I.iii.165–66).

17   **Patch** patch over, cover. Compare IV.i.114, 172, 307.

18   **With Candle-wasters** with those who drown their woes by carousing all night long. Leonato may also be referring to revellers who float flaming raisins or candle-ends ('flapdragons') in tubs of liquor and either swallow them or drink off the liquid while avoiding them. Falstaff refers to this sport in II.iv.266–67 of *2 Henry IV*.

ACT V

Scene 1

Enter Leonato and his Brother.

BROTHER   If you go on thus, you will kill your
        self,
    And 'tis not Wisdom thus to second Grief
    Against your self.
LEONATO   I pray thee cease thy Counsaile,
    Which falls into mine Ears as profitless
    As Water in a Sieve: give not me Counsaile,   5
    Nor let no Comforter delight mine Ear,
    But such a one whose Wrongs do suit with mine.
    Bring me a Father that so lov'd his Child,
    Whose Joy of her is over-whelm'd like mine,
    And bid him speak of Patience,   10
    Measure his Woe the Length and Breadth of mine,
    And let it answer every Strain for Strain
    And thus for thus, and such a Grief for such,
    In every Lineament, Branch, Shape, and Form:
    If such a one will smile and stroke his Beard,   15
    And sorrow, wag, cry hem, when he should
        groan,
    Patch Grief with Proverbs, make Misfortune
        drunk
    With Candle-wasters, bring him yet to me,
    And I of him will gather Patience.
    But there is no such Man, for Brother, Men   20
    Can counsaile and speak Comfort to that Grief
    Which they themselves not feel; but, tasting it,

24   **would . . . Rage**   would prescribe sentences filled with 'moral
        Meaning' (III.iv.80–81) for those in the throes of a fury
        induced by 'Passion' (line 23).

25   **Fetter . . . Thread**   try to shackle mad rage with silk-thin
        thread. Compare IV.i.247–48.

26   **Charm Ache**   control pain. Compare line 36, and see
        III.ii.22–71 and III.iv.53–82. In this line *Ache* is spelled *ach* in
        the Quarto and *ache* in the Folio; in line 36 the word is
        spelled *ake* in both of the early texts. See the note to
        III.iv.56–57.

28   **wring**   struggle, are crushed. *Office* (role, function) echoes
        IV.i.266.

29   **Virtue nor Sufficiency**   strength or patient endurance.

32   **Advertisement**   advice, instruction.

34   **I . . . Blood**   I'll make no effort to deny the anger my injury
        provokes, or to restrain the impulse that stirs my arm to
        vengeance.

37   **writ . . . Gods**   adorned their names with godlike titles. Here
        writ the Stile of Gods can mean either (a) emulated (patterned
        a design after) the steps over a wall or fence that the Gods use
        when they travel from one enclosed area to another, or (b)
        appropriated to themselves the prerogatives and dignified
        titles of Gods.

38   **made . . . Sufferance**   sought to withstand fortune and suffering
        by thrusting it aside or putting it down. Leonato is ridiculing
        the pretensions of Stoics who believe themselves capable of
        denying their emotions and ignoring physical maladies.

39   **bend**   direct (as with a bow bent to release an arrow). Compare
        II.iii.236–37, IV.i.184.

41   **thou speakst Reason**   you say something that makes sense to
        me. A judicious Shakespearean audience would have
        recognized that what Leonato calls 'Reason' (his brother's
        counsel that he avenge his grievances by returning injury for
        injury) is in fact a manifestation of 'Passion' (line 23).
        Compare I.i.69–73, I.iii.5, IV.i.256–57.

42   **belied**   slandered, falsely accused. Compare IV.i.143–44, and
        see line 67.

43   **know**   be informed [in such a way as to tell him that he stands
        challenged to defend himself in a duel]. Leonato is eager to
        establish the rightness of his cause and thereby restore the
        reputation of his daughter and his family.

Their Counsaile turns to Passion, which before
Would give preceptial Med'cine to Rage,
Fetter strong Madness in a silken Thread,   25
Charm Ache with Air, and Agony with Words.
No, no, 'tis all men's Office to speak Patience
To those that wring under the Load of Sorrow,
But no man's Virtue nor Sufficiency
To be so moral when he shall endure   30
The like himself: therefore give me no Counsaile,
My Griefs cry louder than Advertisement.

BROTHER   Therein do Men from Children nothing
    differ.

LEONATO   I pray thee peace, I will be Flesh and
    Blood,
For there was never yet Philosopher   35
That could endure the Tooth-ache patiently,
How ever they have writ the Stile of Gods
And made a push at Chancc and Sufferance.

BROTHER   Yet bend not all the Harm upon your
    self,
Make those that do offend you suffer too.   40

LEONATO   There thou speakst Reason, nay I will
    do so;
My Soul doth tell me Hero is belied,
And that shall Claudio know, so shall the
    Prince,
And all of them that thus dishonour her.

Enter Prince and Claudio.

BROTHER   Here comes the Prince and Claudio
    hastily.   45

46 **Good den**   good evening.

47 **We . . . Haste**   we are in a hurry; we have urgent business elsewhere.

49 **hasty now**   Leonato is alluding to an earlier moment when Claudio and Don Pedro were anything but eager to proceed with an appointment. But what Leonato believes to have been a calculated offence was based in fact upon a hasty misjudgement.
all is one   it makes no difference now. See the note on *one* at III.i.92.

52 **Some . . . low**   there are at least two men who would either hide themselves from danger or 'lie low' in death. *Quarrelling* (engaging in a personal dispute, often the prelude to a duel), lines 50–51, recalls II.i.244, II.iii.202–9.

53 **Mary**   marry, indeed. Leonato's use of this epithet (originally an oath in the name of the Virgin) is a reminder that the root of Leonato's grief was Claudio's wrongful refusal to marry Hero. Compare line 55, and see IV.iv.52.
Dissembler   liar. Leonato's name for Claudio recalls Dogberry's reference to 'our whole Dissembly' in the opening line of the preceding scene (IV.ii.1); see the note to IV.ii.58.

55 **beshrew**   shame on, curse.

56 **your Age**   Claudio's scornful variation on 'your Reverence'. Compare I.i.14–16, II.iii.130–31, 253–55, III.iv.32–34, III.v.34–39, IV.i.165–68, 191–98, V.i.324–26, V.ii.82–87, V.iv.125–27.

57 **to**   with reference to.

58 **fleer**   flout, jeer.

59 **Dotard**   doddering old idiot.

60 **under . . . Age**   protected from retaliation because of the courtesy (indulgence) extended to those too old to fight.

62 **to thy Head**   in absolute defiance. Leonato employs an expression equivalent to 'in your face'.

67 **belied**   borne false witness against. 'Trial of a Man' (line 66) echoes IV.i.321; see lines 78–85.

70 **slept**   reposed [in death].

71 **fram'd**   devised, effected. Compare IV.i.185–87.

PRINCE   Good den, good den.
CLAUDIO   Good day to both of you.
LEONATO   Hear you, my Lords?
PRINCE   We have some Haste, Leonato.
LEONATO   Some Haste, my Lord! well, fare you
   well, my Lord,
  Are you so hasty now? Well, all is one.
PRINCE   Nay do not quarrel with us, good Old Man.   50
BROTHER   If he could right himself with
   Quarrelling,
  Some of us would lie low.
CLAUDIO   Who wrongs him?
LEONATO   Mary thou dost wrong me, thou
   Dissembler, thou:
  Nay, never lay thy Hand upon thy Sword,
  I fear thee not.
CLAUDIO   Mary beshrew my Hand,   55
  If it should give your Age some cause of Fear;
  In faith my Hand meant nothing to my Sword.
LEONATO   Tush, tush, Man, never fleer and jest
   at me,
  I speak not like a Dotard, nor a Fool,
  As under privilege of Age to brag,   60
  What I have done being young, or what would do
  Were I not old; know, Claudio, to thy Head,
  Thou hast so wrong'd mine innocent Child and me,
  That I am forc'd to lay my Reverence by,
  And with grey Hairs and Bruise of many Days   65
  Do challenge thee to Trial of a Man;
  I say thou hast belied mine innocent Child.
  Thy Slander hath gone through and through her
   Heart,
  And she lies buried with her Ancestors:
  O in a Tomb where never Scandal slept,   70
  Save this of hers, fram'd by thy Villainy.
CLAUDIO   My Villainy?
LEONATO   Thine, Claudio, thine, I say.
PRINCE   You say not right, Old Man.

74   **prove it**   show it to be true. Leonato seeks a trial by combat in
       which, by definition, might makes right.

75   **Dispight**   despite, notwithstanding. Compare III.iv.90.
       nice Fence   artistry in (a) fencing (sword-fighting), and (b)
       self-defence.

76   **Bloom of Lustihood**   full-bloomed vigour.

77   **have . . . you**   entertain your challenge. Claudio does not regard
       Leonato's challenge as one that a man of youthful strength
       and expertise could accept without dishonouring himself
       because of the overwhelming odds he would enjoy.

78   **daff me**   doff ('do off') me, thrust me aside. Compare
       II.iii.182–84.

82   **Win . . . wear me**   if he can defeat me, he can have any part of
       me he wants.

83   **Boy**   Antonio's term for Claudio insults him by suggesting that
       what his 'Youth' really represents is a lack of mature
       manhood. Compare II.i.205–7, II.iii.1.

84   **foining**   parrying, thrusting (rather than striking in earnest).

88   **a Man indeed**   a genuine man. See the note to line 67.

89   **As . . . Tongue**   Antonio's point is that Claudio and Don Pedro
       are all boast and no bout in the face of certain death. He may
       also be alluding to the commonplace that a fast-moving
       serpent's tongue is forked or 'double'; see lines 167–71, and
       compare III.iv.95–96, IV.i.321–24.

90   **Jacks**   insolent rascals. Compare I.i.190–92.
       Milksops   effeminate cowards.

92   **utmost Scruple**   last particle. A *scruple* is one twenty-fourth of
       an ounce.

93   **Scambling**   quarrelling, scrambling.
       out-facing   defiant, impudent.
       Fashion-monging   prettified, aping the latest fashions in dress
       and manners (including their fencing style). Compare
       IV.i.232–34.

94   **cog**   cheat.
       deprave   insult.

95   **Go antiquely**   walk in a grotesque (antic) manner, one they
       foolishly believe to be frightening in its 'Hideousness'.

LEONATO   My Lord, my Lord,
  I'll prove it on his Body if he dare,
  Dispight his nice Fence, and his active
    Practice,   75
  His May of Youth, and Bloom of Lustihood.
CLAUDIO   Away, I will not have to do with you.
LEONATO   Canst thou so daff me? thou hast kill'd
  my Child,
  If thou kill'st me, Boy, thou shalt kill a Man.
BROTHER   He shall kill two of us, and Men indeed,   80
  But that's no matter, let him kill one first:
  Win me and wear me, let him answer me.
  — Come follow me, Boy; come, Sir Boy, come
    follow me,
  Sir Boy, I'll whip you from your foining Fence,
  Nay as I am a Gentleman, I will.
LEONATO   Brother.   85
BROTHER   Content your self, God knows I loved
  my Niece,
  And she is dead, slander'd to death by Villains,
  That dare as well answer a Man indeed
  As I dare take a Serpent by the Tongue.
  — Boys, Apes, Braggarts, Jacks, Milksops.
LEONATO   Brother Anthony.   90
BROTHER   Hold you content, what Man! I know
  then, yea,
  And what they weigh, even to the utmost
    Scruple,
  Scambling, out-facing, Fashion-monging Boys,
  That lie, and cog, and flout, deprave, and
    slaunder,
  Go antiquely, and shew outward Hideousness,   95

96   **speak of** utter, 'speak off' in a bluff manner. Compare
        Benedick's phrasing in III.ii.71–73.

100   **meddle** intervene. Compare III.iii.35–36, 54–58.

101   **wake your Patience** rouse your impatience (anger), and thus
        require you to call on your patience (self-control) to hold it in
        check. *Patience* echoes lines 10–32.

104   **full of proof** fully demonstrated to be true. Compare line 74.

105   **hear you** attend your words.

106   **I . . . heard** Leonato probably addresses his brother, with the
        implication that he should refrain from any further attempts
        to obtain satisfaction now.

S.D. **ambo** Latin for *both* (Leonato and Antonio).

111   **almost a Fray** what almost developed into a duel.

113   **with** by. *Teeth* echoes lines 34–38; see the note to III.ii.23.

115   **doubt** fear.

116   **too young** Don Pedro means, not (a) too young (inexperienced)
        to win against them, but (b) too young for them to have a
        chance against us.

117   **a false Quarrel** a dispute in which one is in the wrong morally
        or legally. Compare lines 50–52.

120   **high proof** in the highest degree. *Proof* echoes line 104.
        Melancholy recalls III.ii.55, where Leonato and Claudio were
        teasing Benedick about his new love-sickness; compare
        II.i.359–60.

121   **fain** gladly; be pleased to.

124   **wear . . . Side** Don Pedro is alluding to another kind of 'Wit'
        (sword) than the one Benedick was referring to. See the notes
        to II.i.124, 256, and II.iii.248–49. *Scabbard* recalls the
        imagery in I.i.247–52; see the note to III.ii.12. *Draw* echoes
        III.ii.23–26.

And speak of half a dozen dang'rous Words,
How they might hurt their Enemies if they durst.
And this is all.
LEONATO   But Brother Anthony.
BROTHER   Come, 'tis no matter,
Do not you meddle, let me deal in this.   100
PRINCE   Gentlemen both, we will not wake your
    Patience,
My Heart is sorry for your Daughter's Death:
But on my Honour, she was charg'd with nothing
But what was true, and very full of Proof.
LEONATO   My Lord, my Lord.
PRINCE   I will not hear you.   105
LEONATO   No come, Brother, away, I will be heard.
BROTHER   And shall, or some of us will smart for it.
                                        Exeunt ambo.

                    Enter Benedick.

PRINCE   See see, here comes the Man we went to
    seek.
CLAUDIO   Now Signior, what News?
BENEDICK   Good day, my lord.
PRINCE   Welcome, Signior, you are almost come to   110
    part almost a Fray.
CLAUDIO   We had lik'd to have had our two Noses
    snapp'd off with two Old Men without Teeth.
PRINCE   Leonato and his Brother, what thinkst
    thou? had we fought, I doubt we should have   115
    been too young for them.
BENEDICK   In a false Quarrel there is no true
    Valour, I came to seek you both.
CLAUDIO   We have been up and down to seek thee,
    for we are high proof Melancholy, and would   120
    fain have it beaten away; wilt thou use thy
    Wit?
BENEDICK   It is in my Scabbard, shall I draw it?
PRINCE   Doest thou wear thy Wit by thy Side?

126 **beside their Wit** beside themselves (mad, out of their minds).
Claudio's phrase can also mean 'alongside the female "Wit"
to which their male "Wit" drew them'.

127 **as . . . us** in the way that we ask minstrels (musicians) to draw
their bows across the strings of their instruments. Compare
Romeo and Juliet, II.i.20–34, III.i.47–52, 83–85,
IV.iii.187–235.

128 **As . . . Man** to drop this jesting and speak seriously.

130– **though . . . Cat** though its cares proved fatal to a cat (a
31 proverb). Claudio is still urging Benedick to 'pleasure' himself,
his friends, and his sweetheart by drawing his 'Mettle' (metal)
and killing both his own 'Care' (unfulfilled longing) and hers.
Behind Claudio's jest is the notion that intercourse is a burial
and orgasm a death (see III.ii.64–69). Lines 128–32
(especially the words *pale, sick, angry,* and *Cat*) echo
I.i.256–82.

133– **I . . . me** Benedick compares Claudio's 'Wit' to the weapon of a
34 knight on horseback in a jousting tournament; he says that he
will meet Claudio's lance ('Staff', line 136) at full gallop if
Claudio is so foolish as to keep charging forward.

134 **and** if.

137 **broke cross** shattered by hitting his opponent at a glancing
angle rather than thrusting him straight on. Claudio implies
that Benedick's first foray in this battle of wits was a complete
failure. Compare II.i.152–57, II.iii.250–53.

138 **by this Light** by the light of (a) the sun, (b) my eyes, or (c) my
mind.

140– **turn his Girdle** turn his belt so that the buckle is in the back.
41 Claudio may mean 'indicate that he is ready to fight by
putting his buckle behind him, the way a wrestler does'. Or he
may mean 'avoid doing himself harm by removing the buckle
that someone who wishes him ill could seize upon'; if this is
Claudio's implication, its import is that Benedick will need to
restrain his fury and turn it aside.

142 **Shall . . . Ear?** Benedick's question echoes what Dogberry has
said to Borachio in the preceding scene; see IV.ii.30, and
compare III.ii.71–73.

144 **ieast** jest. But here as elsewhere (see *Romeo and Juliet*, I.iii.45,
II.i.43, II.iii.72–73) the Elizabethan spelling hints at wordplay
on *yeast*.

CLAUDIO   Never any did so, though very many have   125
been beside their Wit; I will bid thee draw,
as we do the Minstrels, draw to pleasure us.
PRINCE   As I am an honest Man he looks pale.
– Art thou sick, or angry?
CLAUDIO   What, Courage, Man: what though Care   130
kill'd a Cat, thou hast Mettle enough in thee
to kill Care.
BENEDICK   Sir, I shall meet your Wit in the
Career, and you charge it against me, I pray
you choose another Subject.   135
CLAUDIO   Nay then give him another Staff, this
last was broke cross.
PRINCE   By this Light, he chaunges more and
more, I think he be angry indeed.
CLAUDIO   If he be, he knows how to turn his   140
Girdle.
BENEDICK   Shall I speak a Word in your Ear?
CLAUDIO   God bless me from a Challenge.
BENEDICK   You are a Villain, I jeast not, I will
make it good how you dare, with what you dare,   145
and when you dare: do me right, or I will
protest your Cowardice. You have kill'd a
sweet Lady, and her Death shall fall heavy
on you, let me hear from you.

---

145   **make it good**   sustain my charge in judicial combat. In the
phrases that follow, Benedick notes that, as the man who is
challenged, Claudio may determine the rules of engagement,
the weapons to be employed, and the time of the
confrontation.

146   **Do me right**   respond to my challenge as a man of honour.

147   **protest**   proclaim [dishonouring you if you don't respond].
Compare IV.i.280–88.

151   **good Cheer**   proper entertainment (food and hospitality).

153–   **I' faith . . . too?**   The creatures Claudio lists are all proverbial
57   for stupidity and docility; his implication is that Benedick has
        invited him to the kind of 'Feast' that only a fool and a
        coward would host. See the note to II.i.25.

158   **easily**   with complete abandon. Benedick's point is that
        Claudio's 'Wit' is trotting at a foolhardy pace.

160   **Wit**   Don Pedro is talking primarily about Benedick's ability to
        reply with sharp ripostes in combats of wit. But the sword
        and dagger imagery implicit in many of his remarks in lines
        159–74 gives *Wit* a phallic suggestiveness that echoes lines
        119–37 and recalls III.iv.70–71, III.v.38–39.

163   **gross**   Here the redundancy is made witty by the fact that *gross*
        can mean both (a) large ('great'), and (b) stupid. It can also
        mean (c) coarse.

164   **Just**   both (a) true, and (b) precisely.

166   **a wise Gentleman**   Beatrice uses this term in the ironic sense –
        one that Dogberry doesn't realize he is reflecting when he
        describes himself (perhaps quoting his 'admirers') as 'a wise
        Fellow' in IV.ii.87.

167   **hath the Tongues**   is adept in languages. See the note to line 89.

169   **forswore**   unswore; denied or proved to have been a lie by his
        actions.

172   **trans-shape**   transform; transfigure (by recasting each
        attribute).
        particular   individual (with a hint at genital 'parts'). See the
        note to IV.i.3, and compare *Troilus and Cressida*, II.ii.8–12,
        52–59.

174   **proper'st**   handsomest, finest. Compare I.iii.53, II.iii.196,
        IV.i.172–73, 311–12.

178   **and if**   [that] if.

CLAUDIO   Well I will meet you, so I may have   150
  good Cheer.
PRINCE   What, a Feast, a Feast?
CLAUDIO   I'faith I thank him he hath bid me
  to a Calve's Head and a Capon, the which
  if I do not carve most curiously, say my   155
  Knife's naught. – Shall I not find a Woodcock
  too?
BENEDICK   Sir, your Wit ambles well, it goes easily.
PRINCE   I'll tell thee how Beatrice prais'd thy
  Wit the other Day. I said thou hadst a fine   160
  Wit. 'True,' said she, 'a fine little one.'
  'No,' said I, 'a great Wit.' 'Right,' says
  she, 'a great gross one.' 'Nay,' said I, 'a
  good Wit.' 'Just,' said she, 'it hurts no
  body.' 'Nay,' said I, 'the Gentleman is   165
  wise.' 'Certain,' said she, 'a wise Gentleman.'
  'Nay,' said I, 'he hath the Tongues.' 'That I
  believe,' said she, 'for he swore a thing
  to me on Monday Night, which he forswore on
  Tuesday Morning: there's a double Tongue,   170
  there's two Tongues.' Thus did she an Hour
  together trans-shape thy particular Virtues,
  yet at last she concluded with a Sigh, thou
  wast the proper'st Man in Italy.
CLAUDIO   For the which she wept heartily and   175
  said she cared not.
PRINCE   Yea that she did, but yet for all that,
  and if she did not hate him deadly, she would
  love him dearly: the Old Man's Daughter told
  us all.   180

181– **moreover ... Garden** Claudio implies that Benedick, like the
82   guilty Adam and Eve of Genesis 3:8 (who tried to hide
       themselves in the trees of the Garden of Eden when they heard
       the voice of the Lord), believed that no one else was aware of
       his presence in the arbour as he eavesdropped on his friends'
       remarks in II.iii; if Benedick, hearing Claudio, now registers
       that he knows himself to have been gulled, he says nothing –
       and probably does nothing – to indicate it. Compare V.iv.21–
       27, where he calls 'enigmatical' (mysterious) a later hint to the
       same effect. Lines 183–86 allude to the dialogue in I.i.256–
       82; Claudio and Don Pedro have inserted other quotations
       from this conversation in lines 128–32.

188– **Gossip-like Humour** mirthful disposition to concoct or trans-
89   mit rumours in the manner of garrulous old women. But
       Gossip-like can also refer to the behaviour of gossips in the
       original sense: 'Godsibs' or 'Godparents', baptismal sponsors.

189– **you ... not** Benedick probably means 'you make juvenile
90   wisecracks in the same evasive way that cowardly braggarts
       damage their swords to make it appear that they have escaped
       uninjured from brave combat'. *Break* echoes lines 136–37.

195   **Lack-beard** Like Leonato and Antonio earlier in the scene,
       Benedick is calling Claudio an effeminate boy. See the note to
       II.i.34, and compare II.i.49–50, V.i.15–19.

199   **warrant** wager, guarantee.

202   **pretty** handsome. Compare the verbal irony in Beatrice's use of
       proper in IV.i.311–12.

203   **Doublet and Hose** tight-fitting jacket and breeches.

205   **a Giant to an Ape** a giant in comparison with a monkey or
       chimpanzee (because he is so puffed up with self-importance).

205–6 **but ... Man** but in terms of 'Wit' (intelligence), an ape is a
       learned scholar in comparison with such a giant fool. A rustic
       example of the kind of 'Giant' Don Pedro and Claudio
       describe in this exchange interrupts their conversation at line
       210. *Wit* (line 204) echoes lines 159–74.

207   **Pluck ... Heart** let me retrieve my heart and restore it to its
       proper function.

208   **sad** serious. Compare I.i.189–90, I.iii.59–61.

211   **nere** ne'er. The Quarto spelling could also be construed here to
       mean 'near'.

CLAUDIO   All all, and moreover God saw him when
   he was hid in the Garden.
PRINCE   But when shall we set the savage Bull's
   Horns on the sensible Benedick's Head?
CLAUDIO   Yea and Text underneath, 'Here dwells   185
   Benedick the Married Man.'
BENEDICK   Fare you well, Boy, you know my Mind,
   I will leave you now to your Gossip-like
   Humour: you break Jests as Braggards do their
   Blades, which God be thanked hurt not. – My   190
   Lord, for your many Courtesies I thank you;
   I must discontinue your Company. Your brother
   the Bastard is fled from Messina; you have,
   among you, kill'd a sweet and innocent Lady;
   for my Lord Lack-beard there, he and I shall   195
   meet, and till then Peace be with him.   [*Exit.*]
PRINCE   He is earnest.
CLAUDIO   In most profound earnest, and I'll
   warrant you for the Love of Beatrice.
PRINCE   And hath challeng'd thee.   200
CLAUDIO   Most sincerely.
PRINCE   What a pretty thing Man is, when he goes
   in his Doublet and Hose, and leaves off his
   Wit!

Enter Constables, Conrade, and Borachio.

CLAUDIO   He is then a Giant to an Ape, but then   205
   is an Ape a Doctor to such a Man.
PRINCE   But soft you, let me be. – Pluck up my
   Heart, and be sad. – Did he not say my Brother
   was fled?
DOGBERRY   Come you, Sir, if Justice cannot tame   210
   you, she shall nere weigh more Reasons in her

211– **weigh ... Balance** Dogberry means 'weigh any further cases
12 [and find men guilty] on her balance scales'. *Reasons* would
have sounded like *raisins* in Elizabethan English; it would
thus have suggested *raisings* (uprisings, rebellious treasons).
Weigh echoes lines 91–92.

212 **and** if.

214 **bound** both (a) fettered, and (b) under arrest. Compare
IV.ii.69–72, 77, and see lines 232–33.

216 **Hearken after** ask about.

219 **Mary** truly. Compare lines 53, 55.

221 **Slanders** slanderers.

222 **belied** lied about. See lines 42, 67, 273.

223 **verified Unjust Things** This could mean 'confessed to crimes'
or 'testified about their own crimes in such a way as to
implicate others [Don John]'. But it could also mean 'excused
injustices' or 'shown that what looked like injustices were in
fact "true things" '. What Dogberry probably intends to say is
'told lies'. Since the other items in his list of offences are
redundancies ('one Meaning well suited', lines 230–31), it
would seem most likely that this entry is to be thought of as
indistinguishable in intended implication from the rest.

228 **lay to their Charge** accuse them of. *Charge* echoes line 134
(where the word means 'drive' or 'thrust').

229– **in ... Division** Dogberry's manner of sorting out 'distinctions'.
30 *Division* is a rhetorical scheme of enumeration, classification,
or discrimination.

231 **well suited** both (a) eloquently stated, and (b) amply arrayed in
multiple layers of rhetorical apparel.

233 **bound ... Answer** required to answer charges. Don Pedro
puns on at several senses, among them: (a) bound (on your
way) to your trial, (b) bound up (your hands tied behind your
backs) as you proceed to justice, and (c) bound (imprisoned)
until it is determined how you shall answer (be punished) for
the crimes you have committed. *Bound* echoes line 214;
Answer recalls lines 12, 82, 86–89, and anticipates lines
236–37.

233– **learned Constable** Compare 'wise Gentleman' in line 166 and
34 'wise Fellow' in IV.ii.87.

234 **cunning** clever, crafty. The Prince is speaking ironically.
Compare IV.i.35–36.

Balance; nay, and you be a cursing Hypocrite
once, you must be look'd to.

PRINCE   How now, two of my Brother's Men bound?
Borachio one.   215

CLAUDIO   Hearken after their Offence, my Lord.

PRINCE   Officers, what Offence have these Men
done?

DOGBERRY   Mary Sir, they have committed false
Report, moreover they have spoken Untruths,   220
secondarily they are Slanders, sixt and lastly,
they have belied a Lady, thirdly they have
verified Unjust Things, and to conclude, they
are lying Knaves.

PRINCE   First I ask thee what they have done,   225
thirdly I ask thee what's their Offence, sixt
and lastly why they are committed, and to
conclude, what you lay to their Charge.

CLAUDIO   Rightly reasoned, and in his own
Division, and by my troth there's one Meaning   230
well suited.

PRINCE   — Who have you offended, Maisters, that
you are thus bound to your Answer? This learned
Constable is too cunning to be understood.
What's your Offence?   235

BORACHIO   Sweet Prince, let me go no farther
to mine Answer: do you hear me, and let this
Counte kill me. I have deceived even your very
Eyes: what your Wisdoms could not discover,
these shallow Fools have brought to Light, who   240
in the Night overheard me confessing to this
Man, how Don John your Brother incensed me to

---

237   **Answer**   both (a) reply to your question, and (b) sentence.

239   **discover**   perceive, discern. See the note to III.v.4, and compare
III.ii.94.

240   **shallow**   shallow-witted, stupid.

242   **incensed**   incited, inflamed.

246– **My . . . Villain** Borachio's penitence gives retrospective
51   pertinence to Dogberry's remark (in IV.ii.61–62) that this
      villain would 'be condemn'd into everlasting Redemption for
      this'. It is thus a double reminder that sometimes Providence
      allows 'shallow Fools' to bring 'to Light' what more
      sophisticated people in their 'Wisdoms could not discover'
      (lines 239–40), a doctrine to be found in such biblical
      passages as Psalm 8:2, Matthew 21:16, and especially 1
      Corinthians 1:19, 25–28, where the Apostle Paul says, 'For it
      is written, I will destroy the wisdom of the wise, and will
      bring to nothing the understanding of the prudent. . . .
      Because the foolishness of God is wiser than men; and the
      weakness of God is stronger than men. . . . God hath chosen
      the foolish things of the world to confound the wise; and God
      hath chosen the weak things of the world to confound the
      things which are mighty; And base things of the world, and
      things which are despised, hath God chosen, yea, and things
      which are not, to bring to nought things that are.'

247   **seal** ratify, confirm as true. See IV.i.163–65. *Disgrac'd* (line
      245) echoes IV.ii.58–60.

248   **then** than. But here, as in IV.ii.65, the usual modern sense of
      'then' could also be applicable. *Shame*, here applied for the
      first time to Hero's accuser rather than to Hero herself, recalls
      IV.i.158.

250   **briefly** to be brief.

252   **like Iron** like either (a) molten iron, or (b) a sword blade.
      Compare II.i.256–57, IV.i.148–49, 215–28; and V.i.121–32.

253   **dronk** drunk.

255   **Practice** enactment. Compare line 5.

256   **compos'd and fram'd** put together and constructed. Compare
      IV.i.184–87.

259   **that** in which. See the Friar's prediction in IV.i.220–31.

261   **reformed** informed. Dogberry's phrasing inadvertently hints at
      what has begun to happen in Claudio's heart, and it
      anticipates a related development in 'Signior Leonato'.

268   **note** observe. Leonato defines yet another kind of 'noting'. See
      IV.i.153–68, and compare I.i.264–65, II.iii.55–60, III.ii.55,
      III.iii.28–32.

slaunder the Lady Hero, how you were brought
into the Orchard, and saw me court Margaret in
Hero's Garments, how you disgrac'd her when   245
you should marry her. My Villainy they have
upon Record, which I had rather seal with my
Death, then repeat over to my Shame. The Lady
is dead upon mine and my Master's false
Accusation: and briefly, I desire nothing   250
but the Reward of a Villain.

PRINCE   Runs not this Speech like Iron through
   your Blood?

CLAUDIO   I have dronk Poison whiles he utt'red
   it.

PRINCE   But did my Brother set thee on to this?

BORACHIO   Yea, and paid me richly for the
   Practice of it.   255

PRINCE   He is compos'd and fram'd of Treachery,
   And fled he is upon this Villainy.

CLAUDIO   Sweet Hero, now thy Image doth appear
   In the rare Semblance that I lov'd it first.

DOGBERRY   Come, bring away the Plaintiffs. By   260
   this time our Sexton hath reformed Signior
   Leonato of the Matter: and Masters, do not
   forget to specify, when Time and Place shall
   serve, that I am an Ass.

VERGES   Here, here comes Master Signior Leonato, 265
   and the Sexton too.

Enter Leonato, his Brother, and the Sexton.

LEONATO   Which is the Villain? let me see his
   Eyes,
   That when I note another Man like him
   I may avoid him: which of these is he?

BORACHIO   If you would know your Wronger, look
   on me.   270

271 **Slave**   base-born villain.
   with thy Breath   with the venomous words you've uttered.
   Compare II.i.257–60, II.iii.187–91, and see the biblical
   passage quoted in the note to line 284.

273 **thou . . . self**   you bear false witness against yourself. *Beliest*
   echoes line 222.

274 **honourable Men**   Leonato uses this phrase with something like
   the withering irony of Mark Antony's descriptions of Brutus
   and Cassius in the funeral oration (III.ii.79–113, 124–43,
   146–52, 155–58) of *Julius Caesar*. The title is apt: it was their
   preoccupation with their 'honour' that led Don Pedro and
   Claudio to respond as they did to the offences they believed
   Hero to have committed. See II.ii.22–26, III.ii.115–17,
   IV.i.30–64, 87, 184–98.

278 **bethink . . . it**   think about it carefully. *Record* (line 277) echoes
   lines 246–48, where it relates to the 'high and worthy Deeds'
   that lay behind Claudio's decision to disgrace his betrothed.
   Compare what Leonato has said about his would-be
   son-in-law in I.i.9–20.

279 **pray your Patience**   beg your forbearance. *Patience* echoes line
   101.

281 **Impose me to**   impose upon me (subject me to).
   Invention   imagination, devising. See lines 290–91.

283 **Mistaking**   mis-taking, noting erroneously. Compare I.i.61–65.

284 **satisfy . . . Man**   make amends to this worthy gentleman. Don
   Pedro's phrasing echoes V.i.50 and recalls Dogberry's
   description of Verges in III.v.37; for other instances of *Old
   Man*, see III.v.11, 16, and V.i.73, 112–13. In Shakespeare's
   time some theatregoers might have detected echoes of such
   New Testament passages as Ephesians 4:22–25 and
   Colossians 3:8–11, where the Apostle Paul urges believers to
   'put off' such vices as 'anger, wrath, malice, blasphemy, filthy
   communication out of your mouth' and to 'Lie not one to
   another, seeing that ye have put off the old man with his
   deeds; And have put on the new man, which is renewed in
   knowledge after the image of him which created him', for
   'Christ is all, and in all.'

285 **bend under**   bow to, subject my body to. *Waight* (weight) plays
   on *wait*.

286 **enjoin**   command.

287 **bid**   ask, request that.

LEONATO   Art thou the Slave that with thy Breath
        hast kill'd
    Mine innocent Child?
BORACHIO   Yea, even I alone.
LEONATO   No, not so, Villain, thou beliest thy
        self;
    Here stand a pair of honourable Men,
    A third is fled that had a Hand in it.   275
    — I thank you, Princes, for my Daughter's
        Death,
    Record it with your high and worthy Deeds,
    'Twas bravely done, if you bethink you of it.
CLAUDIO   I know not how to pray your Patience,
    Yet I must speak: choose your Revenge your
        self,   280
    Impose me to what Penance your Invention
    Can lay upon my Sin, yet sinn'd I not
    But in Mistaking.
PRINCE   By my Soul nor I,
    And yet to satisfy this good Old Man
    I would bend under any heavy Waight   285
    That he'll enjoin me to.
LEONATO   I cannot bid you bid my Daughter live,
    That were impossible, but I pray you both,
    Possess the People in Messina here
    How innocent she died; and if your Love   290
    Can labour aught in sad Invention,
    Hang her an Epitaph upon her Tomb,
    And sing it to her Bones, sing it to night.

---

289   **Possess**   inform, notify. Compare III.iii.167–68.

291   **labour aught**   perform any service.
      in sad Invention   in the doing of mournful deeds. *Sad* recalls
          lines 207–8.

292   **Epitaph**   memorial inscription. The Greek meaning of this
          word, 'upon a tomb', completes the line.

293   **to night**   both (a) to night, and (b) tonight. Compare III.iii.155,
          III.v.34, and see lines 294, 304, 305, 338–40.

297   **Copy**   replica. In other contexts this word can mean
'abundance' (from *copia*, the Latin word at the root of
copious). Compare line 301.

299   **Right**   both (a) duty (in keeping with your pledge to marry),
and (b) rite. Compare II.i.374–75, IV.i.203–6, V.iii.22–23,
V.iv.67–71.

301   **over Kindness**   overflowing generosity. Claudio responds to an
act of grace: forgiveness and blessing where condemnation
was the only reward his misdeeds merited. *Wring* echoes lines
27–28.

302   **dispose**   both (a) put at your disposal, place upon your altar,
and (b) make arrangements [to discard]. The penitent
Claudio, in keeping with his name (see the note to I.i.86), and
regarding his natural self (his 'old man' in the New Testament
terminology cited in the note to line 284) as 'poor' (worthless,
humiliated by its proclivity to error), now resolves to forswear
the 'naughty Man' (line 305) he has been and 'embrace' the
'Offer' to be restored to Leonato's grace. From the 'Travail'
that Leonato will impose on him the audience may 'look for
greater Birth' (IV.i.211) in keeping with the teachings in John
3:3–6.

305   **naughty**   wicked.

307   **pack'd**   conspiring, an accomplice.
Wrong   injustice. Compare I.i.252–55, II.i.213–14, 245–46,
II.ii.22–26, III.i.68–70, 87, IV.i.188–90, 258–59, 314–15,
332–33, V.i.6–7, 50–53, 62–63, V.iii.5–6.

309   **knew . . . did**   either (a) was unaware of how her actions were
being presented and employed, or (b) was unaware of what
the consequences of her actions would be. Compare IV.i.20.

311   **by her**   concerning her behaviour.

313   **under . . . black**   recorded in black on white paper.
Plaintiff   Dogberry means 'defendant'.

315   **rememb'red . . . Punishment**   taken into account when he is
sentenced.

317–
18   **a Key . . . it**   Dogberry's garbled interpretation of III.iii.183–84,
itself no doubt an extrapolation from Borachio's observation
that this deformed Fashion 'turns about all the Hot-bloods'
(III.iii.126–48). Dogberry goes on to offer an ingenious
explanation of Fashion's work as a shyster who discourages
charitable lenders by taking their money and then refusing to
repay them.

To morrow Morning come you to my House,
And since you could not be my Son in Law,   295
Be yet my Nephew. My brother hath a Daughter,
Almost the Copy of my Child that's dead,
And she alone is Heir to both of us:
Give us the Right you should have giv'n her
    Cousin,
And so dies my Revenge.
CLAUDIO   O noble Sir!   300
    Your over Kindness doth wring Tears from me.
    I do embrace your Offer and dispose
    For henceforth of poor Claudio.
LEONATO   To morrow then I will expect your
    Coming,
    To night I take my leave. This naughty Man   305
    Shall Face to Face be brought to Margaret,
    Who I believe was pack'd in all this Wrong,
    Hired to it by your Brother.
BORACHIO   No by my Soul she was not,
    Nor knew not what she did when she spoke to
    me,
    But always hath been just and virtuous   310
    In any thing that I do know by her.
DOGBERRY   Moreover, Sir, which indeed is not
    under white and black, this Plaintiff here, the
    Offender, did call me Ass: I beseech you let it
    be rememb'red in his Punishment. And also the   315
    Watch heard them talk of one Deformed; they say
    he wears a Key in his Ear and a Lock hanging by
    it, and borrows Money in God's name, the which
    he hath us'd so long, and never paid, that now
    Men grow hard hearted and will lend nothing for   320
    God's sake. Pray you examine him upon that
    Point.
LEONATO   I thank thee for thy Care and honest
    Pains.
DOGBERRY   Your Worship speaks like a most

182

thankful ... Youth Dogberry's 'praise' is ludicrously
inappropriate for Leonato, of course, but it offers the
audience an inadvertent reminder that as a consequence of the
Watch's service, another character, Claudio, has now been
'trans-shaped' (line 172) from an insolent 'Youth' (line 76)
into the kind of 'thankful and reverent' young man who
qualifies for Leonato's gratification. *Care* (line 323) echoes
lines 130–32; compare I.ii.28–29, II.i.328–30, III.iii.44–45,
V.iv.102–3.

328 **God ... Foundation** Dogberry's version of the thanks a beggar
uttered when he received alms from a religious monastery or
other charitable foundation.

329 **discharge thee of** release you from responsibility for.

333 **correct your self** punish in your own way. Dogberry's phrasing
alludes unwittingly to a reformation that has now begun in
Leonato, one that his brother was trying to initiate with his
counsel at the beginning of the scene (lines 1–40).

335 **God ... Health** Dogberry's prayer is not irrelevant to a
psychological and spiritual process that commenced with the
entry of the Constables and their prisoners in line 210.

335– **give ... depart** Dogberry probably means 'request your leave
36 (permission) to depart'.

337 **prohibit** No doubt Dogberry intends to say 'permit' here.
Although 'God' has already arranged to 'prohibit' one 'merry
Meeting' (the marriage of Claudio and Hero), he may perhaps
be petitioned to allow a suitable rematch.

340 **fail** fail to appear as promised. *To night* echoes lines 293–94,
304–5, 338–39.

341 **these Fellows** Borachio and Conrade.

342 **lewd** base, filthy. Here as occasionally elsewhere, *Acquaintance*
plays on the Latin word (see the note to I.i.335) that relates to
a woman's part in carnal knowledge (see the note to line 309).

V.ii This scene takes place in Leonato's orchard.

2–3 **to ... Beatrice** speak to Beatrice. Benedick's phrasing is
ambiguous; it can also be construed 'to imitate the style with
which Beatrice speaks, or the kind of speech or writing that
she would find appealing'. As Benedick talks, probably with
pen and paper in hand, he is pondering revisions in a poem he
is composing to the lady whose love he seeks.

thankful and reverent Youth, and I praise God   325
for you.

LEONATO   There's for thy Pains.

DOGBERRY   God save the Foundation.

LEONATO   Go, I discharge thee of thy Prisoner, and
I thank thee.   330

DOGBERRY   I leave an arrant Knave with your
Worship, which I beseech your Worship to
correct your self, for the Example of others.
God keep your Worship, I wish your Worship
well, God restore you to Health, I humbly give   335
you leave to depart, and if a merry Meeting may
be wish'd, God prohibit it. – Come, Neighbour.

                              [*Exit with Verges.*]

LEONATO   Until to morrow Morning, Lords, farewell.

BROTHER   Farewell, my Lords, we look for you
to morrow.

PRINCE   We will not fail.

CLAUDIO   To night I'll mourn with Hero.   340

LEONATO   – Bring you these Fellows on, we'll
talk with Margaret,
How her Acquaintance grew with this lewd
Fellow.   *Exeunt.*

Scene 2

Enter Benedick and Margaret.

BENEDICK   Pray thee, sweet Mistress Margaret,
deserve well at my Hands, by helping me to the
Speech of Beatrice.

MARGARET   Will you then write me a Sonnet in
Praise of my Beauty?   5

184

6   **Stile**   Benedick probably means 'style' (manner of discourse), but *come over it* (either 'exceed it' or 'cross over it') in line 7 suggests a conscious pun on the kind of *stile* (steps over a wall or fence) alluded to in V.i.37. Characteristically, Margaret will find 'double Meaning' (II.iii.275–76) in what Benedick says.

7   **come over it**   literally, come higher than it. See the note on *come* at II.iii.268–69, and compare III.i.14.

8   **comely Truth**   good faith (seemly fidelity). The repetition of *come* gives *so high a Stile* (line 6) a hint of more than the kind of elevation that Benedick aspires to achieve with his literary *stilus* (Latin for a pointed writing instrument).

10   **keep below Stairs**   remain in the servants' quarters, and be treated as a 'Mistress' rather than become a gentleman's wife (giving *come over me* a matrimonial sense related to a husband's role as his bride's 'head', as defined in Ephesians 5:23). Compare I.i.115–19, II.i.61–69. Margaret puns on an ejaculative sense of *come over me*. She may also be using *no* with *double entendre*: it can mean both 'no' and 'any'.

11   **Wit**   Benedick refers not only to Margaret's mental quickness, but to the liveliness of her erotic 'Wit' (and the 'Mouth' by which it 'catches' what it desires). Compare III.iv.66–71, and see V.i.158–74, 202–4, for other references to *Wit*.

14   **Foils**   swords with buttons on the ends to blunt their points. Compare *Hamlet*, V.ii.267–69. *Blunt* echoes III.v.10–14.
    hit . . . not   touch but cause no pain. Compare *Troilus and Cressida*, I.ii.280–90 and III.i.120–34, *Love's Labour's Lost*, IV.i.114–46, and *Romeo and Juliet*, I.i.207–17. II.i.33–38, II.iii.56–73, for other references to erotic 'hitting'; see *Antony and Cleopatra*, V.ii.295–96, for a comparison between 'The Stroke of Death' and 'a Lover's Pinch, / Which hurts and is desir'd'.

15   **manly**   both (a) gentlemanly, and (b) upstanding.

17   **I . . . Bucklers**   I grant that you have shielded your 'Wit' from 'hurt'.

21   **Pikes**   spikes in the centre of a buckler (small round shield).
    a Vice   both (a) a screw, and (b) a vise (US spelling) or clamp (to 'catch' or clasp 'Pikes').

24   **Legs**   both (a) legs with which to come to you, and (b) legs that will accommodate your 'Pike'. *Come* echoes lines 7–8.

BENEDICK   In so high a Stile, Margaret, that no
Man living shall come over it, for in most
comely Truth thou deservest it.

MARGARET   To have no Man come over me, why
shall I always keep below Stairs.   10

BENEDICK   Thy Wit is as quick as the Greyhound's
Mouth, it catches.

MARGARET   And yours as blunt as the Fencer's
Foils, which hit, but hurt not.

BENEDICK   A most manly Wit, Margaret, it will   15
not hurt a Woman: and so I pray thee call
Beatrice, I give thee the Bucklers.

MARGARET   Give us the Swords, we have Bucklers
of our own.

BENEDICK   If you use them, Margaret, you must   20
put in the Pikes with a Vice, and they are
daungerous Weapons for Maids.

MARGARET   Well, I will call Beatrice to you,
who I think hath Legs.

BENEDICK   And therefore will come.   *Exit Margaret.*   25
                    'The God of Love
                       That sits above,
                          And knows me,
                          And knows me,
                       How pitiful I deserve.'   30
I mean in singing. But in loving, Leander the
good Swimmer, Troilus the first Imployer of
Pandars, and a whole Book full of these quondam

---

31   **Leander**   the young man who drowned while trying to swim the
         Hellespont to join the beautiful Hero; see the note to IV.i.78.
         Unlike Troilus (line 32), he died for the love of a woman
         whose fidelity was unblemished.

33   **Pandars**   go-betweens. The name derives from Pandarus,
         Cressida's uncle, in Chaucer's *Troilus and Criseyde* and in the
         play that Shakespeare wrote about the same couple.

33-34 **quondam Carpet-mongers** one-time lovers of carpets. Benedick
implies that, compared to him, the most famous lovers of
antiquity were mere carpet-knights (knights whose exploits
were limited to indoor encounters rather than to the kind that
required a display of martial valour); Sir Toby applies this
term to Ague-cheek in III.iv.253–55 of *Twelfth Night*.
Quondam echoes a term for the female 'Buckler'; see the note
to V.i.342. Like Hotspur (*1 Henry IV*, III.i), Henry V (*Henry
V*, V.ii), and Hamlet (*Hamlet*, II.ii), Benedick is presented as
all the more appealing for his bluff ineptitude with poetry.

35 **even Road** smooth pathway. Compare IV.i.262–64, where
Beatrice refers to 'an even way', and see II.i.250–56.

36 **turn'd over and over** (a) turned head over heels, (b) ploughed
and recycled, and (c) jostled and juggled. Compare
III.iv.58–59, V.i.23. Despite his mental cogitations, Benedick
has not 'turn'd into Tongue' (IV.i.323) in any sense that
would transform him into a versifier.

39 **innocent** both (a) babyish, and (b) childishly inept.

40 **hard** both (a) harsh, painful, and (b) stiff (like the tumescent
'Horn' of a cuckolder and the horned brows of his victim).
babling chatting idly, like schoolchildren and babyish heirs to
the legacy of Babel (see Genesis 11:1–9).

41-42 **borne . . . Planet** carried and born under a planet favourable to
and yielding its influence to poetry. Compare II.i.348–53.

43 **Festival Terms** the rhetorical flourishes that are used to adorn
special occasions.

44 **wouldst thou come** were you so good as to. Beatrice alters the
tense. *Come* echoes line 25.

49 **Then** the word *Then*.

50 **that I came** what I came for.

51 **pass'd** (a) been conveyed, and (b) occurred. Benedick's reply
relates to the first sense only.

53 **foul** Benedick means 'unpleasant'; Beatrice pretends he meant
'rotten', 'stinking' or 'tainted' (IV.i.141). Compare
III.i.63–64, IV.i.101–2.

57 **noisome** (a) foul-smelling, and (b) unhealthy, with wordplay
on (c) *noisy*.

Carpet-mongers, whose Names yet run smoothly in
the even Road of a blank Verse, why they were   35
never so truly turn'd over and over as my poor
self in Love. Mary I cannot shew it in Rime,
I have tried. I can find out no Rime to *Lady*
but *Baby*, an innocent Rime; for *Scorn, Horn*, a
hard Rime; for *School, Fool*, a babling Rime;   40
very ominous Endings. No, I was not borne
under a riming Planet, nor I cannot woo in
Festival Terms.

Enter Beatrice.

– Sweet Beatrice, wouldst thou come when I
call'd thee?   45
BEATRICE   Yea Signior, and depart when you bid
me.
BENEDICK   O stay but till then.
BEATRICE   Then, is spoken: fare you well now, and
yet ere I go, let me go with that I came, which   50
is, with knowing what hath pass'd between you
and Claudio.
BENEDICK   Onely foul Words, and thereupon I will
kiss thee.
BEATRICE   Foul Words is but foul Wind, and foul   55
Wind is but foul Breath, and foul Breath is
noisome, therefore I will depart unkiss'd.
BENEDICK   Thou hast frighted the Word out of
his right Sense, so forcible is thy Wit, but

---

59   **his**   both (a) his, and (b) its.
    right Sense   both (a) right mind, and (b) proper (intended)
      meaning. Compare III.i.68–70.
    Wit   Benedick implies that Beatrice's 'Wit' is so 'forcible' that it
      has propelled Benedick's 'right sense' out the wrong orifice,
      turning 'foul Words' into a 'foul Wind'. *Wit* echoes lines
      11–17.

60 **undergoes** is subject to (is obliged to answer).

62 **subscribe** label (literally, underwrite). Compare I.i.40–42.

64 **Parts** qualities (but with a suggestion of bodily parts as well).
    See IV.i.132–33.

66 **so . . . Evil** both (a) so totalitarian a [political] tyranny, and (b)
    so craftily managed a physical condition.

70 **Epithite** epithet, term.

71–72 **against my Will** despite my wish to avoid it. Compare
    II.iii.263–64. In her reply (lines 73–76) Beatrice appears to
    ignore the potential for a bawdy 'double Meaning'
    (II.iii.275–76) in such words as *indeed* (in deed) and *Will*; but
    in fact she uses *Heart* in a way that hints at a genital
    implication while pretending not to note it. Compare the
    suggestiveness with which *Heart* is employed in such passages
    as I.i.128–32, 331–35, II.i.330–31, III.i.111–12, III.ii.12–15,
    III.iv.74–76, and V.ii.110–11.
    wise clever and discerning in our discourse. Benedick's point is
    that they can never allow words to convey a single meaning
    'plainly' (line 60). Beatrice tacitly agrees, even while twisting
    wise in such a way as to extract a 'Confession' (line 79) that
    proves Benedick's assertion self-contradictory.

74 **poor** pitiable. This word echoes V.i.302–3 and recalls
    II.i.209–10, 329–30, II.iii.170–71, III.iii.121–24, and
    III.v.21–31. *Spight* (spite) carries two senses in this sentence;
    in line 73 *In spight of* means 'despite' or 'notwithstanding',
    and in lines 74–75 *spight* means 'injure', 'thwart', or 'treat
    maliciously'.

82 **Instance** maxim.

83 **that . . . Neighbours** that applied in a better era when one's
    neighbours could be trusted to recognize wisdom ('Wit')
    without having it pointed out to them or memorialized
    (erected) by the wise man himself. Benedick plans to 'erect' his
    own 'Monument', among other things, by doing his part to
    see that the world is properly 'peopled' (II.iii.258).

86 **Bell** funeral bell. This image echoes III.ii.12–15. Here, as in
    V.i.248, both *then* (the spelling in the early texts) and *than*
    yield viable readings. Beatrice's reply accords more readily
    with the latter, and that is the sense favoured by most of
    today's editions.

89 **Question** a proper question indeed.
    Clamour outcries of grief.

I must tell thee plainly, Claudio undergoes   60
my Challenge, and either I must shortly hear
from him, or I will subscribe him a Coward. And
I pray thee now tell me, for which of my bad
Parts didst thou first fall in love with me?

BEATRICE   For them all together, which maintain'd   65
so politic a State of Evil that they will not
admit any good Part to intermingle with them:
but for which of my good Parts did you first
suffer Love for me?

BENEDICK   Suffer Love! a good Epithite, I do   70
suffer Love indeed, for I love thee against my
Will.

BEATRICE   In spight of your Heart I think, alas
poor Heart, if you spight it for my sake, I
will spight it for yours, for I will never   75
love that which my Friend hates.

BENEDICK   Thou and I are too wise to woo
peaceably.

BEATRICE   It appears not in this Confession,
there's not one Wise Man among twenty that   80
will praise himself.

BENEDICK   An old, an old Instance, Beatrice,
that liv'd in the Time of good Neighbours: if
a Man do not erect in this Age his own Tomb
ere he dies, he shall live no longer in   85
Monument, then the Bell rings, and the Widow
weeps.

BEATRICE   And how long is that, think you?

BENEDICK   Question, why an Hour in Clamour and

190

90   **a Quarter in Rheum**   a quarter of an hour in weeping.

91   **Don Worm**   Sir Worm. Conscience was traditionally likened to
      a worm (either a gnawing worm in the usual sense, or a
      venomous snake) because of the internal discomfort caused by
      a guilty conscience. Benedick plays on a phallic sense of
      Worm (see III.ii.27–28) that gives *Conscience* a sexual sense:
      literally, *cunnus*-knowledge (see the note to I.i.335, and
      compare Sonnet 151).

92   **Impediment**   reason, objection. See IV.i.12–14.

100   **mend**   be restored to health. Compare II.iii.243–44, III.i.109.

104   **old Coil**   a terrific hubbub. This phrase recalls III.iii.100–3.

106   **abus'd**   both (a) deceived, and (b) misused.

107   **Author**   instigator.

108   **presently**   immediately. Compare IV.i.249; *come* echoes lines
      44–45.

110– **die . . . Lap**   both (a) rest my head in your lap when I die, and
11   (b) 'expire' in your 'good Part' (line 67, echoing line 64).
      Benedick uses *buried* in the sense implied in III.ii.69; and *Eyes*
      echoes III.iv.93–94, IV.i.227, 241, V.i.238–39, 267.

V.iii This scene takes place at 'the Monument of Leonato' (line 1),
       probably on his estate. The 'Tapers' referred to in the opening
       stage direction are long candles or torches.

S.D. EPITAPH   The early texts do not specify who recites or chants
      the 'Epitaph' to be placed over Hero's tomb; modern editions
      normally assign the lines to Claudio. The words in the epitaph
      are clearly meant to represent the penitent Claudio's
      sentiments, and are probably to be thought of as having been
      composed by him; see V.i.290–93. But there may have been
      good reasons for the 'Lord' or some other person to read the
      lines and hang the epitaph upon the tomb while Claudio
      stands by as one of the mourners (paralleling what he does
      after he asks that 'Music sound' in line 11).

a Quarter in Rheum, therefore it is most   90
expedient for the Wise, if Don Worm (his
Conscience) find no Impediment to the contrary,
to be the Trumpet of his own Virtues, as I am
to my self so much for praising my self, who
I my self will bear witness is Praiseworthy.   95
And now tell me, how doth your Cousin?

BEATRICE   Very ill.

BENEDICK   And how do you?

BEATRICE   Very ill too.

BENEDICK   Serve God, love me, and mend; there   100
will I leave you too, for here comes one in
haste.

Enter Ursula.

URSULA   Madam, you must come to your Uncle,
yonder's old Coil at home, it is proved my Lady
Hero hath been falsely accus'd, the Prince and   105
Claudio mightily abus'd, and Don John is the
Author of all, who is fled and gone: will you
come presently?

BEATRICE   Will you go hear this News, Signior?

BENEDICK   I will live in thy Heart, die in thy   110
Lap, and be buried in thy Eyes: and moreover,
I will go with thee to thy Uncle's.   *Exeunt.*

Scene 3

Enter Claudio, Prince and three or four with Tapers.

CLAUDIO   Is this the Monument of Leonato?

LORD   It is, my Lord.

EPITAPH

Done to death by slanderous Tongues

5   **guerdon of** recompense for. Tongues (line 3) recalls
     V.i.167–71.
     her wrongs the injustices done her. Compare V.i.305–8.

7–8 **So . . . Fame** Claudio is yet to learn how aptly his words apply
     to 'the Life that died with Shame'.

10   **domb** dumb (here spelled, and probably pronounced, to rhyme
     with 'Tomb'). This word derives from the Folio text, which
     has *tombe* in line 9 and *dombe* in line 10; the Quarto reading
     is *dead*, the sense that *dumb* implies in the context of the
     epitaph.

11   **Music** Claudio probably addresses this line to the musicians in
     the party (including Balthaser, no doubt, as in II.iii).

12   **Goddess . . . Night** Cynthia (Diana), Goddess of the Moon and
     patroness of virgins.

13   **thy virgin Knight** Hero, here represented as a knight errant in
     the livery of the warring huntress who personifies chastity.

17   **groan** This verb, which echoes V.i.16, is probably meant to
     evoke a New Testament passage in which the Apostle Paul
     says that 'the whole creation groaneth and travaileth in pain
     together until now. And not only they, but ourselves also,
     which have the first-fruits of the Spirit, even we ourselves
     groan within ourselves, waiting for the adoption, to wit, the
     redemption of our body' (Romans 8:22–23). As Claudio and
     his companion 'groan' in an effort to 'yield' their 'Dead' (their
     old selves, as noted at V.i.284, 302), line 19, they are
     simultaneously in a 'labour' (V.i.291) whose 'Issue' (line 32)
     will be 'newness of life' (Romans 6:4).

23   **Right** both (a) rightful deed, and (b) rite, ritual. Compare
     V.i.290–93, 299–300, V.ii.58–59.

24   **Maisters** Don Pedro probably addresses the 'three or four with
     Tapers' (and the musicians, if they are not included in that
     number).

25   **prey'd** hunted. In this context, an association with *prayed* is
     inevitable, suggesting that even the wolves have been
     transformed to gentleness by the solemnity of this ceremony.

26   **Phoebus** one of the names of the God of the Sun, here
     represented as arriving in his chariot.

29   **several** different, individual.

30   **Weeds** apparel.

Was the Hero that here lies;
Death in guerdon of her Wrongs   5
Gives her Fame which never dies:
So the Life that died with Shame
Lives in Death with glorious Fame.

Hang thou there upon the Tomb,
Praising her when I am domb.   10

CLAUDIO   Now Music sound, and sing your solemn
Hymn.

SONG

Pardon, Goddess of the Night,
Those that slew thy virgin Knight,
For the which with Songs of Woe
Round about her Tomb they go: 15
Midnight assist our Moan,
Help us to sigh and groan.
Heavily, heavily.
Graves yawn and yield your Dead
Till Death be uttered,   20
Heavily, heavily.

LORD   Now unto thy Bones good night,
Yearly will I do this Right.
PRINCE   Good morrow, Maisters, put your Torches
out:
The Wolves have prey'd, and look, the gentle
Day   25
Before the Wheels of Phoebus round about
Dapples the drowsy East with spots of grey:
Thanks to you all, and leave us, fare you well.
CLAUDIO   Good morrow, Masters, each his several
Way.
PRINCE   Come let us hence, and put on other
Weeds,   30

32   **Hymen**   the God of Marriage.
      luckier Issue   (a) a more fortunate outcome (including the
        'Issue', children, to result from the union), and (b) a luckier
        daughter.
      speeds   Most editors assume that Claudio means 'speed's':
        speed (bless) us. Compare *troth's* in III.iv.9, 18. The reading
        in the early texts provides no direct support for that
        conjecture. So it seems at least equally likely that Claudio
        means (a) blesses [us], or (b) hastens [to us].

33   **this**   this issue (Leonato's daughter Hero, as opposed to the
        niece he is now to bestow on Claudio). As in V.ii.86, *Then*
        can here mean either (a) 'Than', or (b) 'Then' (to yield a sense
        that the speaker, as opposed to the audience, little suspects).
      rend'red up this Woe   performed these woeful rites.

V.iv   This scene takes place in Leonato's house.

2   **So . . . Claudio**   Leonato is being magnanimous. Even though
        they were deceived, Don Pedro and Claudio are not 'innocent'
        of blame (a) for having been so susceptible to thinking evil of
        their host, (b) for having shamed Hero so shockingly, and (c)
        for having been so callow about the potential consequences of
        their deed.

3   **debated**   discussed in a public forum (see V.i.288–90).

4   **in some Fault**   partially to blame.

5   **against her Will**   This phrase suggests that Margaret was
        somehow coerced into something she had doubts about; but it
        can also be taken to indicate that Margaret's 'Fault' was
        totally unintentional. The phrasing echoes II.iii.263–64 and
        V.ii.70–72 and may be meant to imply that Margaret's
        free-spirited 'Will' was both involved and uninvolved.

6   **In . . . Question**   now that the interrogation has run its course
        and the truth has come to light. *Course* echoes the imagery in
        V.ii.34–35. In this line *Question* functions metrically as a
        three-syllable word.

7   **sorts so well**   come to such a happy conclusion (an echo of
        IV.i.238).

8   **by Faith**   by my fidelity to the vow I made on my honour to
        Beatrice and to Claudio.

And then to Leonato's we will go.

CLAUDIO   And Hymen now with luckier Issue speeds,
Then this for whom we rend'red up this Woe.

Exeunt.

Scene 4

Enter Leonato, Benedick, Margaret, Ursula, Old Man,
Friar, Hero.

FRIAR   Did I not tell you she was innocent?

LEONATO   So are the Prince and Claudio, who
    accus'd her,
Upon the Error that you heard debated:
But Margaret was in some Fault for this,
Although against her Will, as it appears,   5
In the true Course of all the Question.

OLD MAN   Well, I am glad that all things sorts
    so well.

BENEDICK   And so am I, being else by Faith
    enforc'd
To call young Claudio to a Reckoning for it.

LEONATO   Well, Daughter, and you Gentlewomen
    all,   10
Withdraw into a Chamber by your selves,

---

9   **Reckoning** accounting, payment; punishment. The phrase
     young Claudio, repeated in line 16, is yet another reminder
     that the soldier who has acted so immaturely is in fact still
     something of a 'Boy' (V.i.83–85, 90, 93, 187). It is to be
     hoped that the 'baptism' he has experienced in the wake of
     the feigned burial of his abused Hero (a plot device that has
     given additional resonance to the jests in III.ii.64–69) will
     have metamorphosed him into a Claudio who is 'young' in a
     more positive sense (see the notes to V.i.284, V.iii.17).

12   **masked**   with your faces covered. This situation recalls the
        masquerading in II.i.

14   **Office**   function, responsibility; here an actor's part. Compare
        V.i.27–28.

17   **confirm'd Countenance**   a steadfast expression (a straight face).
        Confirm'd recalls IV.i.148.

18   **intreat your Pains**   beg your assistance.

20   **undo me**   Benedick uses this phrase as both a synonym and an
        antonym of *bind me*. *Undo* can mean either (a) defeat or
        destroy (by binding, or fettering, a man), or (b) untie or
        unbind (releasing a captive). Compare II.ii.29, IV.i.314–15.

23   **That . . . her**   Leonato's phrasing can be taken by Benedick to
        mean 'Beatrice was following the example of my daughter'
        (looking at the world through the 'Eye' of love the way Hero
        did). But the audience also recognizes an oblique reference to
        Hero's role in gulling Beatrice. Once again (see V.i.181–82)
        Benedick either fails to register the significance of the remark
        or cagily ignores it.

27   **enigmatical**   riddling, ambiguous. Benedick's answer is
        probably less 'enigmatical' than it appears. By now he no
        doubt recognizes what Leonato is implying; but he declines to
        acknowledge it with even a tacit admission that he has been
        tricked into his 'Sight'.

28   **Will**   desire (request). But in the phrase that follows Benedick
        alludes suggestively to the kind of male 'Will' or 'Heart' (line
        32) that 'may stand'. See the notes to V.ii.71–72 and V.iv.5,
        and compare II.i.15–18, 223–28.

28–29 **your . . . ours**   that we may count on your good wishes [and
        your consent to give away the hand of your niece in a
        wedding ceremony in which you stand beside us at the altar].

29   **conjoin'd**   joined together (with wordplay on *con-* as a syllable
        that echoes the name of the female 'Will'). See the note to
        I.i.335.

31   **desire**   both wish and request. Compare II.i.284, III.iv.1–2,
        III.v.10–14, IV.i.256, V.i.248–51.

32   **your Liking**   what you desire. Compare III.i.85–86.

34   **fair Assembly**   lovely gathering.

And when I send for you come hither masked:
The Prince and Claudio promis'd by this Hour
To visit me. – You know your Office, Brother,
You must be Father to your Brother's Daughter,   15
And give her to young Claudio.   *Exeunt Ladies.*

OLD MAN   Which I will do with confirm'd
  Countenance.

BENEDICK   Friar, I must intreat your Pains, I
  think.

FRIAR   To do what, Signior?

BENEDICK   To bind me, or undo me, one of them.   20
  – Signior Leonato, truth it is, good Signior,
  Your Niece regards me with an Eye of Favour.

LEONATO   That Eye my Daughter lent her, 'tis
  most true.

BENEDICK   And I do with an Eye of Love requite
  her.

LEONATO   The Sight whereof I think you had from
  me,   25
  From Claudio and the Prince, but what's your
  Will?

BENEDICK   Your Answer, Sir, is enigmatical,
  But for my Will, my Will is your good Will
  May stand with ours, this Day to be conjoin'd
  In the state of honourable Marriage   30
  – In which, good Friar, I shall desire your
  Help.

LEONATO   My Heart is with your Liking.

FRIAR   And my Help.
  Here comes the Prince and Claudio.

          Enter Prince, and Claudio, and two or
                    three other.

PRINCE   Good morrow to this fair Assembly.

LEONATO   Good morrow, Prince; good morrow,
  Claudio;   35

36   **attend you** await the opportunity to serve you. Compare III.v.60–62.
       determined resolved.

37   **marry with** Leonato does not repeat the phrasing that signalled the difficulties at the earlier ceremony. Compare IV.i.4–10. Rather than another 'Dissembly' (IV.ii.1), this gathering will prove to be a 'fair Assembly' (line 34). *To day* (today) recalls V.i.293.

38   **I'll . . . Ethiope** I'd adhere to my commitment even if she were as black as an Ethiopian. Renaissance Europeans were wedded to the notion that beauty was synonymous with fair skin (so much so that women shielded themselves to avoid becoming 'Sun-burnt', as Beatrice notes in II.i.334–35). Shakespeare satirizes this notion in Sonnets 127, 130, but he alludes to it in several plays, among them *A Midsummer Night's Dream* (III.ii.257), *Love's Labour's Lost* (IV.iii.120–21, 268), *As You Like It* (IV.iii.35–36), and *The Winter's Tale* (IV.iv.376–79); compare *Romeo and Juliet*, I.iv.160–61, where Romeo says that Juliet 'hangs upon the Cheek of Night / As a rich Jewel in an Ethiop's Ear'.

41   **February Face** wintry countenance (cold demeanour). Compare I.i.95–96, 198–201, V.i.76.

43   **savage Bull** raging cuckold. Claudio reminds Benedick of the exchanges in I.i.243–83 (with particular reference to the predictions in lines 269–79) and V.i.181–86.

45   **Europa** Europe, with wordplay on the name of the maiden whom Jupiter wooed in the form of a bull (a story Ovid tells in Book II of his *Metamorphoses*). *Jove* (line 46) recalls II.i.101–2.

48   **had . . . Low** possessed a seductive, lowing voice. Benedick's words evoke memories of another purportedly 'amiable Encounter' (III.iii.162–63).

51   **Bleat** the cry of a young bull, goat, or sheep. Benedick manages not only to call Claudio a bastard and a cuckold (another bull), but to associate him with folly, lechery, and cowardice. See the notes to II.i.25, V.i.153–57; and compare the exchanges in I.i.106–19, III.ii.74–79.

52   **For . . . you** I'll get even with you for this. Compare III.iii.111.
       Reck'nings accounts to settle (debts I owe). This word echoes lines 8–9.

We here attend you. Are you yet determined
To day to marry with my Brother's Daughter?
CLAUDIO   I'll hold my Mind were she an Ethiope.
LEONATO   Call her foorth, Brother, here's the
    Friar ready.   [*Exit Antonio.*]
PRINCE   Good morrow, Benedick, why what's the
    matter?   40
That you have such a February Face,
So full of Frost, of Storm and Cloudiness.
CLAUDIO   I think he thinks upon the savage Bull.
    — Tush fear not, Man, we'll tip thy Horns with
      Gold,
And all Europa shall rejoice at thee,   45
As once Europa did at lusty Jove,
When he would play the noble Beast in Love.
BENEDICK   Bull Jove, Sir, had an amiable Low,
And some such strange Bull leapt your Father's
    Cow,
And got a Calf in that same noble Feat,   50
Much like to you, for you have just his Bleat.

      Enter Brother, Hero, Beatrice, Margaret,
                Ursula.

CLAUDIO   For this I owe you: here comes other
    Reck'nings.
    — Which is the Lady I must seize upon?
LEONATO   This same is she, and I do give you
    her.
CLAUDIO   Why then she's mine. — Sweet, let me
    see your Face.   55
LEONATO   No that you shall not till you take
    her Hand,
Before this Friar, and swear to marry her.
CLAUDIO   Give me your Hand before his holy
    Friar,

59 **like of me**   are willing to accept me. Compare line 32; line 57 echoes line 37.

60 **And . . . Wife**   As Hero speaks this line, she apparently removes her mask (see line 12) to let Claudio see her face.

63 **One . . . live**   Hero presents herself as having risen from the grave (see the note to IV.i.160). In a sense, Claudio and Don Pedro have undergone a related transformation. The earlier Claudio was in fact an 'other Husband' (line 61), an unregenerate predecessor of the Claudio who now appears to have 'put off concerning the former conversation the old man, which [was] corrupt according to the deceitful lusts' (Ephesians 4:22–24). This Claudio is 'renewed in the spirit of [his] mind'. In Pauline terms, he is a 'new man', and ideally he will prove as worthy of union with 'Another Hero' as if he had drowned and been resurrected as another Leander. See the note to line 9.

66 **but whiles**   only so long as. The repetitions of *liv'd* and *live* in lines 60–66 echo V.ii.110–13 and V.iii.7–8.

67 **Amazement**   the bewilderment of people lost in a maze. Compare II.iii.123–25.
    qualify   relieve, moderate [by explaining what happened].

69 **largely**   in full detail. *Rites* (line 68) echoes V.iii.22–23.

70 **let . . . familiar**   assume that what inspires wonder can be accounted for by natural (familiar) means.

71 **let us presently**   let us proceed at once. Compare V.ii.107–8.

72 **Soft and fair**   just a moment, if you please. Compare V.i.207.

74 **than Reason**   both (a) than is reasonable, and (b) than I love Reason. *Will* (desire), line 73, echoes lines 26–31; *answer* echoes line 27.

75–76 **Why . . . did**   This is Benedick's public acknowledgement that he overheard the orchard conversation in II.iii.

79 **sick**   overcome with illness.

83 **but . . . Recompense**   only in the way one friend reciprocates another's good will.

84 **Cousin**   This term could be applied to any relative.

I am your Husband if you like of me.
HERO   And when I liv'd I was your other Wife,   60
And when you loved, you were my other
Husband.
CLAUDIO   Another Hero.
HERO   Nothing certainer.
One Hero died defil'd, but I do live,
And surely as I live, I am a Maid.
PRINCE   The former Hero, Hero that is dead.   65
LEONATO   She died, my Lord, but whiles her
Slaunder liv'd.
FRIAR   All this Amazement can I qualify,
When after that the holy Rites are ended,
I'll tell you largely of fair Hero's Death,
Mean time let Wonder seem familiar,   70
And to the Chapel let us presently.
BENEDICK   Soft and fair, Friar, which is Beatrice?
BEATRICE   I answer to that Name, what is your
Will?
BENEDICK   Do not you love me?
BEATRICE   Why no, no more than Reason.
BENEDICK   Why then your Uncle, and the Prince,
and Claudio,   75
Have been deceiv'd: they swore you did.
BEATRICE   Do not you love me?
BENEDICK   Troth no, no more than Reason.
BEATRICE   Why then my Cousin Margaret and Ursula
Are much deceiv'd, for they did swear you did.
BENEDICK   They swore that you were almost sick
for me.   80
BEATRICE   They swore that you were well-nigh
dead for me.
BENEDICK   'Tis no such matter, then you do not
love me.
BEATRICE   No truly, but in friendly Recompense.
LEONATO   Come, Cousin, I am sure you love the
Gentleman.
CLAUDIO   And I'll be sworn upon't that he loves her,   85

87 **halting** limping, inept.
of ... Brain obviously the product of no brain but his own.

88 **Fashioned to** both (a) designed for, and (b) addressed to. Compare IV.i.232–34.

91 **Hands** handwritings (with play on the hands that produced them). It is fitting that in a comedy that depicts so many betrayals, Benedick and Beatrice are finally brought together by two betrayals (those of Leonato and Hero) that prove each lover to be self-betrayed. The 'notings' that implicate Benedick and Beatrice draw the plot to an aptly witty conclusion. *Hearts* echoes line 32.

93 **by this Light** both (a) by the light of the sun (Beatrice echoes this sense in lines 94–95), and (b) by the light of this brain of mine. Compare V.i.138.
for Pity only because I feel sorry for someone so sad as you. Compare III.iii.212–23, 234–38.

95 **upon great Persuasion** with immense reluctance, and only because powerful people have imposed their will upon me. See the note to I.i.335, where *amorous Tale* hints at the 'great Persuasion' (tumescent, pulsating 'Heart', I.i.333) of a 'savage Bull' bent on the raptures of a 'strong Encounter'.

97 **in a Consumption** wasting away, like a patient with tuberculosis. Beatrice alludes to what Hero said about Benedick in the second garden scene (III.i.77–78).

98 **Peace ... Mouth** Though both early texts assign this line to Leonato, editors since the eighteenth century have given it to Benedick, with the implication that he seizes Beatrice and kisses her (as Beatrice has urged Hero to do in II.i.325–27). If Leonato does speak it, it is conceivable that he thrusts Beatrice into Benedick's arms.

99 **How ... Man?** Don Pedro seeks to stuff Benedick's craw with the words he spoke so confidently in I.i.269–77.

100 **a College** a society of professional men (such as doctors or bishops).

102 **Humour** disposition to be a lover. Compare V.i.188–90. Lines 100–10 accord with the resolve Benedick has stated in II.iii.250–60.
care for can be bothered by.

103 **Epigram** brief poem or satirical tag, as in I.i.276–77.

For here's a Paper written in his Hand,
A halting Sonnet of his own pure Brain,
Fashioned to Beatrice.
HERO   And here's another,
  Writ in my Cousin's Hand, stol'n from her
    Pocket,
  Containing her Affection unto Benedick.   90
BENEDICK   A Miracle, here's our own Hands
  against our Hearts: come, I will have thee,
  but by this Light I take thee for Pity.
BEATRICE   I would not deny you, but by this
  good Day, I yield upon great Persuasion, and   95
  partly to save your Life, for I was told you
  were in a Consumption.
LEONATO   Peace, I will stop your Mouth.
PRINCE   How dost thou, Benedick the Married Man?
BENEDICK   I'll tell thee what, Prince: a College   100
  of Wit-crackers cannot flout me out of my
  Humour, dost thou think I care for a Satire
  or an Epigram? No, if a Man will be beaten
  with Brains, 'a shall wear nothing hansome
  about him. In brief, since I do purpose to   105
  marry, I will think nothing to any purpose
  that the World can say against it, and
  therefore never flout at me for what I have
  said against it: for Man is a Giddy Thing,

103–5 **No . . . him**   No, if a man will allow himself to be intimidated
          by mere 'Brains' ('Wit-crackers'), he may as well hide himself
          away for fear of asserting his 'good Parts' (V.ii.68).

109   **Man . . . Thing**   man is an unstable creature. Benedick's
          statement echoes what Borachio and Conrade have said about
          the deformations effected by 'Fashion' (III.iii.141–53).

204

110 **my Conclusion** (a) the conclusion I have arrived at after thinking the matter over at length, (b) the last thing I plan to say on the subject, (c) the end of my own story, and my 'at-one-ment'. Benedick's peroration recalls I.i.206–8, 254–55, 331–37, II.iii.7–28, 253–57, III.iv.88–91, V.i.167–74, 202–6.

116 **single Life** both (a) one life (probably an allusion to the proverb that a cat has nine lives), and (b) life as a single man.

117 **double Dealer** both (a) married man, one who 'doubles' himself by taking on a wife (compare II.iii.184), and (b) cheater at 'cards' (marriage).

118– **look . . . thee** keep a very close eye on you. Compare
19 II.i.354–55.

121– **that . . . Heels** that we may rid our hearts of any burdens they
22 may still be carrying, and liberate our wives to lift their legs in merriment, both now (while they are dancing) and later (when they become 'light a' Love' and point their 'Heels' upward, III.iv.47). See note to II.i.34. *Heart* echoes lines 91–92.

124 **of my Word** on my word.

125 **sad** inappropriately solemn. Compare V.i.207–8, 288–93.

126– **there . . . Horn** Benedick refers to horn-tipped walking-sticks
27 and staffs of office; but he also alludes to other kinds of hard-tipped 'horns' (see I.i.264–79, II.i.19–53, II.iii.64, V.i.152–55, 183–84).

128 **ta'en in Flight** has been captured while trying to flee the country.

131 **brave** bold, suitable.

131– **Strike up, Pipers** Benedick has the last word (as he had insisted
32 in line 124), and the play culminates with a dance that prepares for the private joys to follow. *Pipers* recalls II.iii.13–15 and thereby indicates that Benedick's conversion from 'the Drum and the Fife' to 'the Tabor and the Pipe' is complete. It is perhaps significant that the early texts provide no *Exeunt* to conclude this scene. The partying serves, in effect, as the epilogue, and the audience is implicitly invited to applaud while the actors revel on the stage to provide an appropriate 'Finis' (end) to this 'Giddy' comedy (lines 109–10). Shortly before Shakespeare wrote *Much Ado About Nothing*, Sir John Davies had praised the kind of merriment that concludes the action in his poem *Orchestra* (1596):

and this is my Conclusion. – For thy part,   110
Claudio, I did think to have beaten thee, but
in that thou art like to be my Kinsman, live
unbruis'd, and love my Cousin.

CLAUDIO   I had well hop'd thou wouldst have
denied Beatrice, that I might have cudgell'd   115
thee out of thy single Life, to make thee a
double Dealer, which out of Question thou wilt
be, if my Coosin do not look exceeding narrowly
to thee.

BENEDICK   Come, come, we are Friends, let's have   120
a Dance ere we are married, that we may lighten
our own Hearts, and our Wives' Heels.

LEONATO   We'll have Dancing afterward.

BENEDICK   First, of my Word, therefore play
Music, Prince. Thou art sad: get thee a Wife,   125
get thee a Wife, there is no Staff more
reverent than one tipp'd with Horn.

Enter Messenger.

MESSENGER   My Lord, your Brother John is ta'en
in Flight,
And brought with armed Men back to Messina.

BENEDICK   Think not on him till to morrow, I'll   130
devise thee brave Punishments for him. – Strike
up, Pipers.   *Dance.*

FINIS

Lo, this is Dancing's true Nobility,
Dancing, the Child of Music and of Love;
Dancing it self both Love and Harmony,
Where all agree, and all in Order move;
Dancing, the Art that all Arts do approve,
The Fair Character of the World's Consent,
The Heavens' true Figure, and the Earth's
    Ornament.

PERSPECTIVES ON
Much Ado About Nothing

The earliest reader to comment extensively on *Much Ado About Nothing* was Charles Gildon. In his *Remarks on the Plays of Shakespear* (London, 1710), Gildon observed that *Much Ado* 'is as full of Absurdities, as the Writing is full of Beauties'. On the whole, however, he praised the work, and in an opinion that anticipated the perceptions of such later critics as Samuel Johnson, Sir Arthur Quiller-Couch, and A. P. Rossiter, he argued that it should be categorized as

a Comedy, tho' some of the Incidents and Discourses too are more in a Tragic Strain; and that of the Accusation of Hero is too shocking for either Tragedy or Comedy; nor cou'd it have come off in Nature, if we regard the Country without the Death of more, than Hero. The Imposition on the Prince and Claudio seems very lame, and Claudio's conduct to the Woman, he lov'd, highly contrary to the very Nature of Love, to expose her in so barbarous a Manner and with so little Concern, and struggle, and on such weak Grounds without a farther Examination into the Matter, yet the Passions this produces in the old Father make a wonderful amends for the Fault. Besides which there is such a pleasing Variety of Characters in the Play, and those perfectly maintain'd, as well as distinguish'd, that you lose the Absurdities of the Conduct in the Excellence of the Manners, Sentiments, Diction and Topics. Benedict, and Beatrice are two sprightly, witty, talkative Characters, and, tho' of the same Nature, yet perfectly distinguish'd, and you have no need to read the Names, to know who speaks. . . .

The Character of Don John the Bastard is admirably distinguish'd, his Manners are well mark'd, and every where convenient, or agreeable. Being a sour melancholly, saturnine, envious, selfish, malicious Temper, Manners Necessary to produce these villainous Events, they did; these were productive of the Catastrophe, for he was a Person brought in to fill up the Number only, because without him the Fable could not have gone on.

To quote all the comic Excellencies of this Play would be to transcribe three Parts of it. For all that passes betwixt Benedict and Beatrice is admirable. His Discourse against Love and Marriage in the later End of the second Act is very pleasant and witty, and that which Beatrice says of Wooing, Wedding, and repenting. And the Aversion that the Poet gives Benedict and Beatrix for each other in their Discourse, heightens the Jest of making them in Love with one another.

For Charlotte Lennox, writing nearly half a century later, there was little to commend in *Much Ado About Nothing*. As she noted in *Shakespear Illustrated; or, The Novels and Histories, on Which the Plays of Shakespear Are Founded* (London, 1754), the plot for this 'absurd and ridiculous' comedy came from the

Story of Genevra, in Ariosto's *Orlando Furioso*, a Fiction, which as it is managed by the Epic Poet, is neither improbable nor unnatural; but by Shakespear mangled and defaced, full of Inconsistencies, Contradictions, and Blunders. The defaming a Lady, by means of her Servant personating her at her Chamber-window, is the Subject pursued by both.

Shakespear, by changing the Persons, altering some of the Circumstances, and inventing others, has made the whole an improbable Contrivance, borrowed just enough to shew his Poverty of Invention, and added enough to prove his want of Judgment.

The Scheme for ruining the Lady in the Original, is formed and executed by a rejected Lover, who sees a Rival, his inferior in Rank and Fortune, preferred before him, and loses at once the Object of his Wishes, and the Prospect of increased Honours, by that Preference. Ambition, and the Desire of Revenge, are Passions strong enough in a Mind not very virtuous, to produce Acts of Baseness and Villainy....

Don John [in *Much Ado About Nothing*] is a Villain merely through the love of Villainy, and having entertained a capricious Dislike to Claudio, closes eagerly with his Confidant's horrid Scheme for breaking off his Marriage with Hero....

Claudio only is the Object of Don John's Hatred, yet the chief Force of the intended Injury is to fall on Hero and Leonato her Father, towards whom he has no Malice; and he is made to engage in this wicked Enterprize, to procure the Ruin and Death of two Persons he hates not, to give a little Vexation to one he does. These Absurdities have their Rise from the injudicious Change of the Characters. The Contrivance to slander Hero is not less ridiculous; and this also is occasioned by the Poet's having deviated from the Original to introduce his own wild Conceits.

Borachio tells Don John, that he is highly favoured by Margaret, Hero's waiting Woman; that he will persuade her to dress in her Lady's Cloaths, assume her Name, and talk to him out of her Chamber-window, all which Don Pedro and Claudio being Witnesses of, would effectually convince them that Hero was dishonoured.

But Borachio does not acquaint Don John, and through him the Audience, what Colour he will give to this strange Request, in order to induce Margaret to grant it: Margaret is all along represented as faithful to her Mistress: it was not likely she would engage in a Plot that seemed to have a Tendency to ruin Hero's Reputation, unless she had been imposed on by some very plausible Pretences; what those Pretences were we are left to guess, which is indeed so difficult to do, that we must reasonably suppose the Poet himself was as much at a Loss here as his Readers, and equally incapable of solving the difficulty he had raised.

That Borachio should be the suspected Gallant of Hero, is a Circumstance also highly improbable. Borachio, a mean Dependant on a Man whose Vices had made him the Object of universal Hatred and Contempt, a Stranger almost in Messina, and, as well on Account of the Meanness of his Situation, as the Profligacy of his Manners, excluded from any Acquaintance with a Lady of Hero's Quality.

Yet how easily does Don Pedro the Friend, and Claudio the Lover of the Lady, swallow this gross Scandal, that must even derive Improbability from the Person who utters it; for he is neither an honest Man nor a Friend of Claudio, who is thus solicitous to prevent his dishonouring himself by marrying a bad Woman, but a Wretch noted for his Propensity to all kinds of Mischief and Villainy, an inveterate Hater of Claudio, and but a little while before at open Enmity with Don Pedro his Brother.

Surely these Circumstances were sufficient to make the Prince and Claudio doubt the Truth of this Story, which the Character of the Teller considered, as well as the Improbability of the Facts, seemed much more likely to be contrived to produce Mischief than prevent it. . . .

Margaret having done her Part towards defaming her Mistress, without knowing any Thing of the Matter, though her Discourse with Borachio was calculated to raise the most injurious Suspicions, assists her next Morning to dress for the Wedding, attends her to the Church, hears the designed Bridegroom refuse her Hand, proclaim her a Wanton, and urge her last Night's loose Discourse with Borachio from the Chamber Window as a Proof: Yet all the while she appears wholly insensible of what had happened, neither concerned for her Mistress, whom she had ruined without Design, nor anxious for her own Safety, that seemed to depend upon a candid Confession; for it was not likely her Treachery could be long concealed. Thus supernaturally (if what is out of Nature may be called above it) is the Plot brought to perfection, nor is the unravelling of it less happily imagined. . . .

Shakespear has deviated from the Original, as much in the drawing his Characters, as the Disposition of his Plan. Nothing can be more different than the Sentiments and Behaviour of Ariodant [in *Orlando Furioso*] and Claudio, in Circumstances nearly alike. Both are represented as passionate Lovers, happy in the Possession of their Mistresses Affections, yet prevailed upon to think them false through the Treachery of a Villain; but Ariodant yields only to the strongest Conviction, Claudio to the grossest Artifice.

Ariodant's Grief, Rage and Jealousy, terminate in a fixed Despair: which prompts him to lay violent Hands on his own Life. Claudio is actuated by a Desire of Revenge, and that of the meanest Sort, for he suffers the supposed Gallant to escape, and only mediates the Ruin of the Lady.

Ariodant fights with his own Brother, to preserve the Life of her who had injured him: Claudio without any necessity, exposes his Mistress publickly in Church, brings Ruin and Contempt on her, and everlasting Shame and Affliction on her poor Father, to whom he had been obliged, for an hospitable Reception, and an intended Benefit.

Claudio is mean, selfish, ungenerous and cruel: Qualities, that are seldom found in the Heroe and Lover, and he is represented as both.

Ariodant is always consistent with his Character, too brave, to be actuated by a mean Desire of Revenge, too much in love, to be guided by Reason; hence arise the several Extravagancies he is guilty of, but in all, the Manners of the Soldier and Lover are inviolably preserved.

A few years after Charlotte Lennox published her comments on the playwright's use – or, in her view, misuse – of his source material, Samuel Johnson, the most eminent of the eighteenth-century critics, completed an edition of Shakespeare's works (London, 1765) to which he prefaced a strikingly original essay about his treatment of the dramatic genres. According to Dr Johnson,

Shakespeare's plays are not in the rigorous and critical sense either tragedies or comedies, but compositions of a distinct kind; exhibiting the real state of sublunary nature, which partakes of good and evil, joy and sorrow, mingled with endless variety of proportion and innumerable modes of combination; and expressing the course of the world, in which the loss of one is the gain of another; in which, at the same time, the reveller is hasting to his wine, and the mourner burying his friend; in which the malignity of one is sometimes defeated by the frolic of another; and many mischiefs and many beliefs are done and hindered without design.

Out of this chaos of mingled purposes and casualties the ancient poets, according to the laws which custom had prescribed, selected some the crimes of men, and some their absurdities; some the momentous vicissitudes of life, and some the lighter occurrences; some the terrors of distress, and some the gayeties of prosperity. Thus rose the two modes of imitation known by the names of *tragedy* and *comedy*, compositions intended to promote different ends by contrary means, and considered as so little allied that I do not recollect among the Greeks or Romans a single writer who attempted both.

Shakespeare has united the powers of exciting laughter and sorrow not only in one mind but in one composition. Almost all his plays are divided between serious and ludicrous characters, and, in the successive evolutions of the design, sometimes produce seriousness and sorrow, and sometimes levity and laughter.

That this is a practice contrary to the rules of criticism will be readily allowed; but there is always an appeal open from criticism to nature. The end of writing is to instruct; the end of poetry is to instruct by pleasing. That the mingled drama may convey all the instruction of tragedy or comedy cannot be denied, because it includes both in its alternations of exhibition, and approaches nearer than either to the appearance of life, by showing how great machinations and slender designs may promote or obviate one another, and the high and the low cooperate in the general system by unavoidable concatenation. . . .

Shakespeare engaged in dramatick poetry with the world open before him; the rules of the ancients were yet known to few; the publick judgement was unformed; he had no example of such fame as might force him upon imitation, nor criticks of such authority as might restrain his extravagance; he therefore indulged his natural disposition; and his disposition, as Rymer has remarked, led him to comedy. In tragedy he often writes, with great appearance of toil and study, what is written at last with little felicity; but, in his comic scenes, he seems to produce without labour what no labour can improve. In tragedy he is always struggling after some occasion to be comick; but in comedy he seems to repose, or to luxuriate, as in a mode of thinking congenial to his nature. In his tragick scenes there is always something wanting, but his comedy often surpasses expectation or desire. His comedy pleases by the thoughts and language, and his tragedy for the greater part by incident and action. His tragedy seems to be skill, his comedy to be instinct.

Like Charlotte Lennox, but with much less acerbity, the German critic August Wilhelm Schlegel opened his comments on Shakespeare's most sparkling comedy with a reference to the playwright's Italian source. In *A Course of Lectures on Dramatic Art and Literature* (1808), edited by A. J. W. Morrison and translated by John Black (London, 1846), Schlegel noted that

> The main plot in *Much Ado About Nothing* is the same with the story of *Ariodante and Ginevra* in Ariosto; the secondary circumstances and development are no doubt very different. The mode in which the innocent Hero before the altar at the moment of the wedding, and in the presence of the family and many witnesses, is put to shame by a most degrading charge, false indeed, yet clothed with every appearance of truth, is a grand piece of theatrical effect in the true and justifiable sense. The impression would have been too tragical had not Shakspeare carefully softened it in order to prepare for a fortunate catastrophe. The discovery of the plot against Hero has been already partly made, though not by the persons interested; and the poet has contrived, by means of the blundering simplicity of a couple of constables and watchmen, to convert the arrest and the examination of the guilty individuals into scenes full of the most delightful amusement. There is also a second piece of theatrical effect not inferior to the first, where Claudio, now convinced of his error, and in obedience to the penance laid on his fault, thinking to give his hand to a relation of his injured bride, whom he supposes dead, discovers on her unmasking, Hero herself. The extraordinary success of this play in Shakspeare's own day, and ever since in England, is, however, to be ascribed more particularly to the parts of Benedict and Beatrice, two humoursome beings, who incessantly attack each other with all the resources of raillery. Avowed rebels to love, they are both entangled in its net by a merry plot of their friends to make them believe that each is the object of the secret passion of the other. Some one or other, not over-stocked with penetration, has objected to the same artifice being twice used in entrapping them; the drollery, however, lies in the very symmetry of the deception. Their friends attribute the whole effect to their own device; but the exclusive direction of their raillery against each other is in itself a proof of a growing inclination. Their witty vivacity does not even abandon them in the avowal of love; and their behaviour only assumes a serious appearance for the purpose of defending the slandered Hero. This is exceedingly well imagined; the lovers of jesting must fix a point beyond which they are not to indulge in their humour, if they would not be mistaken for buffoons by trade.

An English comtemporary of Schlegel's, William Hazlitt, commended *Much Ado About Nothing* as 'an admirable comedy'. In *Characters of Shakespear's Plays* (London, 1817), Hazlitt described Hero as 'the principal figure' of the comedy and said that she

> leaves an indelible impression on the mind by her beauty, her tenderness, and the hard trial of her love. The passages in which Claudio first makes a confession of his affection towards her, conveys as pleasing an image of the entrance of love into a youthful bosom as can well be imagined. . . .
>
> In the scene at the altar, when Claudio, urged on by the villain Don John, brings the charge of incontinence against her, and as it were divorces her in the very marriage-ceremony, her appeals to her own conscious innocence and honour are made with the most affecting simplicity. . . .
>
> The justification of Hero in the end, and her restoration to the confidence and arms of her lover, is brought about by one of those temporary consignments to the grave of which Shakespear seems to have been so fond. . . .
>
> The principal comic characters in *Much Ado About Nothing*, Benedick and Beatrice, are both essences in their kind. His character as a woman-hater is admirably supported, and his conversion to matrimony is no less happily effected by the pretended story of Beatrice's love for him. It is hard to say which of the two scenes is the best, that of the trick which is thus practised on Benedick, or that in which Beatrice is prevailed on to take pity on him by overhearing her cousin and her maid declare (which they do on purpose) that he is dying of love for her. . . .
>
> The beauty of all this arises from the characters of the persons so entrapped. Benedick is a professed and staunch enemy to marriage, and gives very plausible reasons for the faith that is in him. And as to Beatrice, she persecutes him all day with her jests (so that he could hardly think of being troubled with them at night); she not only turns him but all other things into jest, and is proof against every thing serious. . . .
>
> Dogberry and Verges in this play are inimitable specimens of quaint blundering and misprisions of meaning; and are a standing record of that formal gravity of pretension and total want of common understanding, which Shakespeare no doubt copied from real life, and which in the course of two hundred years appear to have ascended from the lowest to the highest offices in the state.

Another early nineteenth-century British writer, Dublin-born Anna Brownell Jameson, penned an acute analysis of the heroine of the wit-combats in *Much Ado About Nothing*. In *Characteris-*

tics of Women: Moral, Poetical, and Historical (London, 1832), Jameson said that

> Shakspeare has exhibited in Beatrice a spirited and faithful portrait of the fine lady of his own time. The deportment, language, manners, and allusions, are those of a particular class in a particular age; but the individual and dramatic character which forms the groundwork, is strongly discriminated; and being taken from general nature, belongs to every age. In Beatrice, high intellect and high animal spirits meet, and excite each other like fire and air. In her wit (which is brilliant without being imaginative) there is a touch of insolence, not unfrequent in women when the wit predominates over reflection and imagination. In her temper, too, there is a slight infusion of the termagant; and her satirical humor plays with such an unrespective levity over all subjects alike, that it required a profound knowledge of women to bring such a character within the pale of our sympathy. But Beatrice, though wilful, is not wayward; she is volatile, not unfeeling. . . .
>
> In Beatrice, Shakspeare has contrived that the poetry of the character shall not only soften, but heighten its comic effect. We are not only inclined to forgive Beatrice all her scornful airs, all her biting jests, all her assumption of superiority: but they amuse and delight us the more, when we find her, with all the headlong simplicity of a child, falling at once into the snare laid for her affections; when we see *her*, who thought a man of God's making not good enough for her, who disdained to be o'ermastered by a 'a piece of valiant dust', stooping like the rest of her sex, vailing her proud spirit, and taming her wild heart to the loving hand of him whom she had scorned, flouted, and misused, 'past the endurance of a block'. And we are yet more completely won by her generous enthusiastic attachment to her cousin. When the father of Hero believes the tale of her guilt; when Claudio, her lover, without remorse or a lingering doubt, consigns her to shame; when the Friar remains silent, and the generous Benedick himself knows not what to say, Beatrice, confident in her affections, and guided only by the impulses of her own feminine heart, sees through the inconsistency, the impossibility of the charge, and exclaims, without a moment's hesitation. 'O, on my soul, my cousin is belied!'
>
> Schlegel, in his remarks on the play . . . , has given us an amusing instance of that sense of reality with which we are impressed by Shakspeare's characters. He says of Benedick and Beatrice, as if he had known them personally, that the exclusive direction of their pointed raillery against each other 'is a proof of a growing inclination.' This is not unlikely; and the same inference would lead us to suppose that this

mutual inclination had commenced before the opening of the play. . . .

Infinite skill, as well as humor, is shown in making this pair of airy beings the exact counterpart of each other; but of the two portraits, that of Benedick is by far the most pleasing, because the independence and gay indifference of temper, the laughing defiance of love and marriage, the satirical freedom of expression, common to both, are more becoming to the masculine than to the feminine character. Any woman might love such a cavalier as Benedick, and be proud of his affection; his valor, his wit, and his gayety sit so gracefully upon him! and his light scoffs against the power of love are but just sufficient to render more piquant the conquest of this 'heretic in despite of beauty'. But a man might well be pardoned who should shrink from encountering such a spirit as that of Beatrice, unless, indeed, he had served an apprenticeship to 'the taming school' [*The Taming of the Shrew*, IV.ii.54]. The wit of Beatrice is less good-humored than that of Benedick; or, from the difference of sex, it appears so. It is observable that the power is throughout on her side, and the sympathy and interest on his: which, by reversing the usual order of things, seems to excite us *against the grain*, if I may use such an expression. In all their encounters she constantly gets the better of him, and the gentleman's wits go off halting. . . . Beatrice, woman-like, generally has the first word, and will have the last. . . .

In the midst of all this tilting and sparring of their nimble and fiery wits, we find them infinitely anxious for the good opinion of each other, and secretly impatient of each other's scorn: but Beatrice is the most truly indifferent of the two; the most assured of herself. The comic effect produced by their mutual attachment, which, however natural and expected, comes upon us with all the force of a surprise, cannot be surpassed: and how exquisitely characteristic the mutual avowal! But here again the dominion rests with Beatrice, and she appears in a less amiable light than her lover. Benedick surrenders his whole heart to her and to his new passion. The revulsion of feeling even causes it to overflow in an excess of fondness; but with Beatrice temper has still the mastery. The affection of Benedick induces him to challenge his intimate friend for her sake, but the affection of Beatrice does not prevent her from risking the life of her lover. . . .

. . .On the whole, we dismiss Benedick and Beatrice to their matrimonial bonds rather with a sense of amusement than a feeling of congratulation or sympathy; rather with an acknowledgment that they are well-matched, and worthy of each other, than with any well-founded expectation of their domestic tranquillity.

At approximately the same time that Anna Jameson was publishing her insights on Beatrice and Benedick, Samuel Taylor

Coleridge, the most celebrated of the English Romantic critics, was drawing on Dr Johnson to suggest that in Shakespeare's comic scripts the 'plot interests us on account of the characters, not vice versa; it is the canvas only'. In a comment he seems to have made around 1834 – reprinted here from *Shakespearean Criticism*, edited by Thomas Middleton Raysor (London, 1960) – Coleridge said:

> Take away from *Much Ado About Nothing* all which is not indispensable to the plot, either as having little to do with it, or at best, like Dogberry and his comrades, forced into the service when any other less ingeniously absurd watchmen and night-constables would have answered; take away Benedict, Beatrice, Dogberry, and the reaction of the former on the character of Hero, and what will remain? In other writers the main agent of the plot is always the prominent character. In Shakespeare so or not so, as the character is in itself calculated or not calculated to form the plot. So Don John, the mainspring of the plot, is merely shown and withdrawn.

For one of the principals of *Much Ado About Nothing* an early Victorian critic had even harsher strictures than had Anna Jameson. In *The Dramatic Works of Shakespeare* (London, 1838), Thomas Campbell asserted that

> during one-half of the play, we have a disagreeable female character in that of Beatrice. Her portrait, I may be told, is deeply drawn, and minutely finished. It is; and so is that of Benedick, who is entirely her counterpart, except that he is less disagreeable. But the best drawn portraits by the finest masters may be admirable in execution, though unpleasant to contemplate, and Beatrice's portrait is in this category. She is a tartar, by Shakespeare's own showing, and, if a natural woman, is not a pleasing representative of her sex. In befriending Hero, she almost reconciles us to her, but not entirely; for a good heart, that shows itself only on extraordinary occasions, is no sufficient atonement for a bad temper, which Beatrice evidently shows. . . .

In the estimation of Charles Cowden Clarke, Thomas Campbell deserved to be pilloried for denouncing Beatrice as 'an odious woman'. Writing in *Shakespeare Characters: Chiefly Those Subordinate* (London, 1863), the ever-earnest Clarke depicted the heroine as

> one of those who wear their characters inside out. They have no

reserves with society, for they require none. They may, perhaps, presume upon, or rather forget they possess a mercurial temperament, which, when unreined, is apt to start from its course and inconvenience their fellow-travellers; but such a propensity is not an 'odious' one – it is not hateful. . . . [Beatrice] is warm-hearted, generous; has a noble contempt of baseness of every kind; is wholly untinctured with jealousy; is the first to break out into invective when her cousin Hero is treated in that scoundrel manner by her affianced husband at the very altar, and even makes it a *sine qua non* with Benedick to prove his love for herself by challenging the traducer of her cousin. . . .

. . . And here again, it is impossible to forego a passing remark upon the generous, indeed, the chivalrous conduct of Shakespeare in portraying his heroines. Of all the writers that ever existed, no one ought to stand so high in the love and gratitude of women as he. He has indeed been their champion, their laureate, their brother, their friend. He has been the man to lift them from a state of vassalage and degradation, wherein they were the mere toys, when not the she-serfs, of a sensual tyranny; and he has asserted their prerogative, as intellectual creatures, to be the companions (in the best sense,) the advisers, the friends, the equals of men. He has endowed them with the true spirit of Christianity and brotherly love, 'enduring all things, forgiving all things, hoping all things'; and it is no less remarkable, that with a prodigality of generosity, he has not unfrequently placed the heroes in his stories at a disadvantage with them. Observe, for instance, the two characters of Hero and Claudio in this very play. She is the absolute perfection of sweetness and generosity, quenching in forgiveness all the injuries she has received, and bestowing her heart and confidence where she had every reason to be mistrustful. Claudio, on the other hand, is a selfish manoeuvrer. He tells the prince that he is in love with Hero, but he opens the conversation about her by inquiring of him whether Signior Leonato *has a son*; he had an eye to the cash first, and then the girl, and the circumstance of her being an only child confirms him in his suit. Claudio is a fellow of no nobleness of character, for instead of being the last, he is the first to believe his mistress guilty of infidelity towards him, and he then adopts the basest and the most brutal mode of punishment by casting her off at the very altar. Genuine love is incapable of revenge of any sort, that I assume to be a truism, still less of a concocted and refined revenge. Claudio is a scoundrel in grain.

In the same year that Clarke was extolling Shakespeare's portrayal of women, an American scholar named Richard Grant White was proffering what would become a widely accepted perspective on the title of *Much Ado About Nothing*. In an introduction to the play in his collected edition of the *Works of William Shakespeare* (Boston, 1863), White said:

> We call this play *Much Ado about Nothing*; but it seems clear to me that Shakespeare and his contemporaries called it *Much Ado about Noting*; a pun being intended between 'nothing' and 'noting', which were then pronounced alike, and upon which pun depends by far the more important significance of the title. . . . Balthazar uses the words 'note', 'notes', and 'noting', and Don Pedro replies, 'Note, notes, forsooth, and *nothing*'. Here, if 'nothing' were pronounced *nothing*, the Prince might as well have said 'any thing'; but both quarto and folio give him his pun as well as his jeer. . . .
>
> But as to the significance of the title. The play is *Much Ado about Nothing* only in a very vague and general sense, but *Much ado about Noting* in one especially apt and descriptive; for the much ado is produced entirely by noting. It begins with the noting of the Prince and Claudio, first by Antonio's man, and then by Borachio, who reveals their conference to John; it goes on with Benedick noting the Prince, Leonato, and Claudio in the garden, and again with Beatrice noting Margaret and Ursula in the same place; the incident upon which its action turns is the noting of Borachio's interview with Margaret by the Prince and Claudio; and finally, the incident which unravels the plot is the noting of Borachio and Conrade by the Watch. That this sense, 'to observe', 'to watch', was one in which 'note' was commonly used, is quite needless to show by reference to the literature and the lexicographers of Shakespeare's day. . . .

A little more than a decade later, with words that echoed the remarks of both Thomas Campbell and Anna Brownell Jameson, the German critic G. G. Gervinus reflected on the aftermath of 'the heartless scene which Claudio prepares for Hero in the church'. In *Shakespeare Commentaries*, a work translated by F. E. Burnett (London, 1877), Gervinus observed that

> . . . Beatrice places before Benedick the cruel choice between her esteem and love and his connection with his friend. His great confidence in her, and in *her* unshaken confidence in Hero, lead him to make his difficult decision, in which he acts with vigour and prudence, very differently to Claudio in his difficulties. Beatrice, the untamed colt, learns at the same time how the most masculine woman cannot dispense with assistance in certain cases; she has moreover seen her Benedick in a position in which he responds to her ideal of a man, in whom mirth and seriousness should be justly blended. Even Schlegel considered it well-conceived that Shakespeare, in order to prevent

these friends of mirth from being confounded with jesters by profession, brought them to a point upon which they understood no trifling. . . . Benedick goes off the stage with a confession of his giddiness, but it is a giddiness overcome, and we have no reason to be anxious either for the constancy or peaceableness of this pair. The poet has bestowed upon them two names of happy augury.

Shortly after Gervinus' book appeared in English, Edward Dowden published *Shakspere* (London, 1877), which included an eloquent reminder that

Much Ado about Nothing was popular on the stage in Shakspere's day, and has sustained its reputation. Its variety, ranging from almost burlesque to almost tragedy, and from the euphuistic speech of courtiers to the blundering verbosity of clowns, has contributed to the success of the play. The chief persons, Hero and Claudio, Beatrice and Benedick, are contrasted pairs. Hero's character is kept subdued and quiet in tone, to throw out the force and colour of the character of Beatrice; she is gentle, affectionate, tender, and if playful, playful in a gentle way. If our interest in Hero were made very strong, the pain of her unmerited shame and suffering would be too keen. And Claudio is far from being a lover like Romeo; his wooing is done by proxy, and he does not sink under the anguish of Hero's disgrace and supposed death. Don John, the villain of the piece, is a melancholy egoist, who looks sourly on all the world, and has a special grudge against his brother's young favourite Claudio. The chief force of Shakspere in the play comes out in the characters of Benedick and Beatrice. They have not a touch of misanthropy, nor of sentimentality, but are thoroughly healthy and hearty human creatures: at first a little too much self-pleased, but framed by-and-by to be entirely pleased with one another. The thoughts of each from the first are preoccupied with the other, but neither will put self-esteem to the hazard of a rebuke by making the first advances in love; it only needs, however, that this danger should be removed for the pair to admit the fact that nature has made them over against one another – as their significant names suggest – for man and wife. The flouting of Benedick by Beatrice reminds us of scenes between an earlier pair of lovers, Rosaline and Berowne, in *Love's Labour's Lost*. The trick which is played upon the lovers to bring them together is one of those frauds practised upon self-love which appear in several of the comedies of the period. But neither is an egoist except in a superficial way. Beatrice is filled with generous indignation against the wrongers of her cousin, and she inspires Benedick to become (not without a touch of humorous self-consciousness) champion of the cause. Dogberry and Verges, as well as Beatrice and Benedick, are creations of Shakspere. The blundering watchmen of the time are a source of fun with several Elizabethan playwrights; but Dogberry and good Verges are the princes of blundering and incapable officials. It is a charming incongruity to find, while Leonato rages and Benedick offers his challenge, that the solemn ass Dogberry is the one to unravel the tangled threads of their fate.

For the Danish scholar Georg Brandes – in *William Shakespeare: A Critical Study*, a collection of essays translated by William Archer *et al.* (London, 1898) – the heart of *Much Ado About Nothing* was the coupling of Benedick and Beatrice.

. . . In virtue of a profound and masterly psychological observation, Shakespeare presently makes these two fall suddenly in love with each other, over head and ears, for no better reason than that their friends persuade Benedick that Beatrice is secretly pining for love of him, and Beatrice that Benedick is mortally enamoured of her, accompanying this information with high-flown eulogies of both. Their thoughts were already occupied with each other; and now the amatory fancy flames forth in both of them all the more strongly, because it has so long been banked down. And here, where everything was of his own invention and he could move quite freely, Shakespeare has with delicate ingenuity brought the pair together, not by means of empty words, but in a common cause, Beatrice's first advance to Benedick taking place in the form of an appeal to him for chivalrous intervention in behalf of her innocent cousin.

The reversal in the mutual relations of Benedick and Beatrice is, moreover, highly interesting in so far as it is probably the first instance of anything like careful character-development which we have as yet encountered in any single play of Shakespeare's. In the earlier comedies there was nothing of the kind, and the chronicle-plays afforded no opportunity for it. . . . And the real substance of the play lies not in the plot from which it takes its name, but in the relation between these two characters, freely invented by Shakespeare.

With a wilful perversity that mimicked the characters he found most intriguing in *Much Ado About Nothing*, the Irish playwright and critic George Bernard Shaw refused to admit that he was impressed by the same qualities in them that less prepossessing critics of the comedy thought to be the secret of their charm. Thus, in a review that appeared in a London newspaper on 16 February 1898 and was later collected in a volume entitled *Our Theatre in the Nineties* (London, 1932), he began:

The main pretension in *Much Ado* is that Benedick and Beatrice are exquisitely witty and amusing persons. They are, of course, nothing of the sort. Benedick's pleasantries might pass at a sing-song in a public-house parlor; but a gentleman rash enough to venture on them in even the very mildest £52-a-year suburban imitation of polite society today would assuredly never be invited again. From his first joke, 'Were you in doubt, sir, that you asked her?' to his last, 'There is no staff more reverend than one tipped with horn', he is not a wit, but a blackguard [a coarse, scurrilous reviler and ne'er-do-well]. He is not Shakespear's only failure in that genre. It took the Bard a long time to grow out of the provincial conceit that made him so fond of exhibiting his accomplishments as a master of gallant badinage. . . . When he at last got conviction of sin, and saw this sort of levity in its proper light, he made masterly amends by presenting the blackguard *as* a blackguard in the person of Lucio in *Measure for Measure*. Lucio, as a character study, is worth forty Benedicks. . . . His obscenity is not only inoffensive, but irresistibly entertaining, because it is drawn with perfect skill, offered at its true value, and given its proper interest, without any complicity of the author in its lewdness. . . .

Precisely the same thing, in the tenderer degree of her sex, is true of Beatrice. In her character of professed wit she has only one subject, and that is the subject which a really witty woman never jests about, because it is too serious a matter to a woman to be made light of without indelicacy. Beatrice jests about it for the sake of the indelicacy. There is only one thing worse than the Elizabethan 'merry gentleman', and that is the Elizabethan 'merry lady'.

Why is it then that we still want to see Benedick and Beatrice, and that our most eminent actors and actresses still want to play them? . . . Simply because [like Mozart in *Don Giovanni*, Shakespear] clothed [the characters' thoughts] with wonderful music, which turned . . . worthless words . . . into a magical human drama of moods and transitions of feeling. . . . Paraphrase the encounters of Benedick and Beatrice in the style of a bluebook, carefully preserving every idea they present, and it will become apparent to the most infatuated Shakespearean that they contain at best nothing out of the common in thought or wit, and at worse a good deal of vulgar naughtiness. . . . Not until the Shakespearean music is added by replacing the paraphrase with the original line does the enchantment begin. When a flower-girl tells a coster [costermonger, fruit vendor] to hold his jaw, for nobody is listening to him, and he retorts, 'Oh, you're there, are you, you beauty?' they reproduce the wit of Beatrice and Benedick exactly. But put it this way. 'I wonder that you will still be talking, Signior Benedick: nobody marks you.' 'What! my dear Lady Disdain, are you yet living?' You are miles from costerland at once. When I tell you that Benedick and the coster are equally poor in thought, Beatrice and the flower-girl equally vulgar in repartee, you reply that I might as well tell you that a nightingale's love is no higher than a cat's. Which is exactly what I do tell you, though the nightingale is the better musician. You will admit, perhaps, that the love of the worst human singer in the world is accompanied by a higher degree of intellectual consciousness than that of the most ravishingly melodious nightingale. Well, in just the same way, there are plenty of quite second-rate writers who are abler thinkers and wits than William, though they are unable to weave his magic into the expression of their thoughts.

Among the early twentieth-century commentators on *Much Ado About Nothing*, few were as incisive as Sir Arthur Quiller-Couch. In an introduction he supplied to the *New Shakespeare* text of the play (Cambridge, 1923) under the editorship of John Dover Wilson, Quiller-Couch defended 'Lady Disdain' from some of her nineteenth-century detractors.

It is, after all, pedantic and pickthank work to belittle Beatrice's part in the play. She may not, herself, achieve the solution, or see the way to it: but emotionally she dominates it with her great loyalty, and from the moment she takes charge we know that she will win somehow. Her cast of the die is not a light one, for she truly loves Benedick. To Shakespeare and to his Elizabethan audience her 'Kill Claudio' was probably a far more dangerous, more fatal, cast than in our day we readily understand; the obligation of a lover to his mistress being, in comparison with any convention of our own times, so far weaker than that of a man to his friend. This has to be allowed for if we would understand Beatrice's strength – and Benedick's devotion.

'Kill Claudio.' These words *nail* the play, and may well seem overpoweringly too strong to be converted by Comedy into 'hey nonny nonny'. But we are always lost with Shakespeare if we attempt to define Comedy in categories deduced from Menander or Plautus before him, or from Calderon or Molière or Congreve or Sheridan after him. All Shakespeare's 'comedies' lie close to sorrow; close at least to heart-ache, sometimes close to heart-break.

In *The Shakespearean Tempest* (London, 1932), G. Wilson Knight reinforced Quiller-Couch's insistence that '*Much Ado* treads close, all the while, upon tragedy.' Knight admitted that a lot of the play 'is given over to light-hearted wit'.

But Benedick and Beatrice are more than jesters: their wit is often merry, sometimes bitter, but never scatterbrained. When the action becomes tragic, they know how to act. And though they scoff at love, when love overtakes them, they know how to love.

For Mark Van Doren, writing on *Much Ado About Nothing* in
his one-volume study *Shakespeare* (New York, 1939), the most
'convenient starting-point for any discussion' of the play was Dr
Johnson, whose remark about the differences between Shakespeare's work in serious and lighter veins helped explain why the
'comedy of Benedick and Beatrice is so flexible, so instinctive',
while the 'tragedy of Claudio and Hero is so strangely stiff'.

'Much Ado' begins and ends with Beatrice and Benedick, whose prose
thus describes the circumference of Shakespeare's comic circle. The
first interesting thing of which we hear is the 'merry war' between the
two; 'they never meet', Leonato explains to Don Pedro's messenger
whom Beatrice has so much bewildered, 'but there's a skirmish of wit
between them' (I, i, 64–5). . . .
    Benedick and Beatrice are to be induced to fall in love with each
other – or, since they are already in love, to confess that they are – by
overhearing conversations prepared for the purpose. . . . Benedick
and Beatrice, in other words, are to be turned into lovers by hearing
themselves talked about – a common occurrence in the world, but
they are not common. The ruse is sure to succeed, we want to see it
succeed, and the play pauses while we do. There is no attempt on
Shakespeare's part to complicate the business with plausible delays.
The one charming scene follows hard upon the other; the lovers are
converted schematically in turn; and a brisk vocabulary of sporting
terms brightens and speeds this portion of the play. Benedick had
likened Claudio, jealous of Don Pedro, to a poor hurt fowl creeping
into sedges (II, i, 209–10), but he himself is now a fish on a hook (II, iii,
118–19), a fowl to be stalked (II, iii, 99–100); and Beatrice is a golden
fish to be angled for (III, i, 26–7), a bird to be limed (III, i, 104), a
lapwing who runs close by the ground to hear the ladies' conference
(III, i, 24–5), a coy wild haggard of the rock (III, i, 35–6). The tone of
comedy would seem then to be firmly set, not only by the prattle but by
the kind of brittle action that belongs to comedy everywhere. . . .
    Meanwhile [we are introduced to] Dogberry, Verges, and the
Watch. If nothing else had directed the audience how to feel, and
whether to feel deeply, the ineffable presence of these simpletons
would have done so. Only a comedy could contain such harmless and
irrelevant officials, such senseless and fit men for constables of a
solemn watch. Their dunderheadedness remains indefinable; their
nature is as resistant to analysis as that of the somehow sublime
Bottom; and yet their destiny on any stage would be as clear as day.
Their minds are muddy but their course is charted. They will blunder
about in their tedious and stubborn 'vigitance' till they have made all
well. Fools like that cannot fail. What the wisdoms of gentlemen

would never discover they bring to light, mopping about with their hiccups and their lanterns, and stumbling into the grace of our loud laughter. Benedick and Beatrice draw a clear circle of wit about the play to keep its tragedy in place. Dogberry and his fellows are a coarse tallow candle burning near the center, keeping the comic peace.

Talk is the business of 'Much Ado'. Most of its merit is therefore in its prose, compared with which the verse is generally insignificant. . . . Beatrice can scarcely be imagined in love with a man who is a poet all the time. Benedick never is. Finding himself in love he tries to show it in rhyme, but he can think of nothing better than 'baby' to go with 'lady', 'horn' with 'scorn', and 'fool' with 'school'. 'Very ominous endings', he concludes. 'No, I was not born under a rhyming planet, nor I cannot woo in festival terms' (V, ii, 41–3). He is of course not far distant from Hotspur, who with him helps to say for Shakespeare that verse, at any rate for the time being, seems limited as a channel when the full tide of life comes pouring through.

The prose of Benedick and Beatrice is a brilliant brocade of artifice. But its counterpoint of antithesis and epithet is natural to two such desperate defenders of pride against the leveling guns of love, of personality against passion. It is a logical language for persons who seldom say what they mean, and who, since they love nothing better than talk, must talk always for effect. It is the inevitable idiom for lovers who would deny their love.

Donald A. Stauffer agreed with Van Doren about Benedick and Beatrice's rejection of any role for themselves that had been predefined by convention. In *Shakespeare's World of Images: The Development of his Moral Idea* (Bloomington, Indiana, 1949), Stauffer argued that the dramatist was

no believer in the classroom. Copybook maxims, admirable as they may be, are ineffective. The only school is experience, and axioms are proved upon the pulses. Believing this, Shakespeare finds the drama a most excellent moral instrument, since in the drama characters reach conclusions by putting their various conflicting beliefs into action. Their passions and philosophies are forced to work out practicable solutions, in conflict with a larger world and with unsympathetic alien forces or personalities. . . .

The main interest of [*Much Ado About Nothing*], then, starts in the world of common sense. Raillery and wit will protect light hearts. 'There is measure in everything', says Beatrice, and lest that remark on moderation sound immoderately serious, she makes it into a pun and dances out her conviction. The lovers are too clear-eyed not to be self-critical. . . .

[As for the object of Beatrice's affection,] the integrity and sincerity of his love, based so broadly, make him in the end impervious to mockery, and it is 'Benedick, the married man' who, after kissing Beatrice heartily, replies in all surety, 'I'll tell thee what, Prince: a college of wit-crackers cannot flout me out of my humour', who demands music and dancing, and who advises Pedro: 'Prince, thou art sad. Get thee a wife!' In the wedding of Benedick and Beatrice, humor has been married to love on both sides of the family. Since humor presupposes a greater consciousness of the world and of one's self, the wedding promises more stability and happiness than in any of Shakespeare's previous imaginings. 'Man is a giddy thing', says Benedick, 'and this is my conclusion.' Man is less giddy, surer in his moral sense, in direct proportion to his awareness of his own giddiness.

In *Shakespeare and Elizabethan Poetry* (London, 1951), a study of the playwright's art in the context of literary and theatrical conventions that informed it, Muriel C. Bradbrook observed that

If *Romeo and Juliet* was a tragedy with its full complement of comedy, and *The Merchant of Venice* a comedy with an infusion of tragic pity and fear, *Much Ado About Nothing* is a comedy of Masks where the deeper issues are overlaid with mirth, and appear only at the climax of the play, the church scene. It is for this reason that so very mechanical a villain as Don John becomes a necessity of the plot. A true villain, like Shylock or Edmund or Richard III, would destroy the comedy: those who protest at the insufficiency of Don John should consider what would happen to the total composition if he were other than he is. . . .

Both Benedick and Beatrice are comic without being ridiculous, and they provide the audience with the same kind of mirth that they are supposed to provide their friends. Their transparent attempts at disguising their feelings under the form of a toothache and a cold in the head, their slight peevishness and their extreme gullibility, Benedick's halting sonnet and February face, and Beatrice's extraordinary taciturnity, allow their friends to tease them, and the audience to indulge that particularly pleasing kind of superiority which arises when one's own predicaments are recognizably displayed in larger forms than life. If the two were not so admirable in all their more important actions – if Benedick were not so honest and soldierly, Beatrice so constant and loyal – there would be a good deal less pleasure in this identification. But to see characters in all other respects heroic reduced to such complete helplessness by Nature's ruthless device for ensuring that 'the world must be peopled' is exhilarating in the extreme. . . . To an age brought up on the Platonic politenesses, such a display of Nature must have been doubly engaging. The frank bawdiness and the human inconsistencies of Benedick and Beatrice must be seen against the proprieties of Valentine and Silvia [in *The Two Gentlemen of Verona*], the stately splendour of Belmont [in *The Merchant of Venice*], to win their full value.

To make the human relationship between two lovers display itself through the wit-combat of courtly love, by the simple process of extending the role of 'unwilling' lover to the [gentleman] as well as the [lady], was a stroke of genius which, once achieved, takes on the appearance of the obvious. To quarrel was the stock recipe for comedy. Beatrice may indeed have owed something to the earlier Kate of *The Taming of the Shrew*, for her wit was certainly more forcible as well as more nimble than stage tradition would allow the court. . . .

[After the aborted wedding] Claudio's flippancy about the pitiful insults of Leonato and Antonio (though he behaved admirably in their presence) and his readiness to take a second bride in reparation for the first create difficulties for the modern reader where they are not likely to have existed for an Elizabethan. Leonato's challenge in the presence of the Prince was a social outrage which would have landed the greatest nobleman in prison (Benedick draws Claudio aside to make his defiance). As for the marriage, it may rank with other fictions; by this time the audience and everyone but Claudio can see the happy conclusion, and to treat Claudio as an independent character at this point, and upbraid him for his failure to lodge an objection – like Bassanio [in *The Merchant of Venice*] when he was asked for the ring – is to abandon all sense of theatrical propriety and comic decorum for the sake of a psychological consistency which would defeat its own ends. Claudio cannot now be made into a tragic character or allowed more than a pretty lyric by way of remorse. In the church scene he had spoken out, and spoken the words which his earlier character warranted. There is no further role for him, or for Hero, save to make a pair in the final dance. They each sink back into the kind of formality which the plot allowed, and the conclusion belongs to Benedick and Beatrice. . . .

In both *Much Ado* and *The Merchant of Venice* the clowns are ingeniously but loosely attached to the main plot by a few lines of intrigue – Gobbo acts as go-between for Jessica, Dogberry serves to keep Borachio in safe custody till Act V. Their real function is to act as parody or, in musical analogy, as undersong. . . . Dogberry and Verges are clearly reincarnations of Gobbo and his father, and their role of comic policeman was one of the oldest and most assured cards in popular comedy. But their parts are confined to scenes immediately preceding and following the church scene, where the relief of their broad comedy is most tellingly juxtaposed with the straightforward drama of the main plot. As interludes between the wit combats of

Benedick and Beatrice they would have been unnecessary.

In *The Meaning of Shakespeare* (Chicago, 1951) Harold C. Goddard essayed to derive epistemological implications from the title of *Much Ado About Nothing*.

If I draw a circle on the sand or on a piece of paper, instantly the spatial universe is divided into two parts, the finite portion within the circle (or the sphere if we think of it in three dimensions) and the infinite remainder outside of it. Actuality and possibility have a similar relation. Actuality is what is within the circle. However immense it be conceived to be, beyond it extends not merely the infinite but the infinitely infinite realm of what might have been but was not, of what may be but is not. In this realm are all the deeds that were not done when the other choice was made, all the roads that were not traveled when the other fork was taken, all the life that did not come into existence when its seeds failed to germinate. And in it no less is all that still may be: all the possible combinations of chemical elements that have never been made, all the music that is still uncomposed, all the babies that have not yet been born. This is the realm of NOTHING. In one sense it has no existence. In another, existence is nothing without it. . . .

Shakespeare delighted in using the word 'nothing' in this high metaphysical sense. It is easy to see why an artist might. . . .

Now if our eyes are not so dazzled by Beatrice and Benedick and the glitter of their wit, or our risibilities so tickled by Dogberry and his companions, that we cannot attend to the play as a whole, we shall see that it is dedicated to this area of Nothing. It is full of lies, deceptions (innocent, and not so innocent), and imagination, and these things grade into one another as imperceptibly as darkness does into light. Yet, notwithstanding that fact, the extremes – namely, lies and imagination – are seen to be as opposite as night and noon. . . .

The main plot of *Much Ado* is founded on two deceptions. Don John and his fellow-conspirators spread the lie that Hero is false to Claudio, when she is really true to him. Friar Francis gives it out that Hero is dead, when she is still alive. The first deception is false in fact and false in purpose and intention. It is a lie in the fullest sense. The second deception is false in fact, but is imaginatively and symbolically true. The Hero whom Claudio maligned *is* dead, never to revive. Out of the illusion of her death a new Hero emerges not only in herself but in Claudio's heart and imagination. And so the illusion turns into fact, and looking retrospectively we see there was no deception. . . .

Much Ado About Nothing is saturated with this idea of the power of Nothing (of the creative ingredient of the imagination, that is) to alter the nature of things for good or ill, for, as Shakespeare's History Plays so abundantly show, fear and hate, as well as faith and love, have the capacity to attract facts to them and so, temporarily at least, to confirm their own hypotheses. But the changes fear and hate effect are destructive and pointed in the direction of chaos, whereas imagination integrates, makes for synthesis and reconciliation of clashing interests. The play is full of phrases that imply this fluidity of facts, their willingness to flow for good or evil into any mold the human mind makes for their reception. Antonio brings news to Leonato. 'Are they good?' asks the latter. 'As the event stamps them', the former replies. . . .

But it is the underplot, or, as we might call it, the second main plot, that confirms the theme and proves that we are not reading things into Shakespeare's play in making it center about Nothing.

Beatrice and Benedick are in love with each other without knowing it. Their friends contrive to have them overhear conversations in which Benedick listens in one scene to reports of Beatrice's hopeless passion for him and she listens in the next to similar accounts of his for her and, in addition, to condemnations of her pride and scorn. The effect in both cases is instantaneous. . . . Where faith in the fact can help create the fact, says William James, it would be an insane logic that would deny our right to put our trust in it. If the friends of Beatrice and Benedick had concocted their whole plot out of nothing, as Don John did his against Hero, their means of bringing the two together would not have been 'justified'. But sensing the existence of the seed they brought just enough 'nothing' to bear on it in the form of imaginative sunshine to bring it to the flower of actuality, to give to that 'airy nothing' a local habitation and a name. . . .

And so, paradoxically, *Much Ado* is in the end a sort of repudiation of itself and of the very thing that has given it its immense theatrical reputation. And that, in turn, is our excuse in discussing it for stressing a single word in its title at the price of saying little about the pair who always packed the theater in Shakespeare's own day, whom actors and actresses will long love to impersonate, and about whom so many critics have had so many witty things to say. . . . [Of these critics, one of the cleverest] expresses the hope that the very thought of Benedick covered Shakespeare with shame in later years. But so far from having to be contrite, my guess would be that, quite without the benefit of Bernard Shaw and without going to the extreme of his dissenting opinion, the creator of this incomparable pair was perfectly aware, at the time he made them, of the superficiality of their wit and the shallowness of most of their talk, however brilliant the style in which it is dressed.

Finally, it remains for Dogberry and his fellows, who to some readers are the top of the play, to put the last seal of approval on this way of interpreting it. Dogberry likes to hear himself talk as well as Beatrice and Benedick do, and he, too, is interested in words for their own sake. The parody is apparent. Verbality for verbality, loquacity for loquacity, it sets us wondering how much there is to choose between the repartee of the wits and the mental meanderings of the constable, between the polishing of the King's English by Beatrice and Benedick and the murdering of it by Dogberry. The latter has at any rate contributed more than the former to posterity's stock of familiar quotations.

And the realistic clowning of this part of the story ties in with the theme as well as with the plot of the rest. What culture could not compass, the dumb luck or instinct of the unlettered brings to light. Here sheer witlessness becomes the highest wit, the ridiculous almost sublime; here dulness is sublimated into philosophy. It is all a perfect commentary on the antithesis drawn by Dostoevsky between intelligence and stupidity. 'The stupider one is', says Ivan Karamozov, whose prime gift was intelligence, 'the closer one is to reality. The stupider one is, the clearer one is. Stupidity is brief and artless, while intelligence wriggles and hides itself. Intelligence is a knave, but stupidity is honest and straightforward.' How in keeping with this Shakespeare is in having these plain watchmen in the routine performance of their duty uncover the truth that has evaded the clever and sophisticated. Dogberry himself is loquacious and inane, anything but 'straightforward', it would seem. Yet he is straightforward in Dostoevsky's sense, right on the fundamentals, that is, and when it comes to these he can hit the nail on the head. 'Write God first', he commands. And to Borachio he says, 'I do not like thy look', which, while it may not constitute legal evidence, does credit to his perception. His instant distrust of the man is the counterpart of Beatrice's instant faith in her cousin. Shakespeare even imparts to some of his most muddleheaded blunders overmeanings that seem like nature uttering unconscious wisdom through his mouth. 'Master constable', says the Sexton at the end of the preliminary examination, 'let these men be bound.' 'Let them be opinioned', says Dogberry, rejecting as not dignified enough for his office the Sexton's simpler word. 'Opinioned': is it a slanting glance at the main theme of the play? It might well be. To be a sophisticated man is to be opinioned, and to be opinioned is to be bound. It is the stupid and the imaginative, at the extremes, who are unopinioned and therefore free, free like the Creator and like the creator of the characters in this play, to make something out of NOTHING.

Two years after the publication of Harold Goddard's book, T. W. Craik offered a more mundane exposition of the 'Nothing' in

Much Ado About Nothing in the 1953 volume of *Scrutiny*. For Craik,

> The play is, in a sense, a comedy of errors. The theme is 'The course of true love never did run smooth', and it is by errors, either self-created or the fruit of deliberate villainy, that love's course is impeded. Don John twice promotes error by exploiting the deceitful possibilities of appearances (at the masked ball and at Hero's window). The stage technique of the play, by employing at least five overhearings, one apparent disguise (Margaret's) and several masked encounters, underlines the theme of errors springing from appearances. The thematic connexion between the two plots is that both are love-plots hindered by the deceit of appearances: from evidence which only 'seems' satisfactory, Claudio wrongly deduces that Hero's virtue is only 'seeming'; the other plot deals with Benedick who 'seems' a woman-hater and with Beatrice who 'seems' unmarriageable, while each 'seems' to be particularly averse to the other.
>
> It is my contention that the title, *Much Ado about Nothing*, relates to this tangled web of errors and in particular to those of the fourth and fifth acts.

For A. P. Rossiter, as for Craik, 'Deception by appearances in *love* is patently what most of *Much Ado* is "about".' In *Angel with Horns and Other Shakespeare Lectures* (London, 1961), Rossiter says:

> If I were to answer in a word what the Benedick and Beatrice plot turns on, I should say *misprision*. Benedick and Beatrice misapprehend both each other *and* themselves; each misprizes the other sex, and misapprehends the possibility of a complete agreement between them, as individuals, on what causes that misprision: love of freedom and a superior conceit of themselves as 'wise' where others are fools: as 'free' and 'untied' and as having a right to enjoy kicking other people's traces. They fancy they are quite different *from*, and quite indifferent *to* each other. Indifferent they are not; and the audience is 'superior' in seeing their humours: and in being aware that the opposite to love (as passionate, obsessive interest) is not hate (another passionate interest), but cool or unnoting indifference. How little Beatrice's 'disdain' for Benedick is truly disdainful is shown in her immediately thinking of him as a measure for Don John.
>
> Because the mind of each runs on the other, they can both be simply gulled by hearsay; provided that it is overheard and includes the sort of freedom of comment we all use on absent friends: mildly malicious in tone, unspiteful in intent, and near enough true on their recognizable oddities and shortcomings. The overhearers, for all their sharpness of wit, know that the *comments* have some truth, and

naturally accept the rest as also true. Thus the introduction of love-thoughts into both results from a species of misapprehension. They take the *sense* of the words, but totally fail to apprehend their *intention*. The two gulling scenes belong to the comedy of advertisement. Even the advertisers' nice touches of flattery are not lacking. The criticism is spiced with proper appreciation, as when Don Pedro hints – a very subtle inducement – that he would quite like to have Beatrice himself.

That the 'main' plot of Hero and Claudio turns on misapprehension leading to the misprision of violent misprizing, is too obvious to need commentary: but much of the play's total effect hangs on the structural mainness of this plot being displaced. As in Mannerist pictures sometimes, the emphasis is made to fall on what appears structurally to be a corner. This displaced emphasis helps to maintain the sense that the 'Ado' is about 'Nothing' (it is only through the distortion that reading gives, that much attention is given to the 'character' of Claudio). . . .

Much Ado is not a 'serious' play: it is 'limited' in managing potentially serious matters with a deft nonchalance which passes by the possibility of some being sharp things that might cut. At the same time, it is a play full of themes which are to have sufficiently serious explorations and consequences in Shakespeare's later work. Othello's situation, for example, is a variant of Claudio's; just as Claudio's behaviour to Hero is a sketch of Bertram's [in *All's Well That Ends Well*]. . . .

Much Ado is a fantasy of equivocal appearances in a glittering world of amiable fools of all sorts. As naturally as Italians talk Italian, the Messinans talk 'equivocal'; but their 'double tongues' are as harmless as those of the 'spotted snakes' in *A Midsummer Night's Dream*. This equivocal quality, moreover, is deftly restricted to appearances: there are only the slightest touches of suggestion of any intrinsic equivocation in things themselves (in love, for example). Ambivalence is not a term to apply here.

Just how the dramatist manipulates those 'appearances' in *Much Ado* is the subject of *Shakespeare's Comedies* (Oxford, 1960), a study in which Bertrand Evans asserts that

No [play] of Shakespeare's is more aptly named than *Much Ado About Nothing*, all the ado of which, from our vantage-point, is indeed about nothing. The Prince of Arragon and his party arrive to visit the Governor of Messina. If guests and hosts saw with our eyes, nothing memorable would occur during the visit. Claudio would marry Hero and remain at Messina. The other visitors, including Benedick, would go their way at month's end – unless monotony dispatched them earlier. Beatrice would die an old maid.

But because the inhabitants of the Messinian world do not see with our eyes, monotony finds no time to afflict them. All the action is impelled by a rapid succession of 'practices' [deceptive intrigues] – eight in all, the first of which is introduced at the end of the opening scene, the last exploited in the final moments. These practices are the means by which multiple discrepancies in awareness are created and sustained, some briefly, some over long periods. Sharing the practisers' confidence in each case, we hold advantage over some participants during fourteen of seventeen scenes, and at some time we hold advantage over every named person. Not only heroines and villains – the inveterate practisers in Shakespearian comedy – but very nearly all participants, including old fathers, uncles, and the Friar, take turns at deceiving others; and, conversely, each takes a turn at being deceived. No crowd of characters in a Shakespearian world exhibits more universal predilection for the game, such readiness to exchange and then exchange again the roles of deceiver and deceived. Nor does any play demonstrate more conclusively the dramatist's devotion to situations characterized by exploitable differences in awareness. . . .

At the opening of Act II [for example], we share our vantage-point only with villains, other participants being ignorant both of Don John's threats and of other aspects of the suddenly complex situation. The Prince and Claudio suppose themselves sole proprietors of their innocent plot, not knowing that it has been misunderstood by Leonato and perverted by Don John; Leonato and Hero, believing a false report, are of course ignorant of the Prince's true purpose and know nothing of Don John's malicious interest. . . .

[By] the opening of Act V three large facts, the residue of practices, occupy our minds: that Hero was slandered; that Dogberry is on the way to Leonato's with the truth; that Hero, reported dead, is living. Two secondary facts reside with these: that Benedick and Beatrice were victimized by practices; and that Beatrice has bound Benedick, on his love for her, to kill Claudio. Leonato's ignorance of the first two facts is exploited first, in his long lament for Hero's dishonour. But the centre of attention is Claudio, whose reactions to three moments which the dramatist asks us to anticipate follow in quick succession. These are the moments in which he learns of Hero's 'death', in which he learns of her innocence, and in which he learns of her survival. The most powerful effects of Shakespeare's exploitation of discrepant awareness most commonly occur, first, at the time a participant, acting in ignorance, commits a wrong against another and, second, at the time he learns what he has done. In the scene of denunciation at the altar we have already tasted the first of these fruits. Claudio's successive reactions during Act V together represent the second, and the taste is sour. . . .

[In the play's concluding scene] Leonato's household prepares to work a final practice on the visitors. . . . Here, as usual, the dramatist has not trusted us to guess: we must be told plainly that the 'niece' earlier promised Claudio is Hero herself; the surprise is to be Claudio's, not ours. We are required, in advance of every action, to understand its true nature, and we are not allowed to disregard the advantage we hold. Clear in our facts, then, we are able to observe Claudio objectively. . . . When Hero is unveiled, the sum of his reaction is contained in 'Another Hero!' Shakespeare gives him no more words on the matter, either of love, joy, or apology; his only remaining remarks are directed at Benedick and Beatrice. Viewed from our Olympian height, Claudio's conduct during his journey through several stages of ignorance has hardly appeared heroic. Believing Hero false, he was bestial; believing her dead, he gave her no more thought; learning that she had been true, but still supposing her dead, he compromised his formal expressions of grief with protestations that he should not be blamed; and finally, learning that she is both living and innocent, he is relieved to find that the face behind the veil is not an Ethiope's.

It is the affair of Beatrice and Benedick, though suspended and almost unexploited for two acts, that best sustains the comic spirit during this period and finally lifts it for a joyful close. . . . Awareness of their state brings warmth and mirth even to those moments which demand grief and anger for the main action. . . . Unlike Claudio, both Benedick and Beatrice shine as gloriously in their ignorance as in their awareness. Each was won to love the other through a humane and noble sympathy which was not dimmed but made more luminous by error. Theirs is the final misapprehension to be cleared away, and when they perceive how they have been gulled, the revelation makes no difference in their love. . . .

A few years after Evans's analysis of the dramatic ironies that control an audience's responses to the comedy, J. R. Mulryne examined its larger structural patterns in *Shakespeare: 'Much Ado About Nothing'* (London, 1965). According to Mulryne:

The overall design of *Much Ado* is not difficult to grasp. Basically the play is composed of three movements, the first (and longest) establishing the love-relationship between Benedick and Beatrice and between Claudio and Hero; the second portraying a crisis (when Don John's treachery causes the repudiation of Hero and her 'death'); and the third providing a resolution, as the deceit is exposed and a 'new' Hero marries a remorseful Claudio and Beatrice Benedick. The comic thesis of the play in other words takes the form of love begun, love challenged and love confirmed: we are first made sympathetically aware of the love of two young couples (one pair willingly acknowledging love's claims, the other reluctantly); next, a malicious intrigue threatens to wreck all thoughts of joy and love; and finally life sails out into the clear once more, with a new strength and promise of endurance.

Each of Shakespeare's mature comedies holds in some measure a threat to the happiness of the figures for whom our sympathy is invited; in *Much Ado* our sense of comic triumph, of 'pleasurable reassurance' that 'all shall be well', is strong in proportion to the prominence given to the possibility of disaster . . . And so, when the play ends in double marriage (or rather in the dance that symbolises the concord of marriage) we enjoy vicariously a sense of good now established all the more firmly and valuably by virtue of the testing adversity to which it has been subjected . . .

This 'adversity' includes the 'deep grief' that threatens to drown the play in sorrow after Claudio rejects his betrothed at the altar in IV.i. When Hero's father describes her as having 'fall'n/Into a pit of ink', says Mulryne,

the metaphors of 'tainted flesh', 'the wide sea' and 'cleansing' do not recall several of Shakespeare's greatest plays (notably of course *Macbeth* and *Hamlet*) merely by chance. For Shakespeare is here allowing this play to ride as close as he dare to the borders of tragedy; and his purpose evokes the appropriate language. If we are to appreciate the full richness of the *Much Ado* experience we must be prepared to give due emphasis to this 'tragic' aspect; no other comedy embraces anything like such a range of emotional states, from the wholly carefree to the desperately grieved.

But is the play's mixture of moods and modes a successful one? For John Wain, applying 'The Shakespearian Lie-Detector' to *Much Ado about Nothing* in *Critical Quarterly* (1967), the answer is 'not entirely'.

Much Ado about Nothing is a play that might well halt the critic of Shakespeare in his amble through the plays, in much the same way as *Hamlet* halts him: a strong, buoyant, uneven piece of work. It could not possibly be called a failure, and yet it could not be described as a total success either. I believe the play has interesting things to tell us about the nature of Shakespeare's impulses as an artist, and in particular about the state of his mind in the closing months of the sixteenth century. . . .

. . . As an artist, [Shakespeare] is more often commanded by his imagination than commanding it. He is instinctive, spontaneous, lacking in the effrontery which can simulate inspiration in those parts of a large construction where it fails to come naturally. Where

Shakespeare fails, he makes no attempt to varnish the failure. He is always doing several things at once, and if he loses interest in one of them, he leaves it frankly as a mock-up. But always for a good reason. He worked at speed, had to make a rapid choice of materials, and when a situation, or a character, fails to come to life under his hand, the fault is rarely – I think, never – the poet's. Some surfaces will not take a mural; some clay resists life; some situations, which looked neat enough in the blue-print, disintegrate under the weight of actuality and energy that Shakespeare cannot help putting into them.

Shakespeare, to put it in a more pedestrian way, was not a good hack-writer. He lacked the unvarying professional skill that can arrange even the poorest material into a pleasing shape, keeping its weaknesses out of sight ... As a result, the typical Shakespearean failure is a play at once lop-sided and brilliant – so brilliant that the lop-sidedness does not keep it from being acted and read ...

Like virtually every play of Shakespeare's, *Much Ado* is written in a mixture of prose and verse, and one of the first things we notice when we look at it attentively is that the prose is everywhere more memorable and satisfying than the verse, which at its best is workmanlike and vivacious, but never more, and at its all too frequent worst, weak, monotonous and verbose.

The nature of the malaise is clear enough. The verse is weak because the verse-plot is weak. It was Shakespeare's custom, in comedy, to use a verse-plot alongside a prose-plot. In *As You Like It* and *Twelfth Night*, the two are of equal ease and vivacity... But in those plays, as in *A Midsummer Night's Dream*, whose moonlit atmosphere effortlessly embraces a prose-plot and a tight web of three verse-plots, Shakespeare's imagination was equally involved in all parts of the play. In *Much Ado*, it was not. The verse-plot fails to convince or interest us because it failed similarly with Shakespeare himself...

Why did the Hero-and-Claudio plot go so dead on its author? The answer is not easy to find. Because it is not, *per se*, an unconvincing story. Psychologically, it is real enough. .... It begins to look as if the trouble lay somewhere in the presentation of Claudio.

This young man, according to the requirements of the story, has only to be presented as a blameless lover, wronged and misled through no fault of his own; convinced that his love is met with deception and ingratitude, he has no choice but to repudiate the match; later, when everything comes to light, the story requires him to show sincere penitence and willingness to make amends, finally breaking out into joy when his love is restored to him. On the face of it, there seems to be no particular difficulty. But Shakespeare goes about it, from the start, in a curiously left-handed fashion. First we have the business of the wooing by proxy. Claudio confesses to Don Pedro his love for Hero, and Don Pedro at once offers, without waiting to be asked, to take advantage of the forthcoming masked ball to engage the girl's attention, propose marriage while pretending to be Claudio, and then speak to her father on his behalf. It is not clear why he feels called upon to do this, any more than it is clear why Claudio, a Florentine, should address Don Pedro, a Spaniard, as 'my liege' and treat him as a feudal overlord. . . .

The Hero-and-Claudio plot [in short] is a ruin. And what ruined it, in my opinion, was the pull towards psychological realism that seems to have been so strong in Shakespeare's mind at the time. Certainly this made the character of Claudio unworkable, and once that was hopeless it was all hopeless. Because the plot demanded that Claudio should behave ungenerously to a girl he was supposed to love, because Shakespeare could not stick to the chocolate-box conventions but had to go ahead and show Claudio as a real, and therefore necessarily unpleasant, youth, the contradictions grew and grew until they became unsurmountable.

Perhaps so; but what if critics have been incorrect to assume that the 'verse-plot' in a Shakespearean comedy must necessarily be the 'main plot'? What if the playwright self-consciously set out to make the Benedick-and-Beatrice story the central interest in *Much Ado About Nothing*, and devised every aspect of the Claudio and-Hero story (including its less appealing protagonists) to serve the more interesting tale as a dramatic foil? That would seem to be the best way of accounting for the way *Much Ado* fits into what Sherman Hawkins has described as 'The Two Worlds of Shakespearean Comedy' (*Shakespeare Studies*, 1967).

Hawkins begins by summarizing 'The Argument of Comedy', an influential article by Northrop Frye from *English Institute Essays 1948* (New York, 1949). As he lays out his hypothesis, Frye suggests that comedies such as *The Two Gentlemen of Verona*, *A Midsummer Night's Dream*, *The Merchant of Venice*, and *As You Like It* are organized around two discrete settings.

The action begins in a 'normal' world, moves into a 'green' world where the comic resolution is achieved, and then returns to the normal world (though this return is often indicated without being acted out). The drama thus turns on the contrast between two worlds, two orders of experience, two perspectives on reality. . . . The initial action is set in a court or city which is real but long ago or far away. The ruler of the city is a duke, placing this romantic comedy midway between the royalty proper to tragedy and the bourgeoisie proper to satiric comedy like that of Jonson. . . . The hero and heroine are usually of different social or financial standing. They find themselves opposed by an older figure who is parent or prince or both, and sometimes by a law against lovers, as in *Midsummer Night's Dream*. This opposition, like the law which embodies it, is felt to be foolish or tyrannical, but the only way to escape its threat is to leave the old world altogether. For beyond the walls of cities known at least by name to the Elizabethans stretches another and magical world: forests where fairies dance by moonlight, the pastoral landscape where shepherds woo their loves, the beautiful mountain where is a lady richly left, awaiting the right hero. This green world takes on different meanings in the thematic dialectic of each play: it is the order of grace opposed to the old order of law in *Merchant of Venice*, the moonlit world of fancy (in its Elizabethan double meaning of imagination and desire) opposed to Athens, city of reason, in *Midsummer Night's Dream*. But always, it is the world as we wish it were instead of as it is, reality refashioned 'as you like it'. . . .

Frye's green world theory seems to me both true and useful; it isolates a recurring psychological and mythic pattern in Shakespeare's comedies which is clearly deliberate and which helps to account for the perennial fascination of these plays. There is one obvious limitation to the theory, however. It fits only four of the comedies. . . .

. . . [I]t would be surprising if Shakespeare, having constructed half his comedies as variations on a basic pattern, had written all the rest at random. If, on the contrary, he employed another recurring pattern, we might expect it to bear some significant relation of analogy or contrast to the green world motif. What is the essence of that pattern, the basic dramaturgical device? Clearly, the double setting: the whole convention depends on the juxtaposition of two strongly contrasted locales, representing two orders of reality, and the movement of the action from one to the other. What, then, do we find when we examine the use of setting in the remaining comedies? It strikes us at once that the majority are limited to a single basic locale. . . . Against the four comedies of the green world, we can set *The Comedy of Errors*, *Love's Labors Lost*, *Much Ado About Nothing*, and *Twelfth Night*. These belong to what for the present I shall call the 'alternate pattern', whose distinctive mark is unity of place.

. . . In green world comedies, the hero and heroine begin by leaving the old world behind them: whether they are exiled or elope or set off to seek their fortune, the first phase of the action is an exodus. In the comedies we are now describing, the characters stay put, but they are visited by outsiders, who upset the routine of the community into which they come. These plays begin not with expulsion but intrusion, not exodus but advent. Thus the King of Navarre at the beginning of *Love's Labors Lost* receives an untimely visit from the Princess of France, and *Much Ado* opens with the arrival of Don Pedro in

Messina. The Prince himself is Spanish; Claudio is Florentine and Benedick a Paduan: all three young men are aliens, foreigners; and in impact their entrance is more like an invasion than a homecoming. So in *Twelfth Night*, Viola and Sebastian, shipwrecked in Illyria, turn Orsino's dukedom upside down; and Dromio and Antipholus create as great a stir in *Comedy of Errors* when they land at Ephesus. . . .

In any case, there is little social disparity between the lovers to which a tyrannic father might object. Leonato would gladly marry Hero to a prince, but he is contented with a count; and Beatrice and Benedick, as their friends realize, are destined for each other even by alliteration. . . .

The obstacles to love in comedies of this alternate pattern are not external – social convention, favored rivals, disapproving parents. Resistance comes from the lovers themselves. The premise from which the green world comedies begin is sexual attraction: whoever loved that loved not at first sight? The answer is, of course, Benedick and Beatrice. They belong to a different type of comedy, whose premise is sexual antagonism. Instead of the conflict of generations, we watch the war between the sexes. Instead of age versus youth, the dramatic patterning pits male against female. Thus in *Love's Labors Lost* and *Much Ado*, the 'intruders' belong to one sex, the 'natives' to the other; men visit women or women visit men. . . . The developing action of *Much Ado* sets scenes involving women in contrast and parallel with scenes involving men; attempts to bring the sexes together in a masque or marriage produce comic mistakes or tragic mishaps almost to the end of the play. . . .

. . . In plays of the alternative pattern, the lovers, free from external frustrations and restrictions, proceed to bind themselves with their own wilful bonds. . . So Navarre and his bookmen swear not to see a woman for three long years: Olivia has 'abjured the company and sight of men' to live like a 'cloistress' for seven. Less formally articulated but just as binding is Benedick's determination to die a bachelor. In these vows, as in the attitude that begets them, there is inhibition as well as exclusion, 'shutting in' as well as 'shutting out'. . . . The father's jealous hostility towards his daughter's wooer has likewise been internalized, transferred to the heroine herself. So Beatrice scoffs at Benedick and Katherina rages against the whole race of men. It needs no Bradley to detect the real interest Beatrice feels for Benedick; no Freud to see that Katherina, jealous of Baptista's fondness for her sister, yearns for someone who will combine the dominating authority of a father with the exclusive absorption of a lover. Their surface aggressions are 'humors', forms of compulsive and irrational behaviour which deny and thwart their deepest wishes, their natural selves. In the green world comedies . . . the humor characters are the opponents of the hero. In comedies of the alternate pattern, the heroes and heroines themselves resemble humor characters, imprisoned in their own inhibitions and aggressions, isolated by fear or repugnance from the general life, cut off not merely from others whom they ought to love but even from themselves. Their 'laws' are only whims, but to the compulsive personality whims are law: there is no bondage stricter than bondage to the self.

By now it should be clear why these comedies begin with an intrusion into what is in some sense a closed world. . . . The motif of gaining entrance to a closed house or dwelling repeats in miniature the major pattern of these comedies, in which intruders force their way into a closed world and draw its thwarted or random emotional forces to themselves. . . .

The closed world is a metaphor, a symbol for the human heart. The force which knocks at its closed door is love. And in these comedies, love finally gains admittance: Navarre and Olivia renounce their vows: Katherina and Beatrice fall in love with men they thought they despised. The happy ending comes about not by perseverance through trials and changes of fortune, as in the green world comedies, but by a reversal, by conversion, by a change of heart. . . . For Cupid here becomes a Hercules, performing the seemingly impossible task of changing negative to positive, hostility and inhibition to normal human affection. . . . And there is nothing sentimental about the way these unconscious agents of love set to work. They come speaking the language of judgment: 'I see you what you are — you are too proud. . . .' The beginning of regeneration is the conviction of sin:

> What fire is in mine ears? Can this be true?
> Stand I condemn'd for pride and scorn so much?
> Contempt, farewell! And maiden pride, adieu! . . .

What happens to Kate [in *The Taming of the Shrew*] is less a catharsis than an exorcism. She is freed from the spirit of shrewishness which was her curse. Beatrice too is 'cursed', despite her name: she is 'possessed by a fury', and the 'infernal Ate' must be driven out of her if she and Benedick are ever to be blessed. . . .

The dramatic exorcism necessary to subdue or expel the anticomic spirit seems to proceed on two principles. One is 'acting out' its latent impulses. . . . So in *Much Ado*, the pervasive suspicion of women which exploits Claudio's gullibility as well as Benedick's cynicism must be acted out in the accusation of Hero. . . .

The second principle is 'fixing the blame'. 'Acting out' is expansive and cathartic: it allows the anticomic spirit its full and often violent expression. Only after sexual antagonism has expressed and spent itself in the cruel verbal assault which 'kills' Hero can Benedick be detached from the masculine party or declare his love for Beatrice. Fixing the blame, on the other hand, is a focusing; it locates the general lunacy or evil in a criminal or a scapegoat in whom it can be overpowered or driven out. So the blame which attaches itself to Hero is finally traced to Don John. . . .

Reversal, recognition, penance, exorcism: the form of these plays seems closer to the conventions of tragedy or the punitive logic of satire than to romance. . . . Consider, for example, the 'anticomic' figures, those antagonists of love who refuse or are refused the happy ending. Malvolio and Jaques are both anticomic in their melancholy; Shylock and Don John are both branded by their very lineage as villains. . . . Malvolio and Don John in the closed world represent extreme forms of the self-love or skepticism that afflicts the lovers themselves. . . . The new law offers to fulfill and liberate the old, a promise we see prefigured in Jessica [in *The Merchant of Venice*]. But the lonely malice of Don John must be expelled or imprisoned.

In *Shakespeare and the Experience of Love* (Cambridge University Press, 1981), Arthur Kirsch asserts that

At the center [of the play] is the scene in which Claudio carries out his promise to shame Hero, a scene whose original object, in the words of the *Book of Common Prayer*, is the 'forme and solemnization of Matrimony'. . . . Almost all the early action of *Much Ado* moves directly toward it, and the subsequent action is devoted to its clarification and eventual fulfillment. It provides the context in which Benedick and Beatrice come together resolving their own inward impediments and declaring their love, and it forms the focus of the whole comedy of Dogberry and the Watch.

The specific ceremony the scene evokes is still widely used, but its very familiarity has tended to drain it of meaning. The words of the liturgy, as well as the assumptions behind it, are worth rehearsing:

Dearly beloved friends, we are gathered together here in the sight of God, and in the face of this congregation, to join together this man and this woman in holy matrimony, which is an honorable estate, instituted of God in paradise in the time of man's innocency, signifying unto us the mystical union, that is betwixt Christ and his Church: which holy estate Christ adorned and beautified with his presence and first miracle that he wrought in Cana of Galilee, and is commended of Saint Paul to be honorable among all men, and therefore is not to be enterprised nor taken in hand unadvisedly, lightly, or wantonly, to satisfy men's carnal lusts and appetites, like brute beasts that have no understanding, but reverently, discreetly, advisedly, soberly, and in the fear of God, duly considering the causes for which matrimony was ordained. One was, the procreation of children to be brought up in the fear and nurture of the Lord, and praise of God. Secondly, it was ordained for a remedy against sin, and to avoid fornication, that such persons as have not the gift of continency might marry, and keep themselves undefiled members of Christ's body. Thirdly, for the mutual society, help, and comfort, that the one ought to have of the other, both in prosperity and adversity: into the which holy estate these two persons present come now to be joined. Therefore, if any man can show any just cause why they may not lawfully be joined together, let him now speak, or else hereafter forever hold his peace.

The priest then advises the persons to be married 'that if either of you do know any impediment why ye may not be lawfully joined together in matrimony, that ye confess it.' The service continues with the giving away of the bride, the plighting of troths, the recitation of either Psalm 128 or 67, and a number of prayers. It concludes with several scriptural teachings on the duties of marriage, one of them the passage from St. Paul that enjoins men 'to love their wives as their own bodies'. Another citation of the Scripture, from 1 Peter, gives corresponding instruction to wives, including the prescription that they not let their 'apparel. . . . be outward, with broided hair and trimming about with gold, either in putting on of gorgeous apparel, but let the hid man which is in the heart, be without all corruption, so that the spirit be mild and quiet, which is a precious thing in the sight of God.'

The relevance of this ceremony to the church scene in *Much Ado* is obvious. Claudio accuses Hero not only of an act that marriage is specifically ordained to avoid, but of a spiritual and psychological condition in which true marriage is impossible. Claudio's words are closely related to the opening of the liturgy: He accuses Hero of the 'semblance' of 'honour', of 'cunning sin', of being 'an approved wanton' to whom he will not 'knit' his 'soul', of being 'more intemperate' in her 'blood / Than Venus, or those pamper'd animals / That rage in savage sensuality'. He accuses Hero, in short, of sin and faithlessness – of the blush of 'guiltiness, not modesty', of 'pure impiety and impious purity'.

Though Claudio has apparent provocation for these tortured oxymorons, we ourselves know that they do not apply to Hero; and I think we eventually also understand that they constitute an expression of feelings and impulses that are repressed within himself. . . . The heated carnal fantasies that emerge in his charges against Hero suggest the repression of his own sensuality, and his idealistic interest in her tends from the start to be overly self-centered. . . .

Shakespeare represents Claudio as a victim not merely of slander but of his own unconscious disposition to believe it. By denying his senses, he becomes their virtual prisoner, believing only in what he sees and hears, repeatedly misled and repeatedly duped, a man who sees the outward apparel rather than the hid man that is in the heart. But he is not alone in that condition. Everyone in the play, except the villains and the Watchmen, hears or sees wrongly, everyone is vulnerable to slanderous suggestion, and everyone, though in varying degrees, is willing or disposed to believe that faith melts into blood. Intelligent and alert as they are, even Benedick and Beatrice can be fooled, and both are obviously apprehensive about marriage. Don Pedro, who is *Much Ado*'s social leader if not its monarch, is as susceptible to Don John's plot as Claudio is, and even Hero's own father finds it difficult to sustain his faith in her. In fact, the tendentious misinterpretation of sexual appearances that constitutes a primary mode of slander is also the mode of the play. The action of *Much Ado* is particularly marked by conversations that are wrongly heard or overheard and by sights that are mistakenly perceived. The play implies that such misapprehensions represent a spiritual and psychological, as well as a social, condition; virtually all the characters in the play at one point or another nurse wounds to their self-esteem and are radically self-absorbed. Don John, in his total self-conceit, is the sinister paradigm of this condition, as Dogberry is the beneficent one. *Much Ado* undoubtedly celebrates the manners of a civilized society, but it also represents, and deeply, the narcissistic 'impediments' that make the achievement of such a community at once so difficult and so urgent.

The theological implications of these impediments are adumbrated with unusual emphasis in *Much Ado* in the remarkable dialogue between Borachio and Conrade about the plot against Claudio and Hero [in III.iii.105–76] – the dialogue that is overheard by the Watch and that eventually leads to Don John's exposure. . . .

The three allusions that Borachio makes in such quick succession all call attention to their iconographic character – a reechy painting, an old church window, a worm-eaten tapestry – and they have considerable significance. The first refers to the episode in Exodus in which Moses and the Israelites passed through the Red Sea and Pharaoh's soldiers were drowned. The episode was commonly understood to be a figure of baptism. . . . It is significant, considering the plot that is later engineered by the Friar to redeem the marriage of Claudio and Hero, that this profession and communion, in the words of the liturgy of Baptism, 'is to follow the example of our Savior Christ, and to be made like unto him, that as he died and rose again for us, so should we which are baptized die from sin, and rise again unto righteousness, continually mortifying all our evil and corrupt affections, and daily proceeding in all virtues and godliness of living.' As we shall see, this is essentially the process that the Friar describes in his hopes, through Hero's feigned death and rebirth, to mortify Claudio's misapprehension.

The second of Borachio's allusions, to 'god Bel's priests', also focuses strongly on faithlessness and idolatry. . . . The story may have come to Shakespeare's mind because, like *Much Ado*, it specifically associates the capacity to be deceived by appearances with faithlessness, but even wider connotations of idolatry are germane to the play. The medieval commonplace that the lover who is driven by lustful fantasies makes an idol of his mistress and ultimately is guilty, like Narcissus, of a pathological worship of his own image. . . had many Elizabethan counterparts, particularly in the sonnet sequences, and has obvious applicability to Claudio, who also, like most lovers in this tradition, has blind faith in what he himself calls the negotiation of the eye.

Hercules, the subject of Borachio's third allusion, was, of course, one of the most popular mythological figures in Renaissance art and literature. Borachio's description of him as a blatant adolescent is very unusual, but its import is clear. The heroic Hercules of the Renaissance was the Hercules at the crossroads who chose virtue instead of vice, the manly Hercules who through twelve labors rid the world of monsters. His heroic exploits were routinely interpreted in terms of the Christian psychomachia, and he himself was often regarded as a type of Christ. . . . The figure whom Borachio describes, a 'shaven' Hercules whose 'cod-piece is as massy as his club', is obviously of another type altogether. Shakespeare may be thinking of Hercules' subjection to Omphale and may also be conflating that with the cutting of Samson's hair by Delilah. Both episodes were understood in the Renaissance as examples of the kind of radical unmanliness, ultimately a denial of God, that constituted Adam's submission to Eve at the Fall and that occurs in all men when their bodies and souls are not in harmony and when they worship themselves instead of God. I think they also inform the explicit sexual references to Hercules made elsewhere in the play both by Benedick, who fears that Beatrice 'would have made Hercules have turn'd spit, yea, and have cleft his club to make the fire too' [II.i.262–64], and by Beatrice, who in her turn fears that 'manhood is melted into curtsies, valour into compliment, and men are only turn'd into tongue, and trim ones too. He is now as valiant as Hercules that only tells a lie and swears it' [IV.i.320–25]. It is significant, considering this context, that Don Pedro should speak of his plan to 'fashion' a match between Benedick and Beatrice as 'one of Hercules' labours' [II.i.379–85]. . . .

. . . The larger envelope of Borachio's allusions, the whole subject of apparel and fashion, is one that deeply preoccupied Shakespeare, not only in this play but throughout his work. . . .

The seriousness with which [he] treats the issue of apparel may be in part an inheritance from the medieval drama, in which Vices and devils were regularly depicted as dandies, but his conception of fashion was ultimately scriptural and was common in Elizabethan religious thought. In the sermon against excess of dress, for example, the *Homilies* warned against making 'provision for the flesh, to accomplish the lusts thereof, with costly apparel'; rebuked even wives who sought to please their husbands 'with the devil's attire . . . in such painted and flourished visages, which common harlots most do use'; and in a reference to [1 Peter 3] . . . advised women to 'let the mind and the conscience, which is not seen with the eyes, be pure and clean. . . .' Such an association of ideas, I think, lies behind many of the images of painted women in Shakespeare's plays, including Don John's in *Much Ado*, when [in III.ii.108–10] he slanders Hero by saying the word 'disloyal' is 'too good to paint out her wickedness'. . . .

. . . The whole weight of the play's preoccupation with fashion is brought to bear on [the lines in IV.i.224–25 in which the Friar says that the 'reborn' Hero 'Shall come apparel'd in more precious habit / . . . Than when she liv'd indeed'], and it is difficult not to hear in them an allusion to the passage about wives in 1 Peter that is quoted in the marriage liturgy and remarked upon in the *Homilies*. Hero is clearly such a woman as the Epistle describes. Often castigated by critics for her passivity, she is quite literally mild and quiet, and her apparel is never outward even when it seems to be so. Significantly, just prior to the church scene, when Margaret makes a rather conspicuous fuss over the 'rare fashion' of Hero's gown, Hero replies only, 'God give me joy to wear it, for my heart is exceedingly heavy', and it is only when her hid heart is figuratively reborn in Claudio, when she comes appareled in more precious habit into the eye and prospect of his soul, that the play approaches its comic conclusion. . . .

As many critics have observed, Hero's rebirth is presented to Claudio as a gift of grace that he himself does little to earn. The remorse that the Friar predicts, and its accompanying psychological changes, occur only after the falsehood of the slander has been revealed, and then rather perfunctorily. . . . In *Much Ado* . . . the anatomy of transformation is plain enough in the sacrificial overtones of Claudio's and Hero's story, but the actual experience of spiritual and psychological change is displaced onto the comic relationship of Beatrice and Benedick as well as the comedy of Dogberry and the Watch, both of which drain the serious plot of its tragic potential at the same time that they absorb its deeper implications. . . .

. . . Claudio's shaming of Hero, in addition to dramatizing the whole realm of human inconstancy that is invoked in Borachio's digression, specifically acts out the sexual anxieties to which Benedick and Beatrice themselves have been most subject and upon which their wit has consistently played. . . .

And this brings me, finally, to . . . Dogberry. . . . It is no accident that he is the character directly responsible for discovering Don John's plot and saving Claudio and Hero. In a play in which the organs of sense are almost consistently deceived, only two groups hear and see correctly, Dogberry's and Don John's, and Dogberry and the Watch triumph largely because of their exemption from normal hearing and speech. They actually do pursue one Deformed, the vile thief of fashion who threatens to rob Claudio of the ability to love and who haunts the consciousness of Benedick and Beatrice, and they succeed in apprehending him through a power of innocence that Shakespeare comically manifests in their misuse of language. . . .

In *Much Ado* [the playwright's] identification of humor and love, which Benedick makes explicit in his conclusion that man is a giddy thing and that love is a humor, is fundamental to our own experience of the play, for our response to the foolishness of the invincible ego of Dogberry is the precise counterpart of Benedick's humorous response (and ours) to the foolishness of his love. We could not enjoy Dogberry were we not ourselves adult, but at the same time the pleasure he gives us and our deep sympathy with him release us from the constraints of being grown up and allow us to recover for a moment the euphoria of the world of childhood, which is his natural home and was once ours. The same is true of Benedick's and Beatrice's feeling of love: their adult perception of sexual fashion, of the imperatives and difficulties of instinctual life, is not lost, but transformed into pleasure, redeemed by their foolish unwillingness to be beaten with brains and by their capacity to experience and enjoy a regression to that stage in childhood when the ego cannot be betrayed by its object because the two are felt as one. Both follies, theirs and Dogberry's, are associated with the spiritual childishness of faith, Dogberry's directly in the allusion to 1 Corinthians [in V.i.239–51], Beatrice and Benedick's by its symbiotic relation to the whole drama of the figurative death and rebirth of Hero.

For Harry Berger, Jr., the 'Sexual and Family Politics in *Much Ado About Nothing*' suggest that human nature, especially male human nature, is 'Against the Sink-a-Pace.' In a subtle analysis that appeared in the 1982 volume of *Shakespeare Quarterly*, Berger begins by noting that

'Sink-a-pace' is the way Sir Toby Belch [in *Twelfth Night*] pronounces the name of the five-step dance [that Beatrice alludes to in II.i.73–85], and I borrow his pronunciation here because it signifies a slowing-down that beats against the galliard tempo. . . . In Beatrice's formula, marriage, the afterlife of the wedding, is renamed repentance, and its tempo is divided into the two mutually intensifying rhythms suggested by placing Toby's pronunciation in tandem with Beatrice's description: on the one hand, the decelerating sink-a-pace of the yoke of boredom, the long dull anticlimax to the fantastical jig and stately measure; on the other hand, the frenetic reaction in which the penitent tries ever more desperately and vainly to escape back into jigtime, tries to make himself giddy with acceleration and spin himself into forgetfulness. The state and ancientry of the wedding indicate the influence of the older generation, the father's interest in and control of the alliance that seals his daughter's future. Since Repentance is male, the bad-legged dancer may suggest either the husband himself or else the dominant tone which he – the dominant partner – gives to the monogamous relationship he finds himself unnaturally confined in by what Gloucester, in *King Lear*, called 'the order of law'.

Beatrice begins her little lecture with 'hear me, Hero', and it is difficult, on hearing the ear pun, not to add it to the senses of her name. Most of the 'noting' about which there is much ado consists of hearing or overhearing. Hero, who says almost nothing in the first two acts, hears a great deal, probably more than what is good for her. If she notes what we note, she hears enough to make her feel that her fate in life is to be her father's passport to self-perpetuation, a commodity in the alliance market, the spoils of the love wars – inevitably a conquered Hero, 'overmastered with a piece of valiant dust' who guarantees her anonymity by giving her his name and making her the prisoner and trophy that validates the name. Hero's name threatens to be her fate: Mrs. Hero. Yet even this most male-dominated of heroines betrays more than once her sense of her complicity in the sexual politics of Messina.

The first clue to this sense appears in the brief dance scene beginning at II.i.70. When Hero responds to the masked Don Pedro's request for a promenade, the conditions she imposes sound like a self-description: 'So you walk softly and look sweetly and say nothing, I am yours for the walk'. . . . It is as if she is quite conscious of the principle of behavior to which she conforms, and in offering her role to the Prince she may, by a mere shift of the shifters, indicate the value and objective of that behavior. . . .

. . . When Hero next comes on stage, at II.i.272, it is in time to hear herself compared to a stolen bird's nest being returned to its owner, and to be traded to Claudio by her father as part of a package deal that includes Leonato's fortunes. She seems easily to reconcile herself both to the match and to the role of commodity, but I think we are allowed at least a momentary doubt as to whether she and Leonato would not have preferred the Prince to Claudio, especially when she hears the Prince casually offer himself to Beatrice after giving Claudio back his bird's nest.

Even if we do not seriously entertain this doubt, we cannot help noticing something else about these scenes, namely that Hero's silence is the correlative of Beatrice's witty noise. Beatrice hogs the stage, and does not let Hero and Claudio savor their betrothal by basking in the limelight; she manages the scene, gives them their cues, gets the affair quickly settled, and then, pushing it aside with 'Good Lord, for alliance' (II.i.333), redirects attentions to herself and her brief flirtation with the Prince. It is not only that the absence of parents seems to give her a freedom Hero might well envy: since no honorable father's head burdens her shoulders, she can father herself and fight men with their own weapons. It is also that in Hero's presence she continually puts down the norms Hero is trained to respect and the institutional functions Hero is destined to fulfill.

What I find most interesting about all this is that Hero seems both to admire and envy Beatrice and to disapprove of her. . . .

If Hero's behavior during the rest of the play lends support to these narrowly-based interpretive remarks, then she is a much more interesting character than she has been made out to be, for she not only reflects the limitations of her culture but also betrays a dim awareness of them. This comes out more clearly in her behavior during the gulling of Beatrice. . . .

. . . Hero's reciting her part in the Prince's script – she is to speak of Benedick's lovesickness – only prepares us to see how far she strays from it. For she is herself a weapon of the Prince, and of her father, and of the Men's Club of Messina, and what she wants to harp on is Beatrice's disdain. The vigor with which she berates her cousin suggests that she is doing more than pretending for Beatrice's benefit. . . . The implied contrast is of course to her own quiet, reliable, unappreciated girl-scout self. . . .

Hero thinks it wrong to rebel against fathers and husbands. The world must be peopled, and it is disconcerting to be told that marriage is virtue's repentance rather than its reward. Yet something more than her own wounded pride comes through in the language she uses to humble her cousin. There is a touch not only of envy but of grudging admiration in such images as the fish with golden oars cutting the silver stream, and the haggards of the rock whose spirits are 'coy and wild' (III.i.35). . . .

Beatrice's view of marriage as a sink-a-pace is by no means exceptional in *Much Ado About Nothing*. Benedick seems to share it: 'Is't come to this? In faith, hath not the world one man but he will wear his cap with suspicion? Shall I never see a bachelor of threescore again?. . . An thou wilt needs thrust thy neck into a yoke, wear the print of it and sigh away Sundays' (I.i.206–11). Don John agrees: 'What is he for a fool that betrothes himself to unquietness?' (I.iii.48–49). It is conventional male wisdom that women are not to be trusted. . . .

It is difficult, however, to reconcile the opinion that men are more sinned against than sinning with another which seems to have equal weight:

> Sigh no more, ladies, sigh no more!
>   Men were deceivers ever,
> One foot in sea, and one on shore;
>   To one thing constant never. . . .

The Prince acclaims this as 'a good song' (II.iii.81), and I think his behavior throughout the play shows that although in this instance he may be referring to the music, in general he agrees with the sentiment. However playfully, he treats courtship as a military campaign, or a hunt, or a set of behind-the-back maneuvers – *practices*, as he calls them. . . .

The difference between men and women in this respect – so goes the regnant ideology of the play – is that women are responsible for their sins but men are not. Male deception and inconstancy are gifts that God gives, and their proper name is Manhood. But woman has an awesome responsibility. Since she bears her father's fame and fortune into the future as if – to borrow Benedick's image – she wore his head on her shoulders, and since by marrying she assumes the management not only of her husband's household but also of his reputation and honor, she is expected to conquer blood with wisdom even though the odds are ten to one against it. . . .

. . . The play's two scapegoats are a bastard named Trouble and a woman named Hero, and his bastardy tells us where the blame lies: like Edmund, no doubt, [Don John] is a testimony both to his father's prowess and to his mother's sin – a by-product of the frailty named Woman.

If this is how men choose to distribute praise and blame, we can understand why they expect women to fail to live up to their responsibilities. If men are deceivers ever, their first deception will be to trick women into loving them. And since women have to be won by the practices of men who flaunt their God-given powers of deception and inconstancy as the jewels of manhood, there is no reason to expect the ladies to honor their commitments. On the other hand, there is no reason not to demand it of them and chastise them when (as is likely) they betray their menfolk into shame. For women are, after all, in a double bond: they are to be wives as well as lovers. That is, they are not only prizes of war, but also commodities in the marriage market. Daughters are ducats. Marriage is a woman's vocation; it is her formal induction into the Men's Club; it is therefore her salvation; to be condemned into everlasting redemption is the fate she was born for. Man, however, was not born for wedlock. It is an accidental inconvenience of the system that after a man has amused himself in hunting his lawful prey, and succeeded in trapping her, he is then expected to deny his nature and spend his life by her side.

Men have, then, a bad conscience about their use and abuse of women in both love and marriage. They know that they do not deserve the loyalty and respect they command women to give them; *they* suspect their place, and they also suspect that *women* do. But this raises a question: If they are apprehensive about their own ability to be good husbands, is it *because* they choose to believe themselves born deceivers, or does it work the other way around? That is, could it be *because* marriage strikes them as a difficult, confining, and dull sink-a-pace that they choose to accept their fate as deceivers who are by nature unfit for it? . . . For one thing, it means committing their reputation to wives in whom the power of cuckoldry is legally invested. For another, it spells the death of their most precious experience: their companionship with other men. . . . Wooing bonds men together in a competitive or cooperative association that marriage threatens; therefore when marriage beckons, men no less than women have to be forcibly separated from the arms of their loved ones. . . .

. . . *Much Ado About Nothing* is an *endless moniment* for short time, and what it celebrates, as the machinery of the sink-a-pace turns over, is the ending of happiness.

This ending begins 'aspiciously' enough when Claudio addresses his second wedding as one of the reckonings to be settled, a debt he owes and is owed, or a score he must repay. . . . But this time Hero is more than a match for Claudio. . . . Nothing is 'certainer' to Hero than that, although she was defiled by slander, her virtue has triumphed over all efforts – and especially over Claudio's – to kill it. . . .

Hero makes it clear that the new Hero is simply the old with a vengeance, and though Claudio tries to shuffle off the implication with '*another* Hero', the Prince accepts it: 'The former Hero! Hero that is dead!' (V.iv.65). Her words reflect mordantly on the friar's self-delighting penchant for staging spiritual scenarios. They remind us that this community harbors no twice-born souls. The friar's practice is a travesty on religious psychology, conversion, and ethical self-transformation. It conspicuously excludes what it parodies, and substitutes a mere plot mechanism equal in ethical quality or causality to the bed trick. His terms of death and rebirth, being metaphorical and counterfactual, work by contraries to affirm that Hero and Claudio remain the same. No one is new-created by verbal or theatrical magic. The dialogue quoted above glances toward the conventional reconciliation. But the parties to it would have to be reborn in a new heaven and earth, a new Messina, before they could enter into a relationship free of the assumptions of their community. Their words, and the friar's game, evoke this possibility only to dispel it. They do not cut through the bond; they only nick it, and the play happily concludes, for *Much Ado* is a Shakespearean comedy – that is, an experience which ends in the nick of time.

SUGGESTIONS FOR FURTHER READING

Many of the works quoted in the preceding survey, or excerpts from those works, can be found in modern collections of criticism. Of particular interest or convenience are the following anthologies.

Bloom, Harold (ed.), *William Shakespeare's 'Much Ado About Nothing'* (Modern Critical Interpretations), New York: Chelsea House, 1988.

Brown, John Russell (ed.), *'Much Ado About Nothing' and 'As You Like It': A Selection of Critical Essays* (Casebook Series), London: Macmillan, 1979.

Cookson, Linda, and Bryan Loughrey (eds), *Critical Essays on 'Much Ado About Nothing'* (Longman Critical Guides), Harlow, Essex: Longman, 1989 (10 essays, including the ones listed below by Graham Holderness, Peter Hollindale, and John Turner).

Davis, Walter R., *Twentieth Century Interpretations of 'Much Ado about Nothing'*, Englewood Cliffs, NJ: Prentice-Hall, 1969.

Perrin, Jean (ed.), *Shakespeare: 'Much Ado About Nothing'*, Grenoble: ELLUG, 1992.

Scott, Mark W. (ed.), *Shakespearean Criticism*, vol. 8, Detroit: Gale, 1989.

Other studies that include discussions of *Much Ado About Nothing*:

Auden, W. H., 'Music in Shakespeare', in *The Dyer's Hand and Other Essays*, New York: Random House, 1962.

Barish, Jonas A., 'Pattern and Purpose in the Prose of *Much Ado about Nothing*', *Rice University Studies*, 60 (1974), 19–30.

Berry, Ralph, '*Much Ado about Nothing*: Structure and Texture,' *English Studies*, 52 (1971), 211–23.

Branagh, Kenneth, *Much Ado About Nothing*, New York: Norton, 1993 (screenplay for the 1993 film, with a memoir on how it was produced).

Brown, John Russell, *Shakespeare and his Comedies*, London: Methuen, 1962.

Bryant, Joseph A., *Shakespeare and the Uses of Comedy*, Lexington: University of Kentucky Press, 1986.

Burke, Robert R., 'The Other Father in *Much Ado About Nothing*', *Essays in Renaissance Culture*, 19 (1993), 85–96.

Champion, Larry S., *The Evolution of Shakespeare's Comedy*, Cambridge , Mass.: Harvard University Press, 1970.

Charlton, H. B., *Shakespearean Comedy*, London: Methuen, 1938.

Cook, Carol, ' "The Sign and Semblance of Her Honor": Reading Gender Difference in *Much Ado About Nothing*', *PMLA*, 101 (1986), 186–202.

Cox, J. F., 'The Stage Representation of the "Kill Claudio" Sequence in *Much Ado About Nothing*', *Shakespeare Survey*, 32 (1979), 27–36.

Cunningham, Dolora G., 'Wonder and Love in the Romantic Comedies', *Shakespeare Quarterly*, 35 (1984), 262–66.

Dawson, Anthony B., 'Much Ado about Signifying', *Studies in English Literature*, 22 (1982), 211–21.

Drakakis, John, 'Trust and Transgression: The Discursive Practices of *Much Ado About Nothing*', in *Post-Structuralist Readings of English Poetry*, ed. Richard Machen and Christopher Norris, Cambridge: Cambridge University Press, 1987.

Edwards, Gavin, 'Anticipation and Retrospect in *Much Ado About Nothing*', *Essays in Criticism*, 41 (1991), 277–90.

Everett, Barbara, '*Much Ado About Nothing*', *Critical Quarterly*, 3 (1961), 319–35.

Ewbank, Inga-Stina, 'Much Ado About Imagination', *Critical Survey*, 1 (1989), 17–23.

Fergusson, Francis, '*The Comedy of Errors* and *Much Ado about Nothing*', *Sewanee Review*, 62 (1954), 24–37.

Friedman, Michael D., 'The Editorial Recuperation of Claudio', *Comparative Drama*, 25 (1991–92), 369–86.

—— ' "Hush'd on Purpose to Grace Harmony": Wives and Silence in *Much Ado About Nothing*', *Theatre Journal*, 42 (1990), 350–63.

Furness, Horace Howard (ed.), *A New Variorum Edition of Shake-*

speare: 'Much Ado about Nothing', Philadelphia: J. B. Lippincott, 1899.

Garner, Shirley Nelson, 'Male Bonding and the Myth of Women's Deception in Shakespeare's Plays', in *Shakespeare's Personality*, ed. Norman N. Holland *et al.*, Berkeley: University of California Press, 1989.

Haigh, Kenneth, '*Much Ado About Nothing*' in *Shakespeare in Perspective*, vol. 2, ed. Roger Sales, London: Ariel Books (British Broadcasting Corporation), 1985; see the essay by Eleanor Bron in the same collection.

Hale, John K., ' "We'll Strive to Please You Every Day": Pleasure and Meaning in Shakespeare's Mature Comedies', *Studies in English Literature*, 21 (1981), 241–55.

Holderness, Graham, '*Much Ado About Nothing*: Men Without Women', in the Cookson and Loughrey collection cited above.

Hollindale, Peter, 'Serious Voices in a Comic World', in the Cookson and Loughrey collection.

Howard, Jean E., 'Renaissance Antitheatricality and the Politics of Gender and Rank in *Much Ado About Nothing*', in *Shakespeare Reproduced: The Text in History and Ideology*, ed. Jean E. Howard and Marion F. O'Connor, London: Methuen, 1987.

Hunter, G. K., *William Shakespeare: The Later Comedies*, London: Longmans, Green, 1962.

Hunter, Robert Grams, *Shakespeare and the Comedy of Forgiveness*, New York: Columbia University Press, 1965.

Huston, J. Dennis, *Shakespeare's Comedies of Play*, New York: Columbia University Press, 1981.

Jenkins, Harold, 'The Ball Scene in *Much Ado About Nothing*', in *Shakespeare: Text, Language, Criticism: Essays in Honour of Marvin Spevack*, ed. Bernhard Fabian and Kurt Tetzeli von Rosader, Hildesheim: Olms-Weidman, 1987.

Jorgensen, Paul A., 'Much Ado about Nothing', in *Redeeming Shakespeare's Words*, Berkeley: University of California Press, 1962.

Krieger, Elliott R., 'Social Relations and the Social Order in *Much Ado About Nothing*', *Shakespeare Survey*, 32 (1979), 49–61.

Leggatt, Alexander, *Shakespeare's Comedy of Love*, London: Methuen, 1974.

Lewalski, Barbara. 'Love, Appearance, and Reality: Much Ado about Something', *Studies in English Literature*, 8 (1968), 235–31.

McEachern, Claire, 'Fathering Herself: A Source Study of Shakespeare's Feminism', *Shakespeare Quarterly*, 39 (1988), 269–90.

252

McGrady, Donald, 'The Topos of "Inversion of Values" in Hero's Depiction of Beatrice', *Shakespeare Quarterly*, 44 (1993), 472–76.

Neely, Carol Thomas, *Broken Nuptials in Shakespeare's Plays*, New Haven: Yale University Press, 1985.

Nevo, Ruth, *Comic Transformations in Shakespeare*, London: Methuen, 1980.

Ormerod, David, 'Faith and Fashion in *Much Ado About Nothing*', *Shakespeare Survey*, 25 (1972), 93–105.

Osborne, Laurie E., 'Dramatic Play in *Much Ado About Nothing*: Wedding the Italian *Novella* and English Comedy', *Philological Quarterly*, 69 (1990), 167–88.

Palmer, John, *Comic Characters of Shakespeare*, London: Macmillan, 1946.

Phialas, Peter G., *Shakespeare's Romantic Comedies*, Chapel Hill: University of North Carolina Press, 1966.

Prouty, Charles T., *The Sources of 'Much Ado about Nothing'*, New Haven: Yale University Press, 1950.

Ranald, Margaret Loftus, ' "As Marriage Binds, and Blood Breaks": English Marriage and Shakespeare', *Shakespeare Quarterly*, 30 (1979), 68–81.

Richmond, Hugh M., 'Much Ado About Notables', *Shakespeare Studies*, 12 (1979), 49–63.

Roberts, Jeanne Addison, 'Strategies of Delay in Shakespeare: What the Much Ado is Really About', *Renaissance Papers, 1987* (1988), 95–102.

Sales, Roger, *Much Ado About Nothing* (Penguin Critical Studies), London: Penguin Books, 1990.

Siegel, Paul N., 'The Turns of the Dance: An Essay on *Much Ado About Nothing*,' in *Shakespeare in His Time and Ours*, Notre Dame, Ind.: University of Notre Dame Press, 1968.

Spinrad, Phoebe S., 'Dogberry Hero: Shakespeare's Comic Constables in their Communal Context', *Studies in Philology*, 89 (1992), 161–78.

Stevenson, David L., *The Love-Game Comedy*, New York: Columbia University Press, 1946.

Storey, Graham, 'The Success of *Much Ado about Nothing*', in *More Talking of Shakespeare*, ed. John Garrett, London: Longmans, 1959.

Taylor, Mark, 'Presence and Absence in *Much Ado About Nothing*', *Centennial Review*, 33 (1989), 1–12.

Traversi, D. A., *An Approach to Shakespeare*, vol. 1, New York: Doubleday, 1969.

Turner, John, 'Claudio and the Code of Honour', in the Cookson and Loughrey collection cited above.

Vickers, Brian, *The Artistry of Shakespeare's Prose*, London: Methuen, 1968.

Westlund, Joseph, *Shakespeare's Reparative Comedies*, Chicago: University of Chicago Press, 1984.

Williams, Mary C., 'Much Ado about Chastity in *Much Ado about Nothing*', in *Renaissance Papers, 1984* (1985), 37–45.

Background and general critical studies, and useful reference works:

Abbot, E. A., *A Shakespearian Grammar*, New York: Haskell House, 1972.

Allen, Michael J. B., and Kenneth Muir (eds), *Shakespeare's Plays in Quarto: A Facsimile Edition*, Berkeley: University of California Press, 1981.

Andrews, John F. (ed.), *William Shakespeare: His World, His Work, His Influence*, 3 vols, New York: Scribners, 1985 (articles on 60 topics).

Barroll, Leeds, *Politics, Plague, and Shakespeare's Theater*, Ithaca: Cornell University Press, 1992.

Bentley, G. E., *The Profession of Player in Shakespeare's Time, 1590–1642*, Princeton: Princeton University Press, 1984.

Berry, Ralph, *Shakespeare and Social Class*, Atlantic Highlands, NJ: Humanities Press, 1988.

Blake, Norman, *Shakespeare's Language: An Introduction*, New York: St Martin's Press, 1983.

Bullough, Geoffrey (ed.), *Narrative and Dramatic Sources of Shakespeare*, 8 vols, New York: Columbia University Press, 1957–75 (printed sources, with helpful summaries and comments by the editor).

Calderwood, James L., *Shakespearean Metadrama*, Minneapolis: University of Minnesota Press, 1971.

Campbell, O. J., and Edward G. Quinn (eds), *The Reader's Encyclopedia of Shakespeare*, New York: Crowell, 1966.

Cook, Ann Jennalie, *Making a Match: Courtship in Shakespeare and His Society*, Princeton: Princeton University Press, 1991.

—— *The Privileged Playgoers of Shakespeare's London*: Princeton: Princeton University Press, 1981 (an argument that theatre audiences at the Globe and other public playhouses were relatively well-to-do).

De Grazia, Margreta, *Shakespeare Verbatim: The Reproduction of Authenticity and the Apparatus of 1790*, Oxford: Clarendon Press, 1991 (interesting material on eighteenth-century editorial practices).

Eastman, Arthur M., *A Short History of Shakespearean Criticism*, New York: Random House, 1968.

Gurr, Andrew, *Playgoing in Shakespeare's London*, Cambridge: Cambridge University Press, 1987 (an argument for changing tastes, and for a more diverse group of audiences than Cook suggests).

—— *The Shakespearean Stage, 1574–1642*, 2nd edn, Cambridge: Cambridge University Press, 1981 (theatres, companies, audiences, and repertories).

Hinman, Charlton (ed.), *The Norton Facsimile: The First Folio of Shakespeare's Plays*, New York: Norton, 1968.

Muir, Kenneth, *The Sources of Shakespeare's Plays*, New Haven: Yale University Press, 1978 (a concise account of how Shakespeare used his sources).

Onions, C. T., *A Shakespeare Glossary*, 2nd edn, London: Oxford University Press, 1953.

Partridge, Eric, *Shakespeare's Bawdy*, London: Routledge & Kegan Paul, 1955 (indispensable guide to Shakespeare's direct and indirect ways of referring to 'indecent' subjects).

Rabkin, Norman, *Shakespeare and the Common Understanding*, New York: Free Press, 1967.

Righter, Anne, *Shakespeare and the Idea of the Play*, London: Chatto & Windus, 1962.

Schoenbaum, S., *Shakespeare: The Globe and the World*, New York: Oxford University Press, 1979 (lively illustrated book on Shakespeare's world).

—— *Shakespeare's Lives*, 2nd edn, Oxford: Oxford University Press, 1992 (readable informative survey of the many biographers of Shakespeare, including those believing that someone else wrote the works).

—— *William Shakespeare: A Compact Documentary Life*, New York: Oxford University Press, 1977 (presentation of all the biographical documents, with assessments of what they tell us about the playwright).

Spevack, Marvin, *The Harvard Concordance to Shakespeare*, Cambridge, Mass: Harvard University Press, 1973.

Vickers, Brian (ed.), *Shakespeare: The Critical Heritage, 1623–1801*, 6 vols, London: Routledge & Kegan Paul, 1974–81.

Wells, Stanley (ed.), *The Cambridge Companion to Shakespeare Studies*, Cambridge: Cambridge University Press, 1986.

Whitaker, Virgil K., *Shakespeare's Use of Learning*, San Marino, Cal.: Huntington Library, 1963.

Wright, George T., *Shakespeare's Metrical Art*, Berkeley: University of California Press, 1988.

PLOT SUMMARY

I.1 Near his house Leonato, the Governor of Messina, waits with his family to welcome Don Pedro, the Prince of Aragon. A messenger informs them that the Prince will be arriving shortly, having recently defeated his bastard half-brother, Don John, in battle. The two brothers, now apparently reconciled, are accompanied by Claudio, a young Lord of Florence, who distinguished himself in the fighting, and Benedick, a Lord of Padua.

As soon as Don Pedro and his companions arrive, Benedick and Beatrice, Leonato's niece, begin to try scoring points off one another; they are engaged in a long-running war of wits. Leonato welcomes everybody and leads them off to his house.

Claudio and Benedick, however, remain behind. Claudio has fallen in love with Hero, Leonato's daughter, and is mocked by a scornful Benedick. When Don Pedro returns to find out what has kept them, Benedick reveals Claudio's passion to the Prince before going in. Don Pedro agrees to help Claudio win Hero's hand in marriage; Don Pedro will disguise himself as Claudio and declare the young man's love to Hero during the celebrations that evening. If Hero loves Claudio, Don Pedro will ask Leonato to agree to the marriage.

I.2 Inside the house Leonato's brother, Antonio, tells him of Don Pedro's plan, but only as that was inaccurately overheard by a servant. Leonato leaves to inform Hero that Don Pedro loves her, and will declare his love that night.

I.3 Don John, meanwhile, discusses his discontents with Conrade, one of his followers. When another follower, Borachio, brings news of Claudio's love for Hero, Don John sees a way of gaining revenge on the man who so notably contributed to his defeat; he hopes to prevent the marriage.

II.1 In the great hall Beatrice explains why she does not like the idea of having a husband. Leonato reminds Hero to accept Don Pedro if he asks to marry her. They all put on masks when Don Pedro and the others enter, and the revelry begins.

Don Pedro, disguised as Claudio, goes off with Hero, while Benedick and Antonio are mocked by the ladies with whom they dance. Don John, pretending to believe that Claudio is Benedick, begs him to dissuade Don Pedro from his suit for Hero; Claudio's suspicion that he has been betrayed by Don Pedro is confirmed when Benedick returns with the news that the Prince is wooing Hero for himself. Claudio leaves in despair. Don Pedro enters with the news that he has won Hero for Claudio. Benedick, still upset at Beatrice's mockery of him, leaves when he sees her approaching with the others.

Don Pedro breaks the happy news to Claudio, and Leonato decides that the wedding date will be held in seven days' time, on the next Monday. When Beatrice has left, Don Pedro announces that he is going to try to make her fall in love with Benedick before the week is out; the others agree to help.

II.2 Elsewhere in the house, perhaps a day or so later, Borachio explains to Don John how they may still prevent Claudio's marriage. Margaret, a gentlewoman of Hero's, is in love with Borachio. On the night before the wedding, Borachio will persuade her to disguise herself as Hero and declare her love for him from her mistress's window. Don Pedro and Claudio, having been brought to view this scene by Don John, will thus believe Hero to be unfaithful.

II.3 In the orchard Benedick is marvelling at Claudio's transformation from soldier to lover. When he sees him approaching with Don Pedro and Leonato, he hides himself. The others, however, know that he is there and, after Balthasar has sung them a song, they discuss Beatrice's love for Benedick. By the time they leave, Benedick has decided to marry Beatrice, and he treats her civilly when she comes to call him in to dinner.

III.1 It is now the day before the wedding. In the orchard Hero tells Margaret to fetch Beatrice with the news that she is being talked about. When Beatrice arrives to listen, Hero and Ursula talk of Benedick's love for Beatrice. By the time they leave, Beatrice has decided to yield her love to Benedick.

III.2 In the house Don Pedro and Claudio mock Benedick's love-sick melancholy, a mood Benedick pretends to be the result of tooth-ache. Benedick asks Leonato if he can speak with him in private and they leave together. Don John arrives and tells Don Pedro and Claudio that he believes Hero to be unfaithful; if they are willing, he will take them to see Hero meeting her lover that night.

III.3 After midnight on one of Messina's streets Dogberry, the master constable, organizes the watch before turning in. Borachio comes by, boasting to Conrade how he has made Claudio think Hero unfaithful and in the process earned a thousand ducats from Don John. The watch arrest the pair.

III.4 The next morning at a little before five Hero is choosing her wedding clothes with her gentlewomen. Beatrice enters, love-sick, and is teased. The men arrive, ready to take Hero to church.

III.5 Dogberry and Verges, who is also a parish officer, come to tell Leonato of the men arrested by the watch. They do so in such a roundabout fashion that Leonato never learns what Borachio has done. Leonato, who is wanted at the wedding, asks them to examine the men themselves.

IV.1 In the church Claudio denounces Hero for her unfaithfulness and sexual promiscuity. She faints, and Claudio leaves with Don Pedro and Don John. Her father then denounces her, but Benedick, Beatrice and the Friar are unwilling to believe Claudio's story. The Friar persuades Leonato to let it be known that Hero has died; at the least – if Hero is guilty – it will gain her sympathy instead of infamy, and allow her to start her life again, somewhere out of the public gaze. Claudio may also have second thoughts.

When the others have gone, Beatrice and Benedick disclose their love for one another. Beatrice, as a test of Benedick's love, asks him to challenge Claudio to a duel.

IV.2 In the jail Dogberry, with the help of the Sexton, examines Conrade and Borachio. The Sexton recognizes the importance of what the watch has overheard and orders the prisoners to be taken to Leonato.

V.1 Near his house Leonato refuses to allow his brother to console him for Hero's death; he is now, he says, beginning to think his daughter falsely accused. When Claudio and Don Pedro arrive, Leonato challenges Claudio to a duel for having murdered Hero with his slanders. Leonato's brother then challenges Claudio;

neither challenge is accepted, and Leonato and his brother leave.

Benedick arrives and challenges Claudio to a duel. Don Pedro and Claudio tease Benedick about Beatrice, but he refuses to enter into their attempt at light-heartedness. When Benedick leaves, they realize that he was serious in his challenge, and Don Pedro begins to wonder why Don John has left Messina.

The constables enter with Conrade and Borachio, and Don Pedro and Claudio discover how they have been deceived. Leonato returns, and they acknowledge their mistake; he asks them to tell the people in Messina of Hero's innocence and also to sing epitaphs for her at her tomb. They are to come to his house in the morning and Claudio shall marry Beatrice.

V.2 In the orchard Benedick asks Margaret to fetch Beatrice. When she arrives he tells her that he has challenged Claudio. Ursula brings them news of the uncovering of Don John's plot and they leave to find out more.

V.3 Before dawn the next morning Claudio and Don Pedro mourn at what they believe is Hero's tomb. An epitaph is recited, and some lords sing a hymn. Then Don Pedro and Claudio go to change into their wedding clothes.

V.4 Waiting in his house, Leonato makes preparations for the forthcoming dénouement and grants Benedick's request to marry Beatrice. Claudio arrives with Don Pedro, and when the ladies enter masked, Claudio accepts the one he is given. To his joy, she turns out to be Hero. Benedick then asks Beatrice to marry him and, after their usual quibbling, she agrees. A messenger arrives with the news of Don John's capture; Benedick declares the news matter for another day, and orders the musicians to strike up a dance.